BRANDS, COMPETITION LAW AND IP

Brands and brand management have become a central feature of the modern economy and a staple of business theory and business practice. Contrary to the law's conception of trademarks, brands are used to indicate far more than source and/or quality. This volume begins the process of broadening the legal understanding of brands by explaining what brands are and how they function, how trademark and antitrust/competition law have misunderstood brands, and the implications of continuing to ignore the role brands play in business competition. This is the first book to engage with the topic from an interdisciplinary perspective; hence it will be a must-have for all those interested in the phenomenon of brands and how their function is recognized by the legal system. The book integrates both a competition and an intellectual property law dimension and explores the regulatory environment and case law in both Europe and the United States.

DEVEN R. DESAI is Associate Professor of Law and Ethics at the Georgia Institute of Technology, Scheller College of Business.

IOANNIS LIANOS is Professor of Global Competition Law and Public Policy at the Faculty of Laws, University College London (UCL), Director of the Centre for Law, Economics and Society, UCL and Lead Researcher, Skolkovo Laboratory on Law and Development, Higher School of Economics.

SPENCER WEBER WALLER is the Director of the Institute for Consumer Antitrust Studies and Professor at Loyola University Chicago School of Law.

BRANDS, COMPETITION LAW AND IP

Edited by

DEVEN R. DESAI, IOANNIS LIANOS

AND SPENCER WEBER WALLER

CAMBRIDGE
UNIVERSITY PRESS

CAMBRIDGE
UNIVERSITY PRESS

University Printing House, Cambridge CB2 8BS, United Kingdom

Cambridge University Press is part of the University of Cambridge.

It furthers the University's mission by disseminating knowledge in the pursuit of education, learning and research at the highest international levels of excellence.

www.cambridge.org
Information on this title: www.cambridge.org/9781107103467

First published 2015

A catalogue record for this publication is available from the British Library

Library of Congress Cataloguing in Publication data
Brands, competition law and IP / edited by Deven R. Desai, Ioannis Lianos and Spencer Weber Waller.
pages cm
Includes papers from two conferences jointly sponsored by the Institute for Consumer Antitrust Studies of Loyola University Chicago School of Law and the Centre for Law Economics and Society at University College London. – Introduction.
Includes bibliographical references and index.
ISBN 978-1-107-10346-7 (hbk)
1. Brand name products–Law and legislation–Congresses. 2. Branding (Marketing)–Congresses. 3. Trademarks–Law and legislation–Congresses. I. Desai, Deven R., 1975– editor. II. Lianos, Ioannis, editor. III. Waller, Spencer Weber, editor. IV. Loyola University Chicago. School of Law, sponsoring body. V. University College, London, sponsoring body.
K1569.A6B73 2015
343.08–dc23
2015006121

ISBN 978-1-107-10346-7 Hardback

CONTENTS

FIGURES

TABLES

CONTRIBUTORS

KETAN AHUJA is a Member of Oxford University Centre for Competition Law and Policy and Latham & Watkins LLP.

TONY APPLETON is General Counsel at Procter & Gamble UK.

DANIEL A. CRANE is Associate Dean for faculty and research and the Frederick Paul Furth, Sr Professor of Law at the University of Michigan Law School.

PETER DAVIS is Executive Vice President at Compass Lexecon and a visiting professor at the Faculty of Laws, UCL.

DEVEN R. DESAI is Associate Professor of Law and Ethics at the Georgia Institute of Technology, Scheller College of Business.

KIRSTEN EDWARDS-WARREN is Executive Vice President at Compass Lexecon.

ARIEL EZRACHI is Slaughter and May Professor of Competition Law, University of Oxford and Director of the Oxford University Centre for Competition Law and Policy.

ILANAH FHIMA is Senior Lecturer at the UCL Faculty of Laws and Co-Director of the UCL's Institute of Brand and Innovation Law.

ANDREW GRIFFITHS is Professor at Newcastle University.

WARREN S. GRIMES is Professor at Southwestern Law School.

GREGORY T. GUNDLACH is Coggin Distinguished Professor at Coggin College of Business University of North Florida and Senior Research Fellow at the American Antitrust Institute.

JAMES LANGENFELD is a Managing Director of Navigant Economics and Adjunct Professor of Loyola University Chicago School of Law.

WENQING LI is a Director of Navigant Economics.

IOANNIS LIANOS is Professor of Global Competition Law and Policy, Director of the Centre for Law, Economics and Society, UCL Faculty of Laws, London; Principal Research Fellow, Skolkovo Laboratory on Law and Development, Higher School of Economics, Moscow; Alexander von Humboldt Fellow, WZB, Berlin.

JOHN D. MITTELSTAEDT is Professor of Marketing, Chair of the Department of Management and Marketing, and Interim Dean, College of Business, University of Wyoming.

JOHN NOBLE is Director at the British Brands Group.

JOAN M. PHILLIPS is Professor of Marketing at the Quinlan School of Business, Loyola University Chicago.

SPENCER WEBER WALLER is Director of the Institute for Consumer Antitrust Studies and Professor at Loyola University Chicago School of Law.

SOPHIE YANG is an Associate Director of Navigant Economics.

Introduction

DEVEN R. DESAI, IOANNIS LIANOS, AND SPENCER WEBER WALLER

Brands and brand management have become a central feature of the modern economy and a staple of business theory and business practice. In the business world it is common wisdom that brands have important effects on competition and the marketplace. Yet the two areas of law most concerned with competition – trademark and antitrust – have not yet fully come to grips with the importance of branding.

In simplest terms, the law conflates trademarks and brands. Those scholars who contend that this is a mistake argue that brands are seen as indicating source and quality but that the other functions of brands are missed. Marketing and consumer literature brims with studies about the way brands use identity, emotion, and behavioral levers to compete beyond price. A brand-loyal customer may pay a premium for a brand for reasons other than quality and price. If one's brand cannot be copied, one's product may be so differentiated that competitors cannot compete and commodities such as wheat can be sold at higher margins than would otherwise be possible.

Until recently, these effects were lost in trademark and competition law (antitrust) discussions. Part of the problem flows from reliance in both Europe and the USA on price theory for both intellectual property and antitrust law. Embracing other social science perspectives should bridge the gap. Current brand literature tends to describe competitive advantages a brand can offer, but the welfare and consumer effects are less clear. At first, understanding brands may challenge current models of competition law, as it may not offer the seemingly crisp outcomes regarding whether preferences and related market results are endogenous or exogenous. Nonetheless, given the importance of branding, the explicit desire to use brands to compete, and the way in which brands evade price theory, there is a vigorous debate regarding the extent to which competition law and trademark law must delve into these literatures.

Thus the goal of this volume and our broader project on the nature of brands is to bring together scholars and practitioners from all of the relevant disciplines to learn from each other and explore what would constitute an appropriate legal framework for the treatment of brands in the modern economy. Professors Desai and Waller began with their 2010 article in the *BYU Law Review* examining the shortcomings of US antitrust and trademark law in understanding and regulating brands.[1] They continued to analyze the importance of brands as a potential new legal construct both individually and collectively.[2] At the same time, Professor Lianos from the Centre for Law, Economics and Society at UCL was publishing work on the impact of private labels in competition law assessment,[3] following up the discussions arising out of the UK Competition Commission's groceries market investigations and the focus of the European Commission (and some national competition authorities) at the time on retailer power in the process of the revision of the EU regulation on vertical restraints.

The study of brands as an interdisciplinary exercise grew into an ongoing collaboration between the Institute for Consumer Antitrust Studies of Loyola University Chicago School of Law[4] and the Centre for Law Economics and Society at University College London.[5]

The first aspect of this collaboration was a December 2011 conference, held at UCL in London, focusing primarily on the role of brands in UK and EU competition and trademark law.[6] This conference included distinguished panelists from industry, academia, government, the judiciary, and the bar with a special focus on the issues relating to the role of private label brands as well as broader issues of competition and intellectual property.

[1] D. R. Desai and S. Weber Waller, "Brands, Competition, and the Law," *Brigham Young University Law Review* 5(1) (2010), 1425–500.

[2] D. R. Desai and S. Weber Waller, "The Competitive Significance of Brands," *Competition Policy International* 1 (July 2014); D. R. Desai, "Response: An Information Approach to Trademarks," *Georgetown Law Journal* 100 (2012), 2119–31; D. R. Desai, "A Brand Theory of Trademark," *University of Florida Law Review* 64 (2012), 981; D. R. Desai, "Bounded by Brands," *University of California Davis Law Review* 47 (2014), 821.

[3] I. Lianos, "The Vertical/Horizontal Dichotomy in Competition Law: Some Reflections with Regard to Dual Distribution and Private Labels," in A. Ezrachi and U. Bernitz (eds.) *Private Labels, Brands and Competition Policy* (Oxford University Press, 2009), 161–86; I. Lianos, "New Kids on the Block: Retailer-Driven Vertical Practices and the New Regulation of Vertical Restraints in EU Competition Law," *Competition Policy International* 10(1&2) (2010), available online at: www.competitionpolicyinternational.com/new-kids-on-the-block-retailer-driven-vertical-practices-and-the-new-regulation-of-vertical-restraints-in-eu-competition-law/.

[4] www.luc.edu/antitrust. [5] www.ucl.ac.uk/cles.

[6] www.eventbrite.co.uk/e/brands-competition-law-and-ip-law-tickets-2338470428.

This collaboration continued with a follow-up conference in October 2012 at Loyola University Chicago School of Law, which focused primarily on US perspectives. This conference brought together speakers from the business world, business theory, competition and intellectual property law, and economics to reflect on the role of brands in the economy and the differing ways that these fields have defined and regulated brands.[7]

There is a growing recognition that brands are too important a topic to be examined using a piecemeal and fragmented approach. There has been a recent proliferation of conferences and publications in the USA and the EU on this topic including symposia in the *University of California Davis Law Review*[8] and the *Georgetown Law Journal*.[9]

At the same time, competition enforcers in both the United States and the European Union have shown an increased interest in, and sensitivity to, the role of brands in their cases and investigations. In general, the attention to unilateral effects in merger and other investigations is the study of product differentiation, branding, and its effects on competition in the relevant markets. As the authors in this volume discuss in greater detail, the role of brands appear with increasing frequency in the existing guidelines, consent decrees, commitments, and decisions in analyzing questions of market definition, entry barriers, market power, theories of competitive harm, and remedies in both jurisdictions.

This volume is part of the continuing conversation over the current treatment of brands in both competition and trademark law, and whether the law could benefit from a broader perspective on brands drawing on the vast and evolving business and marketing literature used by business theorists and executives in the marketplace. The twelve chapters and comments presented in this volume are drawn from, or inspired by, the two joint LUC and UCL brands conferences and the ideas they have generated.

While the debate in the chapters of this volume will continue, important themes have emerged. First and foremost, competition lawyers, trademark lawyers, business theorists, marketers, and economists all tend to view brands in different terms and often with a different vocabulary.

[7] www.luc.edu/law/centers/antitrust/events/brands_competition_law.html.

[8] Brand New World, http://lawreview.law.ucdavis.edu/symposia/2012-fall/.

[9] M. A. Lemley and M. P. McKenna, "Is Pepsi Really a Substitute for Coke? Market Definition in Antitrust and IP," *Georgetown Law Journal* 100 (2012), 2055–117; D. R. Desai, "Response: An Information Approach to Trademarks," *Georgetown Law Journal* 100 (2012), 2119–131.

We hope that the chapters in the volume will help guide the discussion toward a common understanding and eventually common proposals for improvement of the existing legal regime regarding brands and brand management.

The volume starts with an exploration of the way price theory and business studies have engaged with the concept of brand.

Professor Davis and Doctor Edwards-Warren from Compass Lexecon in their chapter on "An introduction to the competitive effects of branding" question the view that economics does not take brands sufficiently into account. Economics as a discipline is not defined by the very special case of homogeneous product industries where firms compete only in prices, consumers and firms have perfect information, and all industry dynamics happen instantaneously. The phenomenon of differentiated product markets is prevalent in the modern economy; hence the need for economics to develop tools to assess the effect of brands on prices. The chapter provides a brief overview of the different economic theories on the competitive effects of branding. It concludes that brands may play both a positive and negative role for consumer welfare and that public intervention through competition law should not occur without careful investigation of the effects of branding in the market at hand.

In their chapter on "Bayer or Walgreen's? The relationship of premium and value brands in the United States," Doctors James Langenfeld, Wenqing Li, and Sophie Yang of Navigant Economics dive into the world of private label brands and show that national brands and private or store brands compete and operate differently from each other. The authors find that national brands sales are often *more price-sensitive* than store brands; national brands often *compete more closely* with one another than with store brands; price changes in national brands often affect sales of store brands *more than store-brand price changes affect national brands*; the entry of store brands can lead to an increase in the own price elasticities of national brands; and promotions affect sales independently of actual prices in *economically predictable ways*. Their findings offer insights regarding how national and store brands compete and how pricing decisions are made depending on what other brands are offered in a given market.

Tony Appleton from Procter & Gamble and John Noble from the British Brands group, in their chapter on "The value of brands and the challenge of free-riding," discuss the reality of brands from a business perspective, in particular the opposition between national brands and private labels. They lament the fact that notwithstanding the role of brands in markets and the important value they generate for firms and consumers, there is no common understanding of what a brand is. Appleton and Noble take a "consumer-centric" approach to the concept of brand, explaining the role both consumers and brand owners play in the development of the brand value. They acknowledge that the practice of branding, which includes the manufacture, distribution, and sale of products, is highly regulated in a number of different ways. To illustrate this, they take a well-known problem for brand owners – parasitic copying – and explore the different remedies that have been put forward by different regulatory regimes interacting in this area, such as competition law, self-regulation, intellectual property law, and consumer law. Through their highly interesting problem-based study, Appleton and Noble illustrate the benefits of thinking across legal categories and regimes, thus exemplifying one of the major advantages of the concept of "brand law" in organizing the remedial response of these different areas of law.

The second part of this volume engages with the implications of brands and branding on competition law.

Professors Deven Desai of the Georgia Institute of Technology, Scheller College of Business, and Spencer Weber Waller of Loyola University Chicago School of Law present their chapter on "Brands, competition and antitrust law," which is an adaptation of their earlier work. In this chapter they argue that US antitrust law has largely missed the competitive significance of modern brand management because of its focus on neo-classical price theory. They argue that the rise of the brand in the modern economy diminishes the role of price competition and raises issues of market segmentation, price discrimination, and consumer lock-in that antitrust law is only just beginning to analyze directly. They conclude by recommending that antitrust law enforcers and courts engage more directly with marketing literature and business theory to better understand brands and how to apply antitrust principles in a brand-based world economy effectively.

Professors Gregory Gundlach of the Coggin College of Business of the University of North Florida and Joan Phillips of the Quinlan School of Business of Loyola University Chicago apply their marketing expertise in their contribution "Brands and brand management: insights from marketing for antitrust." In their contribution they survey the economics of product differentiation and the key marketing literature and seek to apply these insights to how antitrust policy makers should understand brands and brand management. They conclude that brands involve real product differentiation for both producers and consumers, pose complex effects for competition, and therefore require a greater use of business literature and theory to determine the effects of powerful brands in specific market settings.

Associate Dean Daniel Crane of the University of Michigan Law School offers "Brands and market power: a bird's eye view." In this thoughtful comment, Dean Crane introduces three challenges that brands pose for a coherent and effective antitrust policy. He first surveys the possible pro- and anti-competitive effects of brands. He then rejects the view that excessive branding can create artificial distinctions in the minds of consumers on the grounds that this premise places in jeopardy the underlying consumer sovereignty assumption of antitrust law. Finally he analyzes, but expresses doubt, whether individual brands should ever be defined as their own relevant market.

Professor Warren Grimes of Southwestern Law School continues his long-standing focus on vertical restraints and resale price maintenance in "The two sides of brand marketing: reconsidering competition law governing distribution restraints." In this comment, Professor Grimes considers how brands are an essential part of modern efficient marketing, but at the same time represent a strong risk as a form of non-informational product promotion. In probing the pluses and minuses of modern brand management under the US antitrust laws, Professor Grimes analyzes the legality of three commonly used distributional restraints for branded products: dealer location clauses, exclusive territories, and minimum resale price maintenance.

Turning to competition law in Europe, Professor Ioannis Lianos' chapter on "Brands, product differentiation and EU competition law" explores the way EU competition law has so far integrated the concept of brands in different areas of enforcement. Professor Lianos notes that although EU competition law has engaged with branding and product differentiation in multiple instances, brands do not constitute an operational concept in EU competition law. This is due to an important uncertainty as to the normative choices that need to be made with regard to the relation between brands and the formation of consumer preferences. The concerns raised by retailer power and the development of private labels also indicate that the existing economic theory on product differentiation may also not provide the complete picture of the effects of brands on the competitive process and ultimately on consumers. Competition law will also need to tackle the issues raised by the development of "social branding" and the dialogic interaction between brand owners and consumers in the constitution of their brand identity, which breaks with a unidirectional view of the power relations between brand owners and consumers. Professor Lianos concludes by emphasizing the importance of normative choices and assumptions on the interaction between brands and the formation of consumer preferences, which, according to him, will be a key parameter in the integration of the concept of brands in EU competition law and other related areas of law (e.g. unfair trade practices law).

Professors Ariel Ezrachi and Ketan Ahuja further explore the nature of competition between private labels and brands in their chapter on "Private labels, brands and competition law enforcement." Their contribution considers the unique characteristics of label/brand competition, which combine horizontal, vertical, and market power elements. According to them, these mixed characteristics pose a challenge to traditional competition analysis. The chapter explores the question whether traditional competition analysis may capture the complex competitive landscape and accurately weigh the short- and long-term effects of private labels on competition. The authors conclude that traditional competition analysis suffers from important limitations and suggest some alternatives.

The third part of the volume delves into the implications of brands on intellectual property law and its interaction with competition.

Professor John D. Mittelstaedt of the University of Wyoming, College of Business, brings law and brand management together in "Trademark dilution and the management of brands: implications of the Trademark Dilution Revision Act for marketing and marketing research." In his contribution Professor Mittelstaedt argues that dilution recognizes that producers play an equal role to consumers in creating brand value. He offers that this shift requires that marketing scholarship plays a role in understanding the contours of fame, likelihood of dilution, and potential universal standards or thresholds at which blurring or tarnishment occur. He also offers the challenge that just as the concept of trademark has been constrained by the law, brands – which have not been so constrained – may be limited in the future where trademarks and brands are merged into legal analysis.

In her chapter Doctor Ilanah Fhima explores how "Trade mark law meets branding." She notes that although trademarks and brands are often thought of as synonymous, lawyers and branding experts have different conceptions of how, why, and to what extend the identifying features of goods and services should be protected. Her chapter considers what those different conceptions are, and the extent to which there is common ground in relation to trademark dilution, which protects the image and reputation of the mark, as well as its more traditional distinguishing function. In her thoughtful contribution, Doctor Fhima explores the case law of the Court of Justice of the European Union (CJEU) on dilution and concludes that this takes two directions. The first suggests that the CJEU is moving toward protecting aspects of image and branding in a way that recognizes how consumers respond to trademarks and the brands of which they form a part. This line of case law protects trademarks not just as indications of trade origin but also as carriers of a protectable image built up through promotion and advertising. At the same time, however, the jurisprudence of the CJEU begins to show a willingness to treat aspects of brand image as a holistic whole in judging distinctiveness, use, and infringement, allowing brand owners to more successfully capture the benefit of the entirety of their brand, rather than just the individual elements that are registered as trademarks.

Professor Andrew Griffiths concludes this volume with a chapter on "Brands, firms and competition." The chapter explores the "nebulous relationship" between brands and trademarks. It is acknowledged that the legal entity of the trademark provides the main legal platform for the marketing entity of the brand, yet it does not capture fully the multiple uses of brands by firms and other business organizations to compete with each other at the level of marketing. Professor Griffiths shows that the use firms make of brands may vary considerably. Some brands provide a "personable façade for the firms behind them"; other firms control a range of product-focused brands, and some brands can appear to be distinct and autonomous entities in their own right. Firms may also develop various competitive strategies. They may decide to invest in the emotional impact of their brands rather than directing investment and competitive effort at improving product quality and at building and maintaining a good reputation for product quality with the aim of achieving a sustainable competitive advantage and reinforcing their market power. While the "emotional and cognitive appeal" of branding should be taken into account when calibrating the property rights conferred on brand owners in order to ensure that they provide an optimal incentive, its social costs should also be considered. Professor Griffiths explores the way this balancing was performed by the jurisprudence of the CJEU on trademarks.

We would like to thank Cambridge University Press and in particular Kim Hughes and Rebecca Roberts from the editorial staff for the chance to present this cutting edge work to a broader audience. Thanks also to Chris Nemes and Lisa Penfold for their hard work on the earlier brands conferences, and Kristine Bergman, Nicole Grabianowski, and Peter O'Loughlin for their excellent research assistance in preparing the final version of the chapters for submission for publication. Finally, we would like to thank the Georgia Institute of Technology, the Faculty of Laws at University College London, the Leverhulme Trust, Loyola University Chicago, and Thomas Jefferson School of Law for their support of our research and writings on these topics.

PART I

Brands, price theory and business studies' perspectives

1

An introduction to the competitive effects of branding

PETER DAVIS AND KIRSTEN EDWARDS-WARREN

> Brands allow businesses to reach consumers directly with messages regarding emotion, identity, and self-worth such that consumers are no longer buying a product but buying a brand.[1]

Introduction

The purpose of this chapter is to provide a brief review of the economics of the competitive effects of branding.[2] Since Marshall (1890, 1919), economists have thought about at least two roles that brands can play, one largely positive the other potentially negative:

1. **Informing and Signalling:** Brands may convey information about a product's price or quality to consumers. As such branding may involve choice of names, terms, symbols and designs which signal the quality of the goods of a particular seller and thereby attempt to differentiate them from those of its competitors. Customers may recognize a brand even when they know little about the product.

[1] D. R. Desai and S. Weber Waller, "The Competitive Significance of Brands", *Competition Policy International* (1) (July 2014), 1–8.

[2] At the outset, it is perhaps worth making two introductory remarks. First, while we refer to a variety of articles in this chapter, our literature review is selective rather than exhaustive. A more exhaustive excellent review of the literature is provided in Bagwell (2007) on which we have drawn liberally – but particularly in providing references to the early literature. Second, we should dispense with a straw man that sometimes arises in a discussion of branding and economics – namely, the straw man that economists are not interested in brands because they are far too focussed on the narrowly applicable case involving homogenous goods, perfect information, and competition only in prices. While this may be true of some bad economics courses, it is not true of the discipline.

2. **Persuading:** Branding may seek to persuade customers to buy a product that they would not have otherwise purchased; branding may seek to create new demand.[3]

In terms of the first role, consider, for example, an experience good, such as a new shampoo, where the quality of the product can only be observed after purchase. For such products, a brand may indicate to consumers that a new product is of high quality. Another example is provided by the franchising literature, which seeks to understand why, for example, potential entrepreneurs pay to open a Subway or McDonalds store rather than open an independent restaurant.[4] One reason may be that the brand signals that products will satisfy a minimum quality – such minimum quality levels will be enforceable since they will form a part of the contract between franchisee and franchisor. The result is that customers know that products purchased from outlets with which they do not have experience will not be too different from the products sold by those with which they do. The brand signals a minimum quality, in this case across locations.

In terms of the second role, the potential persuasive effect of advertising has long been a source of concern to both policymakers and economists. Economists would typically welcome an outcome where a customer is persuaded of the merits of a good because it fits with her wants. However, the concern with the persuasive effect of advertising is that consumers may be persuaded to part with their hard-earned money in exchange for goods and services that they do not really want. Such a concern poses a philosophical challenge that has the potential to go to the heart of the rationale for free markets, since it questions the autonomy of the individual in making choices – traditionally the core behavioural assumption of economists.[5]

Moreover, such newly persuaded customer demand may be created through the development of consumers with a perception of product differentiation (even where none physically exists) and seeking to engender customer loyalty. For the competition economist, such effects may provide a firm with market power and so may be of concern, in particular if significant investment is required for other firms to replicate this strategy.

[3] The field of neuro-marketing considers the impact of marketing exposures on neuronal activity. See for example, Lee, Broderick, and Chamberlain (2007).

[4] See for example Mathewson and Winter (1985) and Lafontaine (1992).

[5] The morality of advertising is considered in the business ethics literature. See, for example, Arrington (1982) and Crisp (1987).

We discuss the implications of these two potential effects of branding in the next two sections of this chapter, focussing first on the potential for pro-competitive effects and then on the potential for anti-competitive effects.

The controversy around the normative economics of advertising has raged for at least a century within industrial organization, with authors respectively emphasizing the potentially positive and potentially negative roles of advertising. In the fourth section we therefore briefly outline the work by Ackerberg (2001), who considered how one might distinguish empirically which of these two hypotheses about the effects of branding is driving consumer behaviour. In doing so, we outline a particular example, considering which effect was dominant in a particular fast-moving consumer goods market. We do so in order to illustrate the approach that most good economists will seek to take to understand the effects of branding in a particular market: namely, to understand the market realities and to seek data that will help us distinguish between the potentially concerning or potentially positive effects of branding in a particular market.

Finally, we note that while the effects of branding are a subject of considerable debate, the idea that brands and advertising more generally are important phenomena to understand is widely accepted among industrial economists. The reasons are perhaps empirical. First, we clearly observe significant amounts of money being spent on efforts at branding. And second, when economists estimate demand for differentiated products, we do find that sales are systematically higher for products sold under particular brands than we would expect if sales volumes were driven solely by prices and product characteristics, although the magnitude of the effect varies across industries.

Potential anti-competitive aspects of branding

In this section we outline some of the potentially anti-competitive aspects of branding that have been considered in the economics literature.

Reduced price competition: Branding a product would typically involve seeking to differentiate it from competitive products sold by other brands. Economists since at least Hotelling (1929) have understood that product differentiation may reduce price competition and increase margins in the absence of entry. Branding thus has the potential to reduce inter-brand competition. Kaldor (1950) and Galbraith (1958) in particular argued that advertising could have deleterious effects.

Barriers to entry and expansion: Competition authorities are often concerned that, after successfully building a strong brand over a period of time, firms may have an incumbency advantage over their rivals. If so, then this may allow high prices to be charged without attracting entry or experiencing expansion by rivals.

Consumer protection: In addition, the potential for persuasive advertising raises a potentially significant consumer protection concern, which may also, under some competition regimes, constitute a potential distortion of competition.[6] In essence, should policymakers protect consumers from themselves?

Bronnenberg *et al.* (2014) provide a recent example of an analysis of such a concern. They consider the demand for headache remedies and find that more informed consumers are less likely to buy national brands with, for example, pharmacists choosing national brands over store brands only 9 per cent of the time, compared to 26 per cent of the time for the average consumer. They argue that the results suggest that 'misinformation explains a sizable share of the brand premium for health products'.

Potential pro-competitive aspects of branding

In this section we outline some of the potentially pro-competitive aspects of branding that have been considered in the economics literature.

Reducing Entry Barriers: Economists have noted that not all aspects of branding are necessarily bad for competition; even persuasive effects of advertising could in principle have positive effects on competition. The reason is a simple one: branding may help an existing firm to diversify into a new market area, using its brand as a signal to consumers about the likely quality of the new product. Some potential instances are illustrated in Figure 1.1.

Direct consumer welfare gains from the brand: Direct consumer welfare gains from being able to purchase branded products would clearly be important for a normative evaluation of the appropriate economic policy towards branding. For example, some individuals may enjoy wearing Rolex watches, while others may enjoy their Nike shirts. Veblen (1899)

[6] For example, the UK Market Investigation Regime asks the UK's Competition and Markets Authority (CMA) to consider whether there are features of the market that prevent, restrict or distort competition. In principle, the CMA might decide to consider that branding was such a feature – although for clarity this has not been an issue in recent years. In the Groceries market investigation, the role of copycat brands was considered, although parties were advised by the CMA to seek intellectual property law remedies rather than competition ones.

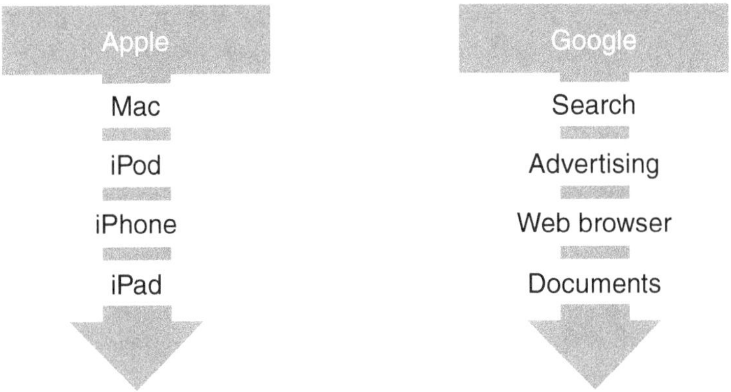

Figure 1.1 Brands may facilitate entry into new market areas

famously studied the extreme version of such preferences wherein consumers might actually enjoy paying more for a more exclusive product because it allows displays of wealth (conspicuous consumption). Branding under this characterization would be an investment in a product characteristic that some consumers care about. However, its welfare effects would need careful evaluation, since a desire for conspicuous consumption may mean that a lot of customers who nonetheless value the product will not get to buy it.

Enhancing intra-brand competition: Branding may enhance intra-brand competition, wherein products from the same brand compete. For example, consider two competing supermarket chains that stock a variety of nationally branded products. To the extent that the supermarkets both stock nationally branded products, their offerings to consumers may be more similar than a situation where one of the supermarkets only carries own label products.[7] The effect may be greatest for specialty retailers who sign exclusive distribution agreements with particular manufacturers. Doing so has the potential to make two retailers who choose the same manufacturers' products appear relatively close substitutes to

[7] For example, Marks and Spencer, a UK retailer, decided publically in 2008 to trial offering some 350 branded products at 19 stores, reportedly for the first time in its history (since 1884). Its chairman Sir Stuart Rose argued: 'This will enable customers to buy "must have" products such as Marmite, Heinz Tomato Ketchup, household products and toiletries.' See www.talkingretail.com/category-news/supermarket/m-and-s-will-stock-branded-products-stuart-rose-confirms/ (accessed 25 February 2015). This trial was subsequently expanded across the UK in 2009; see www.marketingweek.co.uk/ms-to-expand-branded-food-trial/2064661.article (accessed 25 February 2015).

one another in the eyes of consumers. In an extreme case they may differ only by geographic location and, in consequence, we may also observe exclusive territory arrangements with specific brands in order to avoid too much intra-brand competition.[8]

Information: The economics literature has considered a variety of mechanisms whereby advertising generally (and so branding specifically) may potentially have a pro-competitive effect. Some of the most famous examples include:

1. **Reducing search costs:** Stigler (1961: 220) provided a model wherein advertising lowered the search costs faced by consumers, arguing that it 'is clearly an immensely powerful instrument for the elimination of ignorance – comparable in force to the use of a book instead of the oral discourse to communicate knowledge'.
2. **Providing direct utility:** Becker and Murphy (1993) considered a situation wherein advertising and the goods themselves are complementary, so that advertising actually increases the utility obtained from consumption of a good.
3. **Conveying information about product characteristics or product qualities:** The information imparted by a brand can be about product characteristics (for example, business travellers may know what to expect at a Hilton Hotel) or of a certain level of relative quality or style (for example, Apple branded products have many admirers). Telser (1964) and Stigler and Becker (1977)[9] considered the potential role of

[8] Competition specialists may, for example, point to the US Supreme Court's 1977 decision in *Continental TV Inc* v. *GTE Sylvania Inc.*, 433 US 36 (1977), which introduced the rule of reason for non-price vertical restraints, the background to which was Sylvania's termination of a franchise arrangement with Continental to sell TVs after it sold Sylvania's TVs in locations for which it was not the authorized retailer.

[9] In this chapter, Stigler and Becker (1977) argued far more generally that it was neither necessary nor useful for economic analysis to allow the change of consumer tastes over time, since such an economic model cannot then explain consumer behaviour. To the extent that 'persuasive' advertising is a concern that consumer tastes evolve in response to advertising, they do not believe this to be a useful distinction. The reason is that they are arguing that economic models should be built on stable preferences, those that do not change over time, but where consumers' preferences are specified in a manner that is sufficiently rich to capture the important drivers of changes in consumer behaviour. Thus they argue a classical approach to consumer preferences (pre 1950s), which assumed that perfect information does not allow a proper treatment of the role of advertising in conveying information to consumers properly. They write: 'In our analysis … consumers have imperfect information, including misinformation, and a skilled advertiser might well be able to differentiate his product from other apparently similar products' (1977: 85). Thus they note that advertising may have good and bad effects even so.

information from advertising in driving consumers' willingness to pay for a good, but the most famous analysis among economists is perhaps that of Nelson (1974). He considered that advertising can be used to signal the quality of a product to consumers before they purchase the good. If so, firms are able to signal that they produce a high-quality product by essentially burning money, which in certain circumstances only high-quality firms could afford to do. This intuition was later formalized by Milgrom and Roberts (1986).

The implication of such analysis is, for the purposes of this section, that advertising can have pro-competitive effects. For example, advertising prices may lead to more intense competition as consumers become aware of many more available prices prior to purchase.

Such effects may be quite idiosyncratic. Suppose, for example, that it is observed in data from the cinema industry that Arnold Schwarzenegger movies have disproportionally high levels of sales and attendance in theatres when compared to other movies. The Arnold Schwarzenegger brand may convey significant information about the movie to consumers. In this case, a consumer can perhaps safely assume that the movie will be a fairly light-hearted action movie with an abundance of explosions and machine guns. An empirical model will be able to explain this upturn in market share in two ways. It can infer that the movie is either of a high quality, which is why many people are going to see it, or that the movie is of a genre that is popular, which is action movies in this case. In both of these explanations, the presence of Arnold Schwarzenegger has a part to play.

Empirical example: the analysis of the 44 Liquormart decision

Milyo and Waldfogel (1999) studied the impact of this 1996 decision of the US Supreme Court to repeal a Rhode Island law that had banned advertising of alcohol prices in individual liquor stores within the state of Rhode Island (RI) between 1995 and 1997 (the '44 Liquormart' decision). The authors collected information on prices for a variety of products sold at liquor stores near the border of RI and also in Massachusetts (MA), where advertising alcohol prices was legal both before and after the RI ban was repealed.[10]

[10] The data used for the experiment contained 6,480 observations collected from 115 different liquor stores spread between both states and covering 33 different alcoholic beverages. The data was collected at 'approximately quarterly intervals' on 8 different occasions between June 1995 and June 1997. Advertising data was collected on storefront display

The paper showed that, although prices in both markets went up by 2–3 per cent over the period, in four out of the five quarterly observations made by the authors after May 1996 (the date after which advertising was allowed), RI prices rose less than those in MA, which was consistent with a negative effect of advertising on prices. Moreover, the authors found that stores that were advertising prices had approximately 20 per cent lower prices for their advertised products. The results thus suggest that the information obtained from advertising (in this case pricing information) drove down prices in RI compared to MA, which is consistent with the view that the reintroduction of advertising led to pro-competitive effects.

Case-by-case analysis

The analysis described above suggests that the economic effects of advertising generally, and branding specifically, have long been considered potentially ambiguous. Such a conclusion leads most economists to follow in the footsteps of Chamberlain (1933) in concluding that an analysis of whether advertising is playing a positive role or a negative one should be undertaken on a case-by-case basis. Of course, such a conclusion begs the question of whether we can establish empirically whether advertising is having a positive or negative effect. Our next example illustrates that with a little ingenuity such investigations may indeed have a hope of success.

Example: distinguishing informational and persuasive effects

Ackerberg (2001: 317) considered the challenges of distinguishing between the potentially different roles of advertising, and in particular whether it was possible to distinguish empirically informative from persuasive effects of advertising. Three types of effects of advertising are highlighted, namely those that provide (i) 'Information on product existence and search characteristics', (ii) 'Information on experience characteristics', and (iii) 'Prestige and image effects' (Ackerberg 2001: 319).

advertising and print advertising in local newspapers. Information on newsprint price advertising for all liquor stores was collected as opposed to just those of the stores in the sample, since this was used to proxy the extent of rivals' advertising on the sample stores. Finally, while data on sales volumes were unavailable, lottery ticket sales were used as a proxy for customer traffic to the individual liquor stores.

In order to distinguish between these effects, Ackerberg relies on the distinction between experienced and inexperienced consumers, where experienced consumers have already tried the product while inexperienced consumers have not. He argues that informational advertising about product characteristics should only affect inexperienced consumers. This is because experienced consumers have already consumed the product before and so, presumably, know of the product's existence and characteristics, and so should be unaffected by the advertising. Prestige and image effects, on the other hand, should affect both inexperienced and experienced consumers fairly equally as they both gain the same utility bonus from the advertising associated with the product. If so, Ackerberg then argues that it is possible to infer which type of advertising is driving consumer behaviour by examining consumers' purchasing decisions following their repeated exposures to adverts.[11]

Ackerberg examines the effects of advertising exposure upon consumers' tendency to make purchases of Yoplait 150 (a yoghurt product),[12] in particular to test whether the effectiveness of advertising declines over multiple samplings of the product. He finds that, in this case, the effect of advertising on inexperienced consumers is positive and statistically significant while its effect on experienced consumers remains statistically insignificant. This implies that the advertising of Yoplait 150 was only affecting those consumers who had not already tried the product. In fact, he finds that the effect of advertising on consumption rapidly declines after the first sampling and concludes that this is indicative that the advertising is, in fact, informational advertising as opposed to prestige advertising. Therefore, in this particular case the role of advertising appears to be one of informing the customer of the product's characteristics and other information, such as pricing or

[11] The paper uses a consumer-level panel dataset including household-level grocery purchases (via scanner data) and exposure to advertising (using A. C. Nielson TV meter data). The dataset consists of 2,000 households within two separate towns in South Dakota and Missouri for the years from 1986 to 1988 and includes data on prices, redeemed coupons, advertising exposures, and shopping purchases for four different products, but ultimately focusses primarily on consumer behaviour when purchasing a particular type of yogurt.

[12] The authors' empirical analysis focuses on a particular product, Yoplait 150. He chooses this product because it was introduced in the middle of the dataset. That provides an advantage that we can tell which customers have, and which have not, previously purchased the product. In contrast, if one chose a product that entered the market prior to the start of the data series, it would be impossible to distinguish reliably between those customers who have experience of the product and those who do not.

existence, as opposed to explicitly boosting the utility gained from consuming the product.

Conclusions

We began with the observation that branding is clearly important and we have outlined why economists typically consider that the effects of brands on welfare and competition may be potentially either positive or negative, depending on the facts of a particular case. Branding that (i) solves informational problems either by quality signalling or eliminating search costs, or (ii) directly improves consumer welfare because consumers value the brand, or (iii) reduces entry barriers into new markets by diversifying firms, can have significant pro-competitive effects. On the other hand, branding that constitutes a high barrier to entry or expansion and results in significant customer loyalty (reduced consumer price sensitivity as rival products are perceived to be poorer substitutes) has the potential to result in significant anti-competitive effects.

The implication is that competition authorities must take a case-by-case approach to the effect of branding on welfare in a particular market. As always, the economic literature provides both some worrying evidence about the impact of brands on, in particular uninformed, consumer choice and at the same time cautions against intervention without careful investigation of the effects of branding in the market at hand.

In terms of the question posed originally at the 2012 conference 'Economics and Branding: Friend or Foe?', our response is a normative one. Economics should always be a friend to understanding market realities and branding is a part of reality in many markets. Economists and policymakers should endeavour to provide an objective analysis of its effects – which may prove to be positive in some industries and negative in others.

References

Ackerberg, Daniel (2001). 'Empirically Distinguishing Informative and Prestige Effects of Advertising', *RAND Journal of Economics* 32 (2): 316–33.

Arrington, R. L. (1982). 'Advertising and Behavior Control', *Journal of Business Ethics* 1: 3–12.

Bagwell, K. (2007). 'The Economic Analysis of Advertising', in R. Schmalenssee, M. Armstrong and R. D. Willig, *Handbook of Industrial Organization*, Amsterdam: Elsevier, Volume 3, Chapter 28.

Becker, Gary and Kevin Murphy (1993). 'A Simple Theory of Advertising as a Good or Bad', *The Quarterly Journal of Economics* 108(4): 941–64.

Bronnenberg, B., J. P. Dubé, M. Gentzkow and J. M. Shapiro (2014). 'Do Pharmacists Buy Bayer? Informed Shoppers and the Brand Premium', mimeo, Chicago and NBER. Available from: http://faculty.chicagobooth.edu/jesse.shapiro/research/generics.pdf (accessed 26 April 2014).

Chamberlain, E. (1933). *The Theory of Monopolistic Competition: A Re-orientation of the Theory of Value*, Cambridge, MA: Harvard University Press, 1965 8th edn.

Crisp, R. (1987) 'Persuasive Advertising, Autonomy and the Creation of Desire', *Journal of Business Ethics* 6(5): 413–18.

Desai, D. and S. Weber Waller (2014) 'The Competitive Significance of Brands.' Antitrust Chronicle, Competition Policy International, July, No. 2. Available from: www.competitionpolicyinternational.com/the-competitive-significance-of-brands/.

Galbraith, J. K. (1958). *The Affluent Society*, Boston, MA: Houghton Mifflin.

Hotelling, H. (1929). 'Stability in Competition', *The Economic Journal* 29(153): 41–57.

Kaldor, N. V. (1950). 'The Economic Aspects of Advertising', *Review of Economic Studies* 18: 1–27.

Lafontaine, F. (1992) 'Agency Theory and Franchising: Some Empirical Results' *RAND*, 7(1): 263–83.

Lee, Nick, Amanda J. Broderick and Laura Chamberlain (2007). 'What Is "Neuromarketing"? A Discussion and Agenda for Future Research', *International Journal of Psychophysiology* 63(2): 199–204.

Marshall, A. (1890). *Principles of Economics*, London: Macmillan and Co. Ltd, London.

(1919). *Industry and Trade*, McMillan and Co. Ltd, London.

Mathewson, G. F. and R. A. Winter (1985). 'The Economics of Franchise Contracts', *Journal of Law and Economics* 28(3): 503–26.

Milgrom, Paul and John Roberts (1986). 'Price and Advertising Signals of Product Quality', *Journal of Political Economy* 94(4): 796–821.

Milyo, Jeffrey and Joel Waldfogel (1999). 'The Effect of Price Advertising on Prices: Evidence in the Wake of 44 Liquormart', *The American Economic Review* 89(5): 1081–96.

Nelson, Phillip (1974). 'Advertising as Information', *Journal of Political Economy* 82(4): 729–54.

Stigler, George (1961). 'The Economics of Information', *Journal of Political Economy* 69(3): 213–25.

Stigler, George and Gary Becker (1977). 'De Gustibus Non Est Disputandum', *The American Economic Review* 67(2): 76–90.

Telser, L. (1964). 'Advertising and Competition', *The Journal of Political Economy*, 76(6): 537–62.

Veblen, T. B. (1899). *The Theory of the Leisure Class. An Economic Study of Institutions*, London: Macmillan Publishers.

2

Bayer or Walgreen's?

The relationship of premium and value brands in the United States

JAMES LANGENFELD, WENQING LI, AND SOPHIE YANG

1. Introduction

There are substantial sales of 'private label' or 'store brands' for many consumer goods, and relatively modest sales in others. The presence and effects of store brands can have important implications for retail pricing strategy, product positioning, and brand management. For example, if a national brand is considering lowering its price, would the national brand likely take sales away from a store brand and potentially irritate the retailer?

Not surprisingly, a number of researchers have studied various aspects of the competitive interaction between national brand and store brand. To test some of these results, we use store-level scanner data from Dominick's Fine Foods, a large United States retail chain now out of business, to study the interactions of national and store brands. In particular, we see if store brands provide a competitive constraint on national brands similar to the constraint that other national brands provide. We independently estimate own- and cross-price elasticities[1] in bathroom tissues (where several national brands compete with the retailer's brand). In addition, we estimate the independent impact of promotion on own and competitor sales. Finally, we discuss some of the implications of our findings for strategic analysis of pricing and promotion. The analysis of promotions and the effectiveness of store brand competition have not been the primary focus in previous research.

[1] Own-price elasticity measures the change of the quantity demanded of a good to a change in its own prices. Cross-price elasticity measures the change of the quantity demanded of a good to a change in the prices of other goods.

In brief, we find the following:

- National brands sales are often *more price-sensitive* than store brands.
- National brands often *compete more closely* with one another than with store brands.
- Price changes in national brands often affect sales of store brands *more than store brand price changes affect national brands.*
- The entry of store brands can lead to an increase in the own-price elasticities of national brands.
- Promotions affect sales independent of actual prices in *economically predictable ways.*

2. The use of elasticity to assess the competitive interaction between national brands and store brands

Analysis of the competitive interaction of consumer goods can provide useful insights for business pricing and promotional strategies. For example, suppose there are four brands in a product category, three national brands, A, B, and C, and a store brand D. Following Green and Alston,[2] let ε_{ij} represent demand elasticity for brand *i* with respect to the price of brand *j*. That is, ε_{ij} is the percentage change in quantity demanded of good *i* due to a percentage change in the price of good *j*. In short, one expects the 'cross-price' elasticity to be positive, indicating that a price increase in *j* would increase the sales of the substitute good *i*. In contrast, the 'own-price' elasticity of ε_{ii} indicates the impact of a price change in a good on the sales of that good itself. In general, these own-price elasticities are negative. When comparing own-price elasticities, we will discuss them in absolute terms. If ε_{AD} is equal to ε_{AC}, it means that a 1 per cent reduction in the price of store brand D can reduce the sales of the competing brand A by the same percentage as a 1 per cent reduction in the price of national brand C. Similarly, if ε_{DA} is equal to ε_{CA}, it means that if brand A raises its price by 1 per cent, then the sales of store brand D and the sales of the national brand C will increase by the same percentage.

On the other hand, if ε_{AD} is much smaller than ε_{AC}, a decrease in the price of store brand D will have a much smaller impact on the sales of brand A than a decrease in the price of national brand C. If ε_{DA} is much smaller than ε_{CA}, then most of the lost sales by brand A when it raises its

[2] R. Green and J. M. Alston, 'Elasticities in AIDS Models', *American Journal of Agricultural Economics*, 72(2) (1990), 442–5.

price will be diverted to national brand C instead of to store brand D.[3] Similar analyses can be done regarding the impact of promotions, to the extent their effect is in addition to pricing.

In sum, if a national brand's cross-elasticity of demand with respect to the price of store brand is similar to the cross-price elasticity between this national brand and other national brands, it indicates that the store brand can compete with the national brand in question as effectively as other national brands do. If not, the national brand can focus its competitive concerns on the other national brands.

3. Existing Research

Existing research provides some useful information about how national and store brands interact in a number of consumer goods products, focusing on their own and cross-price elasticities. Table 2.1 summarizes their findings, and we next discuss the empirical regularities.

A. *Own-price elasticity of national brands vs. own-price elasticity of store brands*

Table 2.1 shows national brands sales are often *more price-sensitive* than store brands. In effect, we find the own-price elasticity of national brands to be greater than that of store brands in 26 of 36 comparisons.

As discussed in Fong *et al.* (2011), there are reasons for store brands to have a higher own-price demand elasticity (bigger impact on sales in response to price change); for example, price-sensitive customers are more likely to select store brands, store brands are undifferentiated so price is the key differentiator, and store brands may lack brand credibility.[4] However, there are also reasons to expect store brands to have a lower own-price demand elasticity, such as selective entry by retailers and lack of substitutes at lowest price point. The empirical findings summarized in Table 2.1 are more consistent with the latter explanations.

For example, Song and Chintagunta (2006) use Dominick's[5] store-level scanner data to study the cross-category effects of marketing activities

[3] For simplicity, we assume the unit sales of brand C and store brand D are similar before brand A raises its price.

[4] N. M. Fong, D. I. Simester, and E. T. Anderson, 'Private Label vs. National Brand Price Sensitivity: Evaluating Non-Experimental Identification Strategies', working paper (2011), pp. 3–5.

[5] Dominick's Finer Foods used to be a large Midwestern supermarket chain.

Table 2.1 *Summary of own- and cross-price elasticity estimates in the literature*

	Oats[1]	Frozen Pasta[1]	Liquid Detergent[2]	Liquid Softener[2]	Sheet Softener[2]	Toothpaste
Number of National Brands	1	4	3	3	3	8
Share of National Brands	0.927	0.806	0.942	0.947	0.759	NA
Share of Store Brand	0.073	0.194	0.058	0.053	0.241	NA
Number of Cases Where E(N)>E(P)	1 out of 1	4 out of 4	3 out of 3	2 out of 3	3 out of 3	3 out of 8
Number of Cases Where E(PN)>E(NP)	NA	2 out of 4	3 out of 3	3 out of 3	2 out of 3	1 out of 1[6]
Number of Cases Where E(NN)>E(PN)	NA	6 out of 12	E(NN)≈ E(PN)[3]	E(NN)≈ E(PN)[4]	0 out of 6[5]	7 out of 8[7]
Number of Cases Where E(NN)>E(NP)	NA	7 out of 12	6 out of 6	6 out of 6	4 out of 6	8 out of 8[8]
Sources	Chintagunta *et al.* (2002)		Song and Chintagunta (2006)			Kamakura and Kang (2006)

Definitions: E(N): own-price elasticity of national brand; E(P): own-price elasticity of private label; (PN): cross-elasticity of demand of private label with respect to the price of national brand; E(NP): cross-elasticity of demand for national brand with respect to the price of private label E(NN): cross-elasticity between national brands. NA: not available or not applicable.

Notes:

1 For oats and frozen pasta, the shares are based on unit sales per week and per store in Tables 1 and 6 in Chintagunta *et al.* (2002). For the frozen pasta, none of the cross-elasticity is greater than 0.01 in absolute value.

2 For liquid detergent, liquid softener, and sheet softener, the shares are based on the relative volume shares in Table 1 in Song and Chintagunta (2006). In additional to two individual national brands, the researchers combined other national brands into the 'All Other' category. The elasticity comparison is based on the estimates from their discrete choice model.

3 For liquid detergent, although E(NN)>E(NP), none of the differences are greater than 0.01.

4 For liquid softener, none of the differences between E(NN) and E(PN) are greater than 0.02.

5 Although in two cases for sheet softener, E(NN)>E(PN), the differences are only 0.007 and 0.006 respectively so we treat them as roughly equal in these two cases.

6 In the toothpaste category, only one cross-elasticity involving the store brand is positive and statistically significant. In this case, we have E(PN)>E(NP).

Toothbrush	Pool of 125 categories	Milk, Butter, Bread, Pasta, Margarine, and Instant Coffee	Pool of multiple product categories	All-purpose Flour[10]	Bathroom Tissue[10]
7	NA	NA	NA	3	7
NA	0.721	NA	NA	NA	NA
NA	0.279	NA	NA	NA	NA
6 out of 7	E(N)≈ E(P)	3 out of 6	1 out of 1	NA	NA
NA[9]	1 out of 1	5 out of 6	NA	1 out of 3	2 out of 6
NA[9]	NA	NA	NA	2 out of 6	4 out 6[11]
NA[9]	NA	NA	NA	3 out of 6	6 out of 7[11]
	Cotterill *et al.* (2000)	Fong *et al.* (2011)		Blattberg and Wisniewski (1989)	

[7] In the toothpaste category, only one E(PN) is positive and significant and others are all insignificant or negative and significant. Many E(NN)s are also insignificant, but for a given national brand at least one E(NN) is positive and significant, so this cell represents the number of national brands where at least one E(NN) is larger than E(PN).

[8] In the toothpaste category, all E(NP) are either insignificant or negative and significant. Many E(NN)s are also insignificant, but for a given national brand at least one E(NN) is positive and significant, so this cell represents the number of national brands where at least one E(NN) is bigger than E(NP).

[9] In the toothbrush category, none of the cross-elasticity involving the store brand is statistically significant and only three cross-elasticity estimates between national brands are positive and statistically significant, so no meaningful comparison can be made.

[10] The generic brand is excluded from the summary.

[11] Because many cross-elasticities are insignificant, the cell represents the number of national brands where at least one E(NN) is bigger than E(PN) or E(NP).

in four product categories: liquid laundry detergents, powdered laundry detergents, liquid fabric softeners, and sheet fabric softeners.[6] The individual brand's own and cross-price elasticities presented in Song and Chintagunta show that the store brand's own-price elasticity is typically smaller than that of national brands. Only in one case is a national brand's own-price elasticity smaller than that of the store brand.[7] Using both data from a field experiment and historical data at a large retail chain, Fong *et al.* also find that national brands exhibit larger demand elasticity than store brands.[8]

However, for some products store brands exhibit larger or similar demand elasticity than national brands. For example, Cotterill *et al.* (2001) use the Information Resources, Inc. (IRI) data to examine the competition between national and store brands at both the cross-category level and the intra-category level.[9] Cotterill *et al.* examine six product categories in their intra-category study: milk, butter, bread, pasta, margarine, and instant coffee.[10] Unlike many other researchers, Cotterill *et al.* find that the store brand's own-price elasticity is higher than that of national brands in three categories.[11]

B. *Change of sales of national brands in response to price changes in other national brands and store brands*

Previous research indicates that national brands often compete more closely with one another than with store brands, although exceptions do exist, as shown in Table 2.1.

For example, according to Song and Chintagunta (2006), for liquid detergent and liquid softener, demand for a national brand is more

[6] I. Song and P. K. Chintagunta, 'Measuring Cross-Category Price Effects with Aggregate Store Data', *Management Science*, 52(10) (2006), 1594–609.

[7] Song and Chintagunta, 'Measuring Cross-Category Price Effects': 1594, 1605. We only summarize their within-category elasticity estimates in this chapter. All the within-category elasticity estimates are statistically significant at the 5 per cent level in Song and Chintagunta, 'Measuring Cross-Category Price Effects', Table 5: 1605. Unless noted otherwise, we always refer to the absolute value of elasticity when we discuss whether one elasticity is larger than another. In the literature review, we do not assess the statistical significance when we compare two elasticity estimates unless the authors have assessed the statistical significance in their original research.

[8] Fong *et al.*, 'Private Label vs. National Brand Price Sensitivity': 11, 14–15.

[9] R. W. Cotterill, W. P. Putsis, Jr., and R. Dhar, 'Assessing the Competitive Interaction between Private Labels and National Brands', *Journal of Business*, 73(1) (2001), 109–37.

[10] *Ibid.*, Table 5: 125. [11] *Ibid.*, 125–6.

sensitive to the price changes of other national brands than to the price changes of the store brand.[12] For sheet softener, demand for a national brand is sometimes more sensitive to the price changes of store brands than to the price changes of other national brands.[13]

Kamakura and Kang (2007) estimate both the within-category and the cross-category elasticity for toothpaste and toothbrush using Dominick's store-level data. Kamakura and Kang find that in the toothpaste category, the cross-elasticity of demand for all national brands with respect to the price of Dominick's store brand is not statistically different from zero except for the Ultrabrite brand.[14] In contrast, for a given national brand, there is at least one other national brand where the cross-elasticity between these two national brands is positive and statistically significant.[15]

When a national brand raises its price, sometimes its lost sales are mostly diverted to other national brands, as in the case of toothpaste in the study by Kamakura and Kang, while in other cases, such as the laundry detergent and softeners in Song and Chintagunta, its lost sales are diverted evenly to other national brands and the store brand.

C. The asymmetry in the cross-elasticities between national brands and store brands

As summarized in Table 2.1, researchers often find there is asymmetry between the cross-elasticity of demand for national brands with respect to the price of the store brand and for the store brand with respect to the prices of national brands. That is, a decrease in the price of a national brand is more effective in reducing the demand for private labels than vice versa.

In the six product categories studied by Cotterill *et al.* (2001) – milk, butter, bread, pasta, margarine, and instant coffee – they find that price response between national brands and private label products is asymmetric: 'national brand price cuts are generally more effective in

[12] Song and Chintagunta, 'Measuring Cross-Category Price Effects', Table 5: 1605.

[13] *Ibid.*

[14] W. Kamakura and W. Kang, 'Chain-Wide and Store-Level Analysis for Cross-Category Management', *Journal of Retailing* 83(2) (2007), 159–70, at 164. However, in the Ultrabrite case the cross-elasticity with respect to the price of the store brand is negative.

[15] *Ibid.* However, in the Ultrabrite case the cross-elasticity with respect to the price of the store brand is negative.

stealing share from private labels' than vice versa, except for the butter category.[16]

Similarly, among the four product categories (liquid laundry detergents, powdered laundry detergents, liquid fabric softeners, and sheet fabric softeners) studied in Song and Chintagunta (2006), their elasticity estimates suggest that the demand for store brand products are more responsive to price cuts in national brands than vice versa, with the Snuggle brand of sheet softener as the only exception.[17]

D. *The impact of store brand entry on the own-price elasticity of national brands*

Chintagunta *et al.* (2002) conduct within-category analysis to evaluate how the entry of a private label product affects the national brands in the oats product and the frozen pasta product categories, using the scanner data from Dominick's Finer Foods. The oats product category has only one national brand, the Quaker brand, while the frozen pasta category studied by Chintagunta *et al.* has four national brands. Chintagunta *et al.* show that formal statistical tests cannot reject the hypothesis that there is no significant change in the mean value of Quaker's price elasticity after the entry of the store brand.[18] However, the authors find that the own-price elasticity of all four national brands increases with the introduction of the store brand. The increase in elasticity is statistically significant for three national brands at the 5 per cent significant level and at the 10 per cent significant level for one national brand.[19]

E. *Impact of promotion*

When estimating the demand equations for national and store brands, researchers often include promotion variables as a demand shifter, as can be seen in Cotterill *et al.* (2001), Chintagunta *et al.* (2002), and Song and Chintagunta (2006). As expected, researchers often find statistically significant positive own promotion advertising effects and statistically

[16] Cotterill *et al.*, 'Assessing the Competitive Interaction': 125–6.

[17] Song and Chintagunta, 'Measuring Cross-Category Price Effects', Table 5: 1605.

[18] P. K. Chintagunta, A. Bonfrer, and I. Song, 'Investigating the Effects of Store-Brand Introduction on Retailer Demand and Pricing Behavior', *Management Science*, 48(10) (2002), 1258–9. Chintagunta *et al.* also examine the effect of the store brand entry on retailer's mark-up.

[19] *Ibid.*, 1264–5.

significant negative cross-promotion advertising effects. For example, according to Cotterill *et al.*, a 1 per cent increase in the volume of branded products on display at the point of the sales raises the branded product sales by 0.023 per cent, while reducing the sales of the private label products by 0.078 per cent.[20]

4. Analysis of bathroom tissues

To independently check the results of these other researchers, we use the Dominick's store-level scanner data to estimate the own- and cross-price elasticities for bathroom tissue products, and compare our estimates to the research we have reviewed on a variety of different branded products above.

As shown in Table 2.1, Blattberg and Wisniewski (1989) also estimated elasticities of bathroom tissue products.[21] Our study of the bathroom tissue products differs from that in Blattberg and Wisniewski in two aspects. First, Blattberg and Wisniewski use the scanner data from Jewel Food Stores, another leading grocery chain in Chicago. We use more recent data from a different supermarket chain in the Chicago area. Second, Blattberg and Wisniewski use a log linear functional form in their econometric estimation, while we use the almost ideal demand system (AIDS) specification in our estimation. Our study is complementary to Blattberg and Wisniewski, providing a test of robustness of the results regarding bathroom tissue products when different data and econometric specification are used.

A. *Description of the data*

To estimate own and cross-elasticities for bathroom tissue, we used publicly available data from the Kilts Center for Marketing at the University of Chicago Booth School of Business, which is similar to the data used by Blattberg and Wisniewski and other researchers. The data include weekly store-level transaction prices, quantities, percentage mark-ups, and discount information for over 100 stores operated by Dominick's Finer Foods (DFF), which is a major grocery chain in the Chicago area. The data spans September 1989 to April 1997 (399 weeks).[22]

[20] Cotterill *et al.*, 'Assessing the Competitive Interaction': 122–3.

[21] R. Blattberg and K. Wisniewski, 'Price-Induced Patterns of Competition', *Marketing Science*, 8(4) (1989), 291–309.

[22] Although it could be useful to have data for more than one chain, it is likely that inclusion of other chains in our study would have little effect on our estimation of substitution

There are a total of 16 brands in the bathroom tissue category, including Dominick's store brand, during the entire sample period. We have combined brands with less than 5 per cent market shares into the 'Others' brand category. As a result, we estimate the demand equations for 7 brands in the bathroom tissue category: Scott, Charmin, Northern, Cottonelle, Kleenex, Dominick's, and Others.[23]

B. *Econometric model*

We use the linear approximate almost ideal demand system (LA/AIDS) model to estimate the demand for the bathroom tissue products. Previous research often includes a promotion variable as a demand shifter, as seen in Cotterill *et al.* (2001), Chintagunta (2002),[24] Chintagunta *et al.* (2002), and Song and Chintagunta (2006). We also include the percentage of volume of a brand under promotion as an independent variable.[25]

We include store dummies in our regression as well because stores in different areas can have different demographics that can affect demand. We estimate seven equations with the following specification:

patterns (K. Sudhir, 'Structural Analysis of Manufacturer Pricing in the Presence of a Strategic Retailer', *Marketing Science*, 20(3) (2001), 244–64; P. K. Chintagunta, J.-P. Dubé, and S. Vishal, 'Balancing Profitability and Customer Welfare in a Supermarket Chain', *Quantitative Marketing and Economics*, 1(1) (2003), pp. 111–47). In effect, substitution between individual products sold in different stores would require the customer to incur additional transactions costs that may not be worthwhile for a single product in a basket of products typically purchased at a supermarket.

[23] Among the Others brand category, Whitecloud was a relatively large brand. However, Dominick's stopped selling the Whitecloud brand after week 223. In addition, Cottonelle's sales decreased dramatically after week 339 while its price remained at the same level as before. Inspection of the data shows that Cottonelle sales were zero at many stores after week 339, so we suspect the data for Cottonelle are incomplete in the Dominick's data after week 339. Therefore, we use data from week 224 to week 339 (23 December 1993 to 13 March 1996) in our econometric estimation to maintain data consistency. We drop the observations that are flagged as invalid in the Dominick's data and where both sales and quantities are zero. There are a few instances where we have zero bathroom tissue sales for a particular brand for a whole store for a specific week. These observations are dropped in the final regression analysis because they do not contain complete data for all brands, so we have unbalanced panel data. In the period from week 224 to week 339 there are only 11 brands, including the store brand, in Dominick's data and all the brands that are included in the Others brand category account for less than 5 per cent of the market share in the period from week 224 to week 339.

[24] P. K. Chintagunta, 'Investigating Category Pricing Behavior at a Retail Chain', *Journal of Marketing Research*, 39(2) (2002), 141–54.

[25] The promotion variable in the Dominick's data indicates whether the promotion is a bonus buy, coupon, or a simple price reduction. When Blattberg and Wisniewski use

$$s_{int} = \propto_i + \sum_{j=1}^{K} \gamma_{ij} \ln\left(p_{jnt}\right) + \beta_i \ln\left(\frac{X_{nt}}{P_{nt}}\right) + \theta_i \cdot t$$
$$+ \sum_{j=1}^{K} \varphi_{ij}\, prom_{jnt} + \sum_{n=1}^{N} d_{ij} \delta_n + \mu_{int} \quad (1)$$

where s_{int} is the share of brand *i* in store *n* in week *t* and i=1–7;[26] p_{jnt} is the price of brand *j* in store *n* in week *t*; X_{nt} is the customers' total expenditure on bathroom tissue in store *n* in week *t*; $ln\left(P_{nt}\right)$ is Stone's price index and $lnP_{nt} = \sum_{j=1}^{K} s_{jnt} ln\left(P_{jnt}\right)$; *t* is the time trend; $prom_{jnt}$ is the percentage of volume of brand *j* under promotion in store *n* in week *t*; δ_n is the store dummy, and μ_{int} is the unobserved random factor that affects demand. The average price, share, and percentage under promotion of each brand are listed in Table 2.2.

Given (1), the Marshallian elasticity of demand for good *i* with respect to the price of good *j* can be expressed as:[27]

$$\varepsilon_{ij} = \delta_{ij} - \frac{\gamma_{ij}}{\bar{s}_i} - \beta_i \frac{\bar{s}_j}{\bar{s}_i} \quad (2)$$

the Jewel data to estimate cross-elasticities, they note that 'weekly data were collected Monday through Sunday and the price reported on the data tape was the Sunday price'. Blattberg and Wisniewski, 'Price-Induced Patterns of Competition', 298. However, price deals are typically offered Thursday through Wednesday in the Chicago area, so if the price was higher or lower in the first part of the week, this was not recorded. It is not clear if the prices in the Dominick's data include all the price reductions due to promotion. To the extent they do, the coefficient of the promotion variable would measure additional promotional effect on sales beyond the price effect. Although there are potential issues in the endogeneity of the promotional variable, Chintagunta shows that the promotional variable can be assumed as uncorrelated with the unobserved factors that affect price in the Dominick's data. See Chintagunta, 'Investigating Category Pricing Behavior', 147–8. Accordingly, we treat the promotional variable as exogenous.

26 The actual estimation is done on s1–s6 because of the constraint of all market shares summing up to one.

27 As pointed out by Green and Alston, although this elasticity formula treats shares as exogenous, it approximates the fully specified elasticity formula for the LA/AIDS model very well. Green and Alston, 'Elasticities in AIDS Models'. Other researchers have used this simplified formula to calculate the elasticity based on the parameter estimates from the LA/AIDS model. For example, see Cotterill *et al.*, 'Assessing the Competitive Interaction'.

Table 2.2 *Summary statistics by brand*
Weekly Data, 23/12/1993–13/3/1996

	Weighted Average Dollar Market Share	Weighted Average Price	Weighted Average Profit Margin	Per cent of Volume Sold on Promotion
KLEENEX	10.82%	\$0.57	12.39%	31.91%
SCOTT	20.57%	\$0.48	1.43%	48.86%
CHARMIN	26.18%	\$0.29	6.26%	37.11%
NORTHERN	18.54%	\$0.28	7.17%	39.57%
COTTONELLE	11.59%	\$0.28	8.61%	48.50%
DOMINICK'S	5.87%	\$0.27	20.15%	26.25%
OTHERS	6.43%	\$0.23	18.29%	50.82%

where $\delta_{ij} = 1$ if $i = j$, and $\delta_{ij} = 0$ otherwise and $\bar{s}_l$ is sample average market share.

A number of researchers, such as Song and Chintagunta (2006) and Chintagunta (2002),[28] have used the wholesale prices in Dominick's data as instruments when estimating demand functions because of the potential endogeneity of the price variables in equation (1).

However, as discussed in Chintagunta (2002), the manner in which the wholesale price series are constructed in the Dominick's data raises concerns about the validity of using the wholesale prices as the instruments.[29]

Chintagunta (2002) also discusses other circumstances that could make wholesale prices as invalid instruments, such as if manufacturers take into consideration the specific demand drivers in each retail chain while setting the wholesale prices, or if the unobserved term in μ_{int}

[28] See Song and Chintagunta, 'Measuring Cross-Category Price Effects': 1601 and Chintagunta, 'Investigating Category Pricing Behavior': 147–8.

[29] Chintagunta, 'Investigating Category Pricing Behavior': 148. According to Chintagunta, 'The reported wholesale price in week *t* is not the replacement cost in week *t* but the average cost of inventory held by the chain. This implies that the reported wholesale price depends on current and lagged replacement costs and lagged sales. This is problematic if there is serial correlation in the unobserved term μ_{jt}, because it would imply a correlation between μ_{jt} and the wholesale price at time *t*, thereby invalidating these wholesale prices

equation (1) reflects manufacturer-level decision variables such as television advertising.[30]

When using store-level data and the AIDS model to estimate demand functions for beer, Hausman *et al.* (1994) point out that to the extent that supermarkets set their prices under a constant marginal cost assumption in the short run and do not alter their prices to equilibrate supply and demand in a given week, prices in equation (1) may be predetermined and can be treated as exogenous.[31] This condition is likely to be met in the Dominick's data. According to the Kilts Center for Marketing at the University of Chicago, which made the Dominick's data available for the public, 'the chain sets retail prices for the next week and also determines [average acquisition cost] at the end of each week.'[32]

Given the potential issues of using the wholesale prices as instruments and the likelihood that the weekly prices in the Dominick's data can be treated as predetermined, we estimate equation (1) using the ordinary least square (OLS) regression.[33]

C. *Estimation results for bathroom tissue products*

1. Results of price elasticity estimates

Table 2.3 presents regression coefficients and Table 2.4 presents the own- and cross-price elasticity estimates for the bathroom tissue products. All of the estimates of the own-price elasticity are negative and statistically significant. The own-price elasticity of the store brand is lower than that of the national brands, similar to the findings of other researchers for many other products.[34]

as instruments.' The unobserved term in equation (1) in this chapter is μ_{int}. See also information about the wholesale prices in the Dominick's data provided by the Kilts Center for Marketing at the University of Chicago at http://research.chicagobooth.edu/marketing/databases/dominicks/movement.aspx.

30 *Ibid.*, 147–8.

31 J. Hausman, G. Leonard, and J. D. Zona, 'Competitive Analysis with Differentiated Products', *Annales D'Economie ET DE Statistique*, 34 (1994), 195.

32 See information about the Dominick's data provided by the Kilts Center for Marketing at the University of Chicago at http://research.chicagobooth.edu/marketing/databases/dominicks/movement.aspx.

33 Because the regressors are the same for each brand demand equation, OLS and seemingly unrelated regressions produce the same result.

34 Some of the tissue products are double roll or big roll tissue products and the prices of the double roll or big roll tissue products are roughly double the prices of the single roll tissue products. The percentage of the sales accounted for by the double/big roll tissue products

Most of the estimates of the cross-price elasticity are positive and statistically significant, which is consistent with economic theory that different brands of bathroom tissue are substitutes for each other. There are two negative and statistically significant cross-elasticity estimates but, as discussed in Kamakura and Kang (2007), some counter-intuitive negative cross-elasticity estimates are not uncommon in previous research.[35]

The cross-elasticities between national brands and the store brand do not exhibit a clear pattern of asymmetry, as was often found by other researchers. For the Scott, Northern, and Kleenex brands, price changes in national brands affect sales of the store brand more than store brand price changes affect national brands. However, for Charmin, Cottonelle, and 'Others', a price reduction in the store brand can steal more sales from the national brands than vice versa.

Similar to what other researchers have found for many other products, in most of the cases the cross-elasticity of demand for a national brand with respect to the price of the store brand is smaller than between this national brand and another national brand. For example, a 1 per cent decrease in the price of Dominick's store brand can reduce the demand for the Cottonelle brand bathroom tissue by 0.22 per cent. In contrast, if the price of the Northern brand decreases by 1 per cent, this can lower the Cottonelle brand sales by 1.4 per cent. A 1 per cent price reduction in the Charmin and Kleenex brands can also lower the sales of the Cottonelle brand by about 0.77 per cent and 0.85 per cent, respectively.

The cross-elasticity of demand for the Dominick's store brand with respect to the price of a national brand is also often lower than between two national brands. For example, if the Northern brand raises its price by 1 per cent, the sales of the Scott, Charmin, and Cottonelle brands will increase by about 1 per cent or higher. In contrast, Dominick's store brand's sales will only increase by 0.17 per cent.[36]

varies somewhat from week to week for different brands. To investigate if the changes in the product mix of double/big roll vs. single roll have any significant impact on the results of estimation, we convert the double and big rolls into single rolls by dividing the prices of double and big rolls by 2 and multiplying the unit sales of double and big rolls by 2. The price elasticity estimates remain basically the same after the conversion is made. The regression results are available from the authors upon request.

35 Kamakura and Kang, 'Chain-Wide and Store-Level Analysis': 164.

36 However, if the Others brand raises its price by 1 per cent, Dominick's store brand will experience a larger increase in sales than other national brands do.

Table 2.3 *Regression results of LA/AIDS demand equations with fixed store effect*

Weekly Data, 23/12/1993–13/3/1996

	Equation 1 Brand= SCOTT	Equation 2 Brand= CHARMIN	Equation 3 Brand= NORTHERN	Equation 4 Brand= COTTONELLE	Equation 5 Brand= KLEENEX	Equation 6 Brand= DOMINICK'S	Equation 1 Brand= OTHERS
SCOTT Price	−.5162***	.1406***	.128***	.0548***	.0645***	.0397***	.0885***
	(t=−61.49)	(t=19.86)	(t=17.98)	(t=8.97)	(t=15.72)	(t=15.)	(t=)
CHARMIN Price	.1891***	−.574***	.1784***	.0854***	.0115***	.0137***	.096***
	(t=30.49)	(t=−109.78)	(t=33.93)	(t=18.91)	(t=3.79)	(t=7.02)	(t=)
NORTHERN Price	.3189***	.2582***	−.8885***	.1599***	.0239***	.0045	.1231
	(t=28.56)	(t=27.42)	(t=−93.85)	(t=19.67)	(t=4.38)	(t=1.27)	(t=)
COTTONELLE Price	.1204***	.1091***	.1299***	.1599***	.0368***	.0078***	.0748***
	(t=16.27)	(t=17.48)	(t=20.71)	(t=−88.84)	(t=10.16)	(t=3.34)	(t=)
KLEENEX Price	.137***	−.1365**	.2007***	.0967***	−.4217***	.0368***	.0869***
	(t=5.11)	(t=−6.04)	(t=8.83)	(t=4.96)	(t=−32.17)	(t=4.36)	(t=)
DOMINICK'S Price	−.1244***	.1074***	−.0066	.0244***	.0042	−.053***	.0481***
	(t=−19.06)	(t=19.51)	(t=−1.19)	(t=5.13)	(t=1.32)	(t=−25.75)	(t=)
OTHERS Price	.025**	−.0131	.0757***	.0035	.0237***	.0309***	−.1457***
	(t=2.49)	(t=−1.55)	(t=8.91)	(t=.48)	(t=4.84)	(t=9.77)	(t=)

Table 2.3 (*cont.*)

	Equation 1 Brand= SCOTT	Equation 2 Brand= CHARMIN	Equation 3 Brand= NORTHERN	Equation 4 Brand= COTTONELLE	Equation 5 Brand= KLEENEX	Equation 6 Brand= DOMINICK'S	Equation 1 Brand= OTHERS
SCOTT Promotion	.0469***	−.0037	−.0309***	−.0051**	.0009	−.0121***	.0039**
	(t=16.99)	(t=−1.58)	(t=−13.18)	(t=−2.52)	(t=.63)	(t=−13.82)	(t=2.3)
CHARMIN Promotion	−.0091***	.0337***	.006**	−.0081***	−.0093***	−.0016	−.0116***
	(t=−2.67)	(t=11.69)	(t=2.08)	(t=−3.27)	(t=−5.56)	(t=−1.45)	(t=−5.5)
NORTHERN Promotion	.0151***	−.0078***	.0437***	−.0105***	−.0132***	−.0098***	−.0175***
	(t=4.31)	(t=−2.64)	(t=14.7)	(t=−4.1)	(t=−7.72)	(t=−8.86)	(t=−8.18)
COTTONELLE Promotion	−.0159***	−.005**	−.0102***	.0388***	.0019	−.0002	−.0095
	(t=−5.37)	(t=−1.99)	(t=−4.05)	(t=17.97)	(t=1.34)	(t=−.21)	(t=−5.22)
KLEENEX Promotion	.0021	−.0478***	−.0045	.0027	.0576***	−.0042***	−.0059***
	(t=.63)	(t=−17.22)	(t=−1.61)	(t=1.13)	(t=35.74)	(t=−4.03)	(t=−2.91)
DOMINICK'S Promotion	.0027	−.0261***	−.0096***	−.0031	.0196***	.015***	.0014
	(t=.89)	(t=−10.22)	(t=−3.76)	(t=−1.39)	(t=13.28)	(t=15.77)	(t=0.76)
OTHERS Promotion	.0038	.0036	−.0123***	.0038**	−.0072***	−.0008	.0092***

	(t=1.43)	(t=1.62)	(t=−5.55)	(t=1.97)	(t=−5.59)	(t=−.97)	(t=5.75)
Total Expenditure Divided by Stone Price Index	.0499***	.0133***	.024***	−.0133***	−.0563***	−.0285***	.013***
	(t=14.89)	(t=4.02)	(t=8.44)	(t=12.57)	(t=−34.41)	(t=−26.98)	(t=6.35)
Time Trend	.0002***	−.0003***	.0007***	−.0007***	.0003***	.0002***	−.0005***
	(t=5.82)	(t=−8.42)	(t=19.14)	(t=−23.98)	(t=16.66)	(t=17.05)	(t=−18.07)
Intercept	−.033	.209***	−.6208***	.3144***	.4619***	.2948***	.3736***
	(t=−.96)	(t=7.21)	(t=−21.31)	(t=12.57)	(t=27.48)	(t=27.19)	(t=17.82)
Fixed Store Effects	Yes	Yes	Yes	Yes	Yes	Yes	Yes
Observations	8697	8697	8697	8697	8697	8697	8697
R-Square	0.6922	0.8353	0.7842	0.6875	0.6893	0.5651	

Notes:
*** indicates significance at the 1% level; ** indicates significance at the 5% level.
The models were estimated without symmetry or homogeneity assumptions.

Table 2.4 *Own- and cross-price elasticity estimates*

Weekly Data, 23/12/1993–13/3/1996

	SCOTT	CHARMIN	NORTHERN	COTTONELLE	KLEENEX	DOMINICK'S	OTHERS
SCOTT	*−3.5595****	.8558***	1.5054***	.5571***	.64***	−.6193***	.1059**
	(t=−90.53)	(t=30.75)	(t=28.34)	(t=15.59)	(t=4.91)	(t=−19.46)	(t=2.17)
CHARMIN	.5281***	*−3.2042****	.9785***	.4117***	−.5262***	.4077***	−.0529
	(t=20.27)	(t=−173.78)	(t=27.8)	(t=17.38)	(t=−6.09)	(t=19.33)	(t=−1.64)
NORTHERN	.6638***	.9283***	*−5.8161****	.6858***	1.0686***	−.0432	.4001***
	(t=17.95)	(t=35.47)	(t=−116.42)	(t=20.4)	(t=8.72)	(t=−1.44)	(t=8.73)
COTTONELLE	.4966***	.7665***	1.401***	*−5.117****	.8471***	.217***	.0375
	(t=9.77)	(t=21.32)	(t=20.41)	(t=−110.79)	(t=5.03)	(t=5.28)	(t=.6)
KLEENEX	.7032***	.2425***	.3173***	.4***	*−4.8397****	.0696**	.2525***
	(t=19.24)	(t=9.37)	(t=6.43)	(t=12.04)	(t=−39.94)	(t=2.35)	(t=5.58)
DOMINICK'S	.7766***	.3609***	.1662***	.189***	.68***	*−1.8747****	.5572***
	(t=17.87)	(t=11.73)	(t=2.83)	(t=4.78)	(t=4.72)	(t=−53.3)	(t=10.35)
OTHERS	1.3349***	1.4392***	1.8765***	1.1388***	1.3285***	.7358***	*−3.2778****
	(t=17.41)	(t=26.52)	(t=18.11)	(t=16.33)	(t=5.22)	(t=11.85)	(t=−34.49)

Notes:

Effects of column prices on row quantities.

*** indicates significance at the 1% level; ** indicates significance at the 5% level.

The models were estimated with the LA/AIDS model with store fixed effects. No symmetry or homogeneity assumption was applied.

The cross-elasticity estimates based on the OLS regression suggest that for a given national brand bathroom tissue product, other national brands are often closer substitutes than the store brand. However, the store brand does impose a competitive constraint on the national brands, given the relatively large cross-price elasticity estimates between some national brands and the store brand.

2. Results of promotion elasticity estimates

For the promotion variables, we found similar results to the previous research – the promotional effects are all positive and statistically significant as expected as shown in Table 2.3. For example, if the percentage of the volume of the Scott brand under promotion increases by 1 per cent, Scott's dollar sales share will increase by 0.047 per cent if total sales of the bathroom tissue product during the sample period hold constant. This result implies an increase of the unit sales of the Scott brand of 0.23 per cent. Table 2.5 presents the estimates of the promotion elasticities. Unlike the price elasticities, the store brand's own promotion elasticity is higher than three national brands' own promotion elasticities.[37]

As expected, all the statistically significant cross-promotion effects are negative except for three cases, as can be seen in Table 2.3. The corresponding cross-promotion elasticities are shown in Table 2.5. The promotional activities of the Scott, Northern, and Kleenex brands have a bigger negative impact on the store brand than the impact of the store brand's promotional activity has on the national brands. In contrast, the store brand's promotional activity has a greater impact on the Charmin brand than the Charmin brand has on the store brand. The cross-promotion effects between Cottonelle and the store brand are not statistically significant. Accordingly, cross-promotion effects appear to exhibit asymmetry similar to the cross-price elasticity between the national brands and the store brand. That is, the promotional activities of national brands are

[37] Researchers treat the promotion variable as exogenous when they use the Dominick's data to estimate demand elasticities. For example, see Chintagunta *et al.*, 'Investigating the Effects of Store-Brand Introduction', and Song and Chintagunta, 'Measuring Cross-Category Price Effects'. To study if the potential endogeneity of the promotion variable is a serious issue, we use the percentage of the Universal Product Code (UPC) codes under promotion for a given brand as an alternative promotion variable. To the extent that Dominick's decides which product will be under promotion in advance, this alternative promotion variable is less susceptible to the endogeneity issue. The price elasticity estimates using this alternative promotion variable remain basically the same. The regression results are available from the authors upon request.

Table 2.5 *Own- and cross-promotion elasticity estimates*[a]

	SCOTT	CHARMIN	NORTHERN	COTTONELLE	KLEENEX	DOMINICK'S	OTHERS
SCOTT Promotion	*0.2280**	−0.0141	−0.1667*	−0.0440*	0.0083	−.2061*	0.0606*
CHARMIN Promotion	−0.0442*	*0.1287**	0.0324*	−0.0699*	−0.0859*	−0.0273	−0.1803*
NORTHERN Promotion	0.0734*	−0.0298*	*0.2357**	−0.0906*	−0.1220*	−.1669*	−0.2721*
COTTONELLE Promotion	−.0773*	−0.0191*	−0.0550*	*0.3348**	0.0176	−0.0034	−0.1477
KLEENEX Promotion	0.0102	−0.1826*	−0.0243	0.0233	*0.5322**	−0.0715*	−0.0917*
DOMINICK'S Promotion	0.0131	−0.0997*	−0.0518*	−0.0267	0.1811*	*0.2555**	0.0218
OTHERS Promotion	0.0185	0.0138	−0.0663*	0.0328*	−.0665*	−0.0136	*0.1430**

Notes:

[a] The promotion elasticity represents the percentage increase in unit sales of a brand if the per cent of volume under promotion for this brand or another brand increases by 1%, say from 50% to 51%. The table represents the effects of row promotions on column unit sales. The elasticity is evaluated at weight average prices, weighted average shares, and total dollar and unit sales of each brand from week 224 to 339.

* indicates significance at 5% level.

more likely to steal sales from the store brand than vice versa. However, unlike in the case of cross-price elasticities, where the price changes of the store brand often have a smaller impact on the sales of a national brand than the price changes of other national brands, the promotion activities of the store brand can often affect the sales of a national brand as the promotion activities of other national brands do.

5. Implications for business strategy

Although each product market may have different results, our elasticity estimates of the tissue products show relatively large own-price elasticities of the national brands and relatively large cross-elasticities between national brands. The relatively large own-price elasticities of the national brands suggest they are being priced to take advantage of their national brand recognition, and any substantial price increase would not be profitable due to lost sales to other brands and secondarily to store brands.[38] However, store brand competition may be more important in a market with fewer brand name competitors. Store brands in general sell at a discount compared to national brands.

Given the standard discount of store brands against the price of national brands, the store brand should avoid engaging in further discounts or 'price wars' with national brands because of (1) the relatively small own-price elasticity of the store brand compared to the national brands and (2) the relatively low cross-elasticity of demand for national brands with respect to the price of store brand. Under these circumstances, further lowering the price of a store brand will gain relatively few sales from national brands.

To the extent that price reductions associated with Dominick's promotional activities are already reflected in the prices in the Dominick's data, our promotional elasticity estimates imply that promotions can have a noticeable impact on sales beyond the price effect. This additional impact of promotion should be taken into account when the frequency and the magnitude of the promotional activities are determined.

These implications of our research on bathroom tissues should be taken into consideration in pricing national and store brands. However,

[38] Pricing of national brands on the elastic portion of their demand curves with higher prices than store brands is consistent with the national brands being more highly valued by consumers, but they have raised their prices to maximize profits to the point that they would lose substantial sales if they raised prices further.

Table 2.6 *Definitions for variables used in the analysis*

SHARE	Dollar market share
PRICE	Natural log of retail price per-unit volume
PROMOTION	Per cent of volume sold on promotion (Sales flag = B, C, G or S)
EXPENDITURE	Natural log of total expenditure divided by Stone's price index, which is equal to the sum of market share*ln (Price of brand i) across all brands.
TREND	Time trend variable; starting from the week of 23/12/1993
STORE_DUMMY	Dummy variables for each Dominick's store

Table 2.7 *Descriptive statistics*
Weekly Data, 23/12/1993–13/3/1996

	Mean	S.D.	Min.	Max.
SCOTT Price	0.58	0.07	0.25	0.72
CHARMIN Price	0.36	0.07	0.15	0.50
NORTHERN Price	0.31	0.03	0.15	0.36
COTTONELLE Price	0.31	0.04	0.13	0.43
KLEENEX Price	0.58	0.02	0.43	0.65
DOMINICKS' Price	0.29	0.06	0.13	0.58
OTHER BRANDS' Price	0.24	0.03	0.14	0.38
SCOTT Promotion	23.6%	34.4%	0.0%	100.0%
CHARMIN Promotion	21.6%	29.4%	0.0%	99.8%
NORTHERN Promotion	23.0%	30.0%	0.0%	99.9%
COTTONELLE Promotion	35.1%	31.9%	0.0%	100.0%
KLEENEX Promotion	21.4%	32.2%	0.0%	100.0%
DOMINICKS' Promotion	21.4%	30.2%	0.0%	100.0%
OTHER BRANDS' Promotion	49.0%	34.7%	0.0%	100.0%
SCOTT Share	18.5%	13.3%	2.4%	97.2%
CHARMIN Share	25.7%	15.4%	0.7%	84.0%
NORTHERN Share	18.6%	13.5%	0.3%	78.2%
COTTONELLE Share	12.4%	9.6%	0.3%	62.3%

Table 2.7 (*cont.*)

	Mean	S.D.	Min.	Max.
KLEENEX Share	11.5%	6.5%	0.6%	45.7%
DOMINICKS' Share	6.4%	3.5%	0.3%	37.8%
OTHER BRANDS' Share	6.8%	5.5%	0.4%	69.0%
Log (Total Expenditure Divided by Stone Price Index)	8.8274	0.4591	7.2707	11.5135
Observations	8697	8697	8697	8697

as indicated by the results of other researchers for other products, each market can be quite different, depending on the nature of the product and its competitive structure. The best strategic actions for a consumer product will be based on a detailed analysis of the market in question.

3

The value of brands and the challenge of free-riding

TONY APPLETON AND JOHN NOBLE

Introduction

Brands embody strong reputations and feature powerful connections between producers and individual consumers. As such, they are valuable. That value attracts a wide range of commercial operators like bees to a honeypot, ranging from the criminal (in the form of the counterfeiter) to the legitimate (in the form of the welcome joint-venture partner) and everything in between. This chapter provides a perspective on the nature of brands and their value before focusing on a practice that has sat on the boundary between the lawful and the unlawful, that of parasitic packaging (aka lookalikes or copycats). Banned in some countries and implicitly permitted in others, this is a practice that has IP, competition and consumer dimensions. It is of long-standing concern to companies in the UK where there are insufficient remedies to safeguard consumers and protect brand interests.

It is surprising, bearing in mind that brands are present in so many markets, represent such value and influence positively the functioning of markets, that there is no common understanding of what a brand is. For some, 'product' and 'brand' is synonymous. In the IP world, some consider 'brand' and 'trade mark' to be interchangeable. Others talk of 'rebranding' in the sense that brands are no more than logos or simply an element of corporate identity. Differences in perspectives and interpretation inhibit common understanding of the role and significance of brands and thus make appropriate debate on the issues that matter more difficult.

The British Brands Group, a corporate membership organisation of brand owners, champions brands and seeks to ensure that competition is vigorous but fair in the UK. This chapter reflects the Group's perspective on brands and explores some of the many dimensions of parasitic packaging. It is inherently a business perspective but, as it embraces brands, is also consumer-centric in approach as we consider brands to rest in the minds and emotions of each of us. The views expressed focus in particular on fast-moving consumer goods (FMCG).

Exploring further the idea of 'brand' as a consumer-centric concept, the Group considers a brand to be the total understanding of and feeling for a product that rests within an individual, comprising that individual's total experience gained over their lifetime. The influences that make up that experience may be positive or negative and may arise from a wide range of sources, some under the control of the producer, some not. Jeremy Bullmore, the former Chairman of J. Walter Thompson, the global advertising agency, drew the analogy between brand-building and the way birds build nests, using scraps and straws from a variety of different sources.[1] Brands derive their power when individuals behave and purchase as individuals but in common with many others, on a local, regional, national or even global scale, as in the case of McDonalds or Google.

There are myriad definitions of 'brand', but a study by the Westminster Business School captures it particularly well:

> Brand is a reputational asset which has been developed over time so as to embrace a set of values and attributes, resulting in a powerfully held set of beliefs by the consumer and a range of other stakeholders.[2]

While brands may rest in the minds and hearts of individuals, it is brand owners who invest significant sums in 'branding', building that knowledge of and appreciation for a product that will, they hope, drive preference and long-term loyalty. To succeed, the product needs a clear proposition or promise to the consumer, be different from others and be distinctive, standing out from the crowd to be noticed. Many branded products seek to add value over the generic or commodity product, but that is not always the case. Examples of strong brands that rely on value positioning include Dell computers, Ikea home furnishings, Primark clothing and Lidl groceries.

Successful brand-building requires ongoing, profound consumer insights in order to satisfy ever-evolving needs and wants better than

[1] Jeremy Bullmore, 'Posh Spice and Persil', British Brands Group Lecture (2001), p. 5, available at www.britishbrandsgroup.org.uk/upload/File/Lecture-2.pdf (last accessed 26 February 2015).

[2] Peter Urwin, Valeriya Karuk, Philip Hedges, Frank Auton, 'Valuing brands in the UK economy', Westminster Business School for British Brands Group (2008), p. 9, available at www.britishbrandsgroup.org.uk/upload/File/WBS%20VoB%20128.pdf (last accessed 26 February 2015).

competitors. It also requires investment in consistency, ongoing innovation (in order to sustain the brand's promise) and different ways of doing business that resonate with consumers. This may be a business model based on a highly ethical approach to business and the environment adopted by the clothing company Patagonia at one extreme, down to a no-frills, some could say spartan approach adopted by the successful Irish airline Ryanair.

The economic benefits of brands

The brand-led business model requires significant ongoing investment. The Westminster Business School study calculates that UK firms invest some £33 billion per year on branding, a conservative estimate as not all the investments that influence reputation were included due to the nature of the data. This equates to 12 per cent of all intangible investment in the UK economy, comparable to the total annual investment in scientific R&D.[3] A more recent World Intellectual Property Organization (WIPO) report estimated global brand investments to stand at $466 billion in 2011, but highlights data limitations that suggest the actual level of investment may be significantly greater.[4]

Such investment is made possible by the availability of intellectual property rights, notably trade marks, which allow for investments in reputation to be linked to a specific distinctive source or origin.

Such IP rights are granted by the state in return for some wider economic benefit. The Westminster Business School study estimated that companies' investment in brand-building equated to a £16 billion investment in the UK economy, identifying a number of areas of specific benefit:

- providing a surety that new products, ventures or markets are 'safe' for consumers;
- the quicker adoption of new technologies and ways of living and working;
- aligning business with society while allowing firms to compensate for any social costs arising from the consumption of their products;
- a means of regulating the behaviour of large global firms irrespective of borders;

[3] *Ibid.*, pp. 21–4.

[4] WIPO, 'Brands – Reputation and Image in the Global Marketplace', WIPO, Economics & Statistics Series (2013), pp. 35–37, available at www.wipo.int/edocs/pubdocs/en/intproperty/944/wipo_pub_944_2013.pdf (last accessed August 1, 2014).

- a spur to innovation as brand owners strive to maintain their reputational asset;
- enhancing the reputation of British products and services abroad, thus supporting exports.[5]

Other studies have also identified wider benefits. Work by PIMS Associates in 2004 found that branded goods manufacturers invest more, and invest more efficiently, in areas such as innovation that drive economic growth, productivity and employment,[6] while an earlier benchmarking study by the same firm found that brand-focused companies innovate twice as much as non-branded companies[7] and generate more economic value from R&D in comparison to non-branded companies.[8]

A more specific study into firms that register trade marks was undertaken in 2011 by the UK's Intellectual Property Office,[9] which found a positive correlation between such firms and higher productivity, higher employment, higher wages, benefits to households in the form purchasing power, higher quality and increased variety, and ultimately higher growth (in terms of both employment and turnover).

Branding's emphasis on differentiation provides the very basis for competition, enabling consumers to distinguish quickly, accurately and efficiently one offer from another and to evaluate their relative values. Importantly, brands, with their focus on quality, differentiation and intangible values, spur both price and non-price competition.

The brand model also puts consumers in the driving seat. If a branded goods manufacturer misreads the consumer, under-invests or is slow to respond to competitors, punishment tends to be brutal.

Some commentators have argued that brands, by generating a strong, hard-earned consumer franchise that delivers consumer loyalty, may create a barrier to market entry as consumers may be reluctant to switch to a new or less well-known competitor. Such an analysis is over-simplistic, implying that consumer behaviour acts as a barrier and that creating

5 *Ibid.*, pp. 26–38.

6 James Amos, 'Brands, Innovation and Growth', *British Brands*, issue 20 (2004), available at www.britishbrandsgroup.org.uk/library/download/462e24f89b979 (last accessed 26 February 2015).

7 Tony Clayton and Graham Turner, 'Of Brands and Growth – Key Findings', PIMS Associates for AIM, 1998, p. 7.

8 Clayton and Turner, 'Of Brands and Growth', p. 25.

9 Christine Greenhalgh, Mark Rogers, Philipp Schautschick and Vania Sena, 'Trade Mark Incentives', UK Intellectual Property Office, July 2011/1, pp. 7–8, available at www.ipo.gov.uk/ipresearch-tmincentives-full-201107.pdf (last accessed 1 August 2014).

products that consumers value inhibits competition. The success of truly innovative products such as Dyson vacuum cleaners and the Apple iPod were not barred by strong established brands such as Hoover, Electrolux and the Sony Walkman, indicating that incumbent players with strong brands do not pose a barrier to new entrants, even in mature markets. Customer loyalty arising from a good innovative product delivering strong value from a reliable, trusted manufacturer is part of healthy competition.

The evidence points strongly to brands being positive for consumers, productivity, innovation, employment, growth and competition, sustaining their pact with the state in return for the intellectual property rights on which they rely to underpin their distinctiveness and reputational investments.

The regulation of brands

It would be overly narrow to consider the regulation of branding in terms of intellectual property and competition laws alone. The practice of branding, which includes the manufacture, distribution and sale of products, is highly regulated in a number of different ways. Product and category-specific regulations control ingredients, claims and manufacturing processes. Marketing regulations control the presentation of products to consumers, requiring communication to be legal, decent, honest and truthful. Consumer regulations provide a further layer of regulation, protecting against misleading actions, omissions and misrepresentations.

Such regulation presents a compliance hurdle that all companies must clear in order to participate in the market on the one hand, while on the other excluding from the market companies that fail to comply. However, the theory is not matched by reality and this chapter will concentrate on a widespread practice in consumer product markets where brands are not well protected, despite the interplay of a range of laws and regulations.

Parasitic copying

In the early 1990s Sainsbury's supermarket launched its Classic Cola, produced by Cott Corporation, in packaging that closely resembled that of Coca-Cola. This brought into the public spotlight the problem of competitors unduly boosting their sales and reputations by mimicking the packaging designs of familiar, trusted brands. The similar packaging suggests to shoppers they are buying the brand or something closely connected with it when they are not. The practice is often attributed to retailers' private label products, but this is not exclusively the case. There have been examples of suppliers copying other suppliers.

As in the case of 'brand', there is no widely agreed definition of a parasitic copy, with many following the maxim 'you know one when you see one'. Indeed, the practice itself falls under a number of names, including 'lookalikes', 'copycats' and 'parasitic copies'. The European Brands Association (AIM) provides the definition preferred by brand owners:

> Parasitic copying takes many – but not necessarily all – of the marketing properties of a brand and becomes a variation on a theme. Thus the colour and shape of the packaging, the layout and the design of the label, the concept and style of the advertising and promotion and the design of the product itself are closely imitated.

This, however, has been criticised for being broad and not explaining 'concept' and 'style'. An alternative working definition was put forward by the Intellectual Property Institute in its study[10] commissioned by the UK Intellectual Property Office:

> A lookalike product is a product sold by a third party which looks similar to a manufacturer brand owner's product and by reason of that similarity consumers perceive the lookalike to share a greater number of features with the manufacturer brand owner than would be expected by reason of the products being in the same product category alone.

This, however, potentially presents its own problems. A definition that focused only on copies sold by third parties may exclude all those private label products that are both wholly specified and sold by a retailer – the most significant aspect of the problem.

There is a clear distinction between a retailer's private label product that is distinctively packaged, competing on its own merits, and a private label that adopts packaging designs that mimic a familiar brand. The vast majority of private label products are distinctively packaged and do not mislead consumers. The fact that the clear majority are distinctive indicates they do not need to copy to succeed (private label products represent some 46 per cent of the UK grocery market[11]).

[10] Phillip Johnson, Johanna Gibson and Jonathan Freeman, 'The Impact of Lookalikes – Similar Packaging and Fast-moving Consumer Goods', Intellectual Property Institute for the UK Intellectual Property Office, 2013, p. 13, available at www.ipo.gov.uk/ipresearch-lookalikes-main.pdf (last accessed 1 August 2014).

[11] Nathan Gray, 'Private Label Growth: UK Consumer Data Suggests Private Label Trend Is Here to Stay', *Foodnavigator.com*, 27 March 2014, available at www.foodnavigator.com/Market-Trends/Private-label-growth-UK-consumer-data-suggests-private-label-trend-is-here-to-stay (last accessed 26 February 2015).

How copies work

The absence of a widely agreed definition does not inhibit understanding of how such copies operate. This can best be understood in the context of the shopping environment. Copies thrive in supermarkets where consumers self-select products from the shelf. They also tend to be relatively low-price (under £10), low-involvement, regular purchases where much of the consumer decision-making is subconscious. In the UK grocery market, for example, only around 18 per cent of consumers use shopping lists with the remainder relying on products in store to remind them of the purchases they need.[12]

Faced with a shopping environment containing many tens of thousands of products (40,000 in a typical large superstore), shoppers need quick, reliable ways to find the products they want and to discard the rest. They identify and select the products in a matter of seconds, using heuristics (mental shortcuts) to guide their decisions.[13] They tend not to read labels, relying instead on colour and shape to inform their choice.[14]

Deeper understanding of consumer behaviour suggests that shoppers adopt a two-stage process when faced with regular, low-cost choices in a crowded environment. Identification of the product is largely a subconscious act and it is only once the product has been identified that rational analysis takes over, determining the pack size or product variety to be selected.[15] Hence the decision tends not to encompass all possible options but is 'bounded', including only those options of most relevance to the individual.

The copy seeks to hijack the visual cues (or heuristics) of the familiar branded product, prompting a change in the consumer's analysis

[12] Tony Durham, 'Shopper Behaviour and Brands: How Choices Are Made', Report on the Eighth Annual Symposium Trends in Retail Competition: Private Labels, Brands and Competition Policy, 2012, p. 9.

[13] Alexander Carter-Silk and Jane Leighton, 'Confusion, Heuristics and the Consumer', Speechly Bircham for British Brands Group, 2012, pp. 3–5, available at www.britishbrands-group.org.uk/upload/File/Heuristics_doc.pdf (last accessed 26 February 2015).

[14] Paul Dobson and Arvind Yadav, 'Packaging in a Market Economy: The Economic and Commercial Role of Packaging Communication', Norwich Business School for British Brands Group, 2012, p. 18, available at www.britishbrandsgroup.org.uk/upload/File/Packaging%20in%20a%20market%20economy%20NBS%2028062012.pdf (last accessed 26 February 2015).

[15] Carter-Silk and Leighton, 'Confusion, Heuristics and the Consumer', pp. 4–5.

than would have been the case for an unknown distinctively packaged product. To achieve this effect, it is not necessary to copy the packaging elements precisely. Calling to mind the original brand is likely to be sufficient to change the shopper's analytical, and ultimately commercial, behaviour.

Some have argued that such copying is no more than adopting the visual cues of a particular category and that consumers find these useful in navigating the store. Examples may include the colour green being used to denote 'organic' or the colour yellow to denote lemon-flavoured or scented. There is no question that such cues exist or that shoppers may find them useful. However, parasitic copies go much further than copying a single category cue, by copying several features of the familiar brand's design.

Furthermore, the features copied are often those of the brand rather than of the category, and they change and evolve following changes in the brand's packaging.[16] Also, to be a true category cue, such a feature should be expected to be adopted by a reasonable number of products in the category. This may not be the case.

'Category cue' is clearly an imprecise term. Does a product copy a generic indicator of a product type (such as images of bees on honey) or a brand cue that is well known in its category (such as red for cola)? Copying of the latter risks consumer confusion over quality, origin and product, or all three.

Parasitic copying is dismissed by some as just a bit of harmless fun, as Asda presented it at the time of its spat with United Biscuits over its Puffin biscuits that mimicked Penguin biscuits, with actors in Penguin and Puffin suits outside the High Court. Others dismiss copying tritely as being the sincerest form of flattery. Such arguments seek to trivialise the practice, diverting attention from deeper analysis.

The obvious argument that parasitic copying must influence shopper behaviour in favour of the copy, otherwise it would not be such a persistent practice, tends not to be persuasive in the policy debate. Fortunately, extensive research over many decades indicates that there is an effect on consumers, with variances product by product and category by category.

[16] British Brands Group, 'Similar "parasitic" packaging 2012', p. 51, available at www.britishbrandsgroup.org.uk/upload/File/Similar%20pkg%20examples%202012.pdf (last accessed 26 February 2015).

The effect on consumers

There is now compelling evidence that shoppers are more likely to buy products in similar packaging by mistake where packaging designs are similar. Mistaken purchase has been a consistent finding in research since the 1990s[17] and is verified by more recent studies. In 2013 the UK's consumer body Which? researched its members, finding that 20 per cent had bought a product by mistake due to similar packaging.[18] The UK Intellectual Property Institute (IPI) study found an even higher proportion of mistaken purchases, 57 per cent in the UK, 50 per cent in Germany and 60 per cent in the USA.[19]

Equally, there is compelling evidence gathered over many years that similar packaging increases perceptions amongst consumers that there is a connection between the two products, in particular that they come from the same source. Research for the British Brands Group in 2009 indicates that the more similar the packaging, the more the products are perceived to have common origin.[20]

There is a general belief that many private label products are made by a brand manufacturer, generally an incorrect assumption.[21] However, what the evidence shows is that similar packaging will increase this perception while distinctive packaging will reduce it.

In addition to mistaken purchase and perceptions of common origin, research also indicates that in some categories similar packaging increases perceptions of quality[22] and consumers' propensity to buy the product.[23] Research for the British Brands Group in 2009 indicated, for

[17] British Brands Group, 'Similar Packaging – A Summary of Consumer Research 1993–2005', British Brands Group, 2009, available at www.britishbrandsgroup.org.uk/upload/File/Research%20summary%2049.pdf (last accessed 26 February 2015).

[18] 'Spot the Difference: Big Brand or Supermarket Equivalent?', *Which? Magazine*, May 2013.

[19] Johnson *et al.*, 'The Impact of Lookalikes', pp. 89–90.

[20] Don Edwards, 'A Study into the Impact of Similar Packaging on Consumer Behaviour', British Brands Group, 2009, pp. 16–24, available at www.britishbrandsgroup.org.uk/upload/File/BBG%20packaging%20study%20Feb%2009.pdf (last accessed 26 February 2015).

[21] Canadean, 'Shoppers Choose Private Label', February 2014, available at www.canadean.com/news/shoppers-choose-private-label/ (last accessed 26 February 2015).

[22] 'Confusion in the Supermarket? Consumer Reactions And Attitudes', Consumers' Association, 1998, p. 14.

[23] Femke van Horen, 'Breaking the Mould on Copycats: What Makes Product Imitation Strategies Successful?', Narcis, 2010, pp. 52–6, 80, 96, available at www.narcis.nl/publication/RecordID/oai:dare.ubvu.vu.nl:1871%2F50999/id/1/coll/publication/Language/EN/uquery/breaking%20the%20mould (last accessed 26 February 2015).

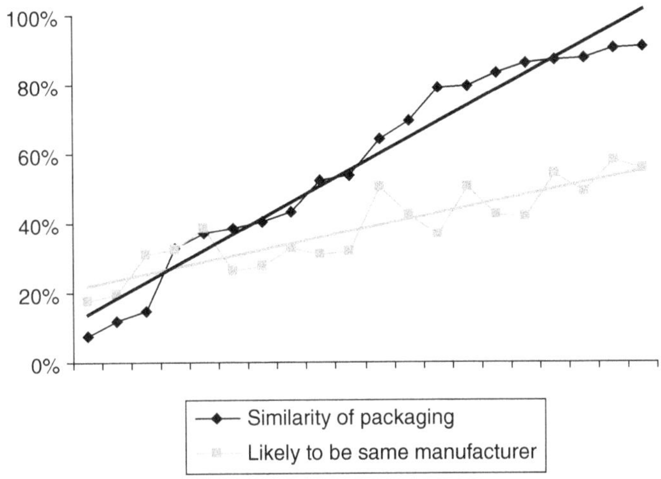

Figure 3.1 Products – ranked by similarity

As product packaging becomes more similar, so more people believe the products to come from the same manufacturer.

ten similarly packaged products tested, a 10 per cent swing in favour of the copy.[24]

The recent IPI study summarised the effect of similar packaging on consumers as follows:

Consumer perceptions

Reception – in the absence of the brand leader, products that look similar to that leader are better received by consumers than those that look distinct;
Comparison – when a lookalike is on the shelf at the same time as the brand leader, the lookalike might be used for comparison purposes;
Mistake – the presence of lookalikes will reduce a consumer's reaction time in selecting a product and will (under time pressure and outside the normal shop environment) increase the chance of mistaken selection.[25]

While the impact of parasitic copying on consumers is one thing, some have queried the extent to which confusion concerns them. At a general

[24] Edwards, 'A Study into the Impact of Similar Packaging', pp. 8–9.
[25] Johnson *et al.*, 'The Impact of Lookalikes', p. 35.

level, there clearly is concern. The research by Don Edwards & Associates Ltd in 2009 found that three times as many shoppers agreed than disagreed that they would be concerned if a product's packaging suggested a connection with an established brand when there was no such connection.[26]

A different perspective was adopted by the IPI study, which explored whether or not consumers who had bought a product by mistake felt advantaged in some way as a result.[27] It found that, while over 40 per cent in the UK felt very or somewhat disadvantaged, slightly fewer considered themselves very or somewhat advantaged. Crucially the research did not explore **why** consumers felt the way they did. It did not explore whether consumers felt they were buying something closely connected to the branded product or whether the packaging suggested a comparable quality, on both of which grounds they may well have been misled.

Some consumers find similar packaging helpful, and this is borne out by the IPI study, which found that some buy the copies deliberately. Again, though, the reasons for such behaviour have not been explored. Some may see similar packaging as a quality/price signal, believing they are buying leading brand quality at a lower price. Whether or not this is true will depend on the specific product, but it is certainly not true that similar packaging is a reliable, consistent indicator of quality.

Similar pack designs that suggest similar product performance are an implicit comparative advertisement, but are not regulated as such. In the UK packaging falls outside the self-regulatory mechanism on advertising, while consumer protection rules are not enforced by public authorities. For a comparative advertisement to comply with the rules, an advertiser must make objective comparisons that can be quantified and verified. Similar packaging that prompts a subconscious belief of similarity need undergo no such rigour.

A consumer who feels advantaged may actually have been duped and be disadvantaged. It is probable that a product that mimics a familiar brand may command a higher price than it would otherwise be able to do were it unknown, untried and have no reputation. The consumer risk in trying such a product would be high and a price discount would need to apply to compensate. Meanwhile a product that hints at all the familiar cues of the trusted brand may well reassure and help overcome any purchasing reticence, pricing higher than would otherwise be possible. Such an effect was shown in

26 Edwards, 'A Study into the Impact of Similar Packaging', pp. 13–15.

27 Johnson *et al.*, 'The Impact of Lookalikes', pp. 90–1.

the *L'Oréal* v. *Bellure*[28] case, where cheap perfumes in similar packaging were able to command a price premium over cheap perfumes in distinctive packaging.

Whether consumers may feel advantaged or may or may not be bothered by copies does not mitigate the finding that many have been confused with other goods – and that alone is evidence of unlawful marketing.

The effect on brands

A market in which copying goes unchallenged weakens brands and brand communication. Similarly packaged products are a commoditising force, suggesting to consumers that the products are essentially the same. Consumer choice is channelled primarily towards price rather than differences in qualities and reputation between products.

Branded products compete by being distinct and differentiated, helping to explain why trade marks (which must be distinct to be registrable) are so crucial in creating the framework for brand creation. This ability to be distinct provides the framework in which companies can invest significant sums in consistency, quality, innovation and responsible business practices, some of the main platforms for brand competition, and to do so over the long term. Such investments build reputation. When packaging designs are copied, the heuristics and signals that consumers use to identify products and their associated reputations are also copied, allowing the copier to free-ride off, and to undermine, the investments that built that reputation in the first place.

The consequent reduced ability for the branded product to communicate clearly and effectively its points of difference, encapsulated in its reputation, represents damage. The branded product has less stand-out on the shelf and is thereby less able to compete effectively for the consumer's attention.[29]

Damage for the original brand and brand owner takes a number of further forms. The 'stolen' reputation enjoyed by the copy increases consumers' propensity to buy it, something that is demonstrated by the evidence already mentioned. That in turn results in lost sales for the original brand. The extent to which this occurs will vary product by product, influenced by such factors as the design of the copy, the strength of the brand in the category and other factors such as shelf position, promotion and price.

28 *L'Oréal SA* v. *Bellure* NV [2007] EWCA Civ 968, para. 6.

29 Dobson and Yadav, 'Packaging in a Market Economy', p. 29.

Identifying precisely the impact on lost sales is fraught with challenges. The IPI study attempted to do this but failed. It used panel data (generated by respondents scanning their purchases at home some time after purchase) rather than by scanner data (generated at the supermarket till). The pack design could not be correlated with the data and the methodology relied on a launch date from which to measure effects. That date also could not be correlated with the data. Scanner data would be a more reliable data source, but this is owned by retailers. It is understood that the IPI, supported by the Intellectual Property Office (IPO), requested such data from UK retailers, but that this request was declined.

Were there access to a reliable data source, challenges would still remain in quantifying sales diversion. The effect of similar packaging would need to be isolated from other effects such as product formulation, promotion, shelf position and on-shelf facings as well as price. However, difficulties of measurement do not mean sales damage can be dismissed. Evidence on mistaken purchase and consumers' increased propensity to purchase products in similar packaging correlates with a reduction in sales of branded products.

It is feasible that it is not only the copied brand that loses sales. Shoppers may switch to the copy from other products in the category, including other (distinctively packaged) private label products, if they believe from the similar packaging design that they are getting leading brand quality for less money. However, quantifying such effects runs into the same evidentiary obstacles.

Further damage to the copied brand owner comes from increasing its costs as it seeks to defend itself against the copy. Costs may be incurred in a number of areas:

- Management time can be spent in seeking to resolve the problem.
- Remedial action to reduce the risk of confusion can be costly. In the 1990s Kellogg's spent an incremental £1 million to broadcast that, if it didn't say Kellogg's on the box, it wasn't Kellogg's in the box. More recently it embarked on a social media campaign to distinguish its products from its copies.[30] In the USA, Vicks states on the shrink-wrap of the cap that 'Vicks do not make store brands'.

The recent IPI study investigated remedial action via interviews with brand owners, finding that companies' strategies varied, with one

[30] Special K Aldi low fat cereal spoof advert, 13 June 2013, available at www.youtube.com/watch?v=fLG5uIhGdUA (last accessed 26 February 2015).

increasing training and another marketing spend. What was clear was a wariness to increase *product* advertising as this would have the effect of also promoting the copy.
- There are costs associated with repackaging, undertaken in order to reassert distinctiveness in the marketplace. Interviews with brand manufacturers reported in the IPI study identified that copying may well prompt revisions to packaging designs, though this would be unlikely to be the sole cause.

The competition effect of parasitic copies was the subject of a discussion paper from Nottingham University, written by Professor Paul Dobson in 1998.[31] This indicated not only the potential effects on competition between manufacturers, but also between retailers.

By undermining the brand owner's product and communication investment that build its reputation in the long term, the copy free-rides off that investment, weakens the brand owner's incentives (and ability) to make such investments in the future and may well directly undermine reputation when the copy disappoints (the consumer is likely to blame the brand owner in instances when the similar packaging is taken to indicate common origin).

Where brands are weakened, so are those retailers who rely on those brands. This tends to be the smaller stores without the scale and scope to develop their own products. Furthermore, retailers who artificially boost the quality perceptions of their private label ranges by mimicking packaging cues, rather than incurring the associated product and communication costs, distort competition vis-à-vis those retailers who incur those costs.

Retailers who copy are able to leverage their advantage further via their control of in-store presentation. In-store promotion, shelf displays and layout, and consumer pricing may affect consumer buying behaviour and rates of sale, diverting sales from the original brand to the copy, while giving the impression to shoppers that they are receiving good value for money.

Remedies

The potential remedies available to brand owners are varied, including unfair competition, intellectual property rights, provisions against

[31] Paul W. Dobson, 'The Competition Effects of Look-alike Products', Nottingham University School of Management & Finance, Discussion Paper, 1998.

misleading comparative advertising and consumer protection rules, but are not necessarily effective. In the UK, for example, many copies go unchallenged.

Competition Law

One area of law that can be quickly ruled out as an area for remedy is competition law, although many may see such mimicry as an issue of rivalry between two companies and therefore as a competition issue. Even though many copies may be specified, promoted and distributed via large retailers with substantial market shares, such retailers rarely have a dominant market share and as a result there is no abuse of dominance. Also the production of such copies does not involve collusion between horizontal competitors.

The UK Competition Commission looked into the matter as part of its 2006 market investigation into the UK groceries market. It stated that similarity of packaging will stimulate private label success, but recognised that there were also other forces at work. It concluded that the matter was more appropriately the subject of consumer protection law.[32]

Self-regulation

The UK Code of Non-broadcast Advertising, Sales Promotion and Direct Marketing (CAP Code)[33] is issued by the Committee of Advertising Practice, an advertising industry group organised to promote and ensure high standards in advertising. Through CAP and the Advertising Standards Authority the advertising industry self-regulates advertising, sales promotion and direct marketing and has specific provisions against 'taking unfair advantage' and misleading consumers (see clauses 3.41 and 3.43, both of which are relevant in relation to parasitic copies). However, the Code does not cover packaging, as there is no enforcement mechanism for such a voluntary initiative to work.

In 1995 the Institute of Grocery Distribution, at the behest of both branded suppliers and retailers, put in place a Dispute Resolution

[32] Competition Commission, 'The Supply of Groceries in the UK Market Investigation' (2006), Appendix 9.10, paras. 11–19, available at http://webarchive.nationalarchives.gov.uk/20140402141250/http://www.competition-commission.org.uk/assets/competition-commission/docs/pdf/non-inquiry/rep_pub/reports/2008/fulltext/538_9_10.pdf (last accessed 26 February 2015).

[33] The UK Code of Non-broadcast Advertising, Sales Promotion and Direct Marketing (CAP Code), (12th Edition, 2010), available at http://webarchive.nationalarchives.gov.uk/20140402141250/http://www.competition-commission.org.uk/assets/competition commission/docs/pdf/non-inquiry/rep_pub/reports/2008/fulltext/538_9_10.pdf.

Procedure in which signatories agreed to 'avoid using any combination of the same or similar name, colour scheme, shape, typeface, design layout or portrayed images so as to convey significant visual features which are essentially similar to those of another product'.[34] While this was seen as a conciliatory move, it proved to be no answer. The presence of parasitic copies continued in the marketplace, introduced even by signatories, while use of the procedure, and eventually the procedure itself, became shrouded in secrecy. Furthermore, not all retailers were prepared to sign it. It has long believed to have fallen into disuse.

IP remedies

In a parliamentary debate[35] in 2013 the Minister for IP, Viscount Younger, claimed that existing IP remedies in the UK were sufficient to tackle parasitic copying, a statement at odds with the practical experiences of brand owners and the conclusion of an earlier review into the UK's intellectual property framework, the Gowers Review.[36] This review concluded that brands in the UK were not well protected against misappropriation.

In relation to trade mark rights, the question first arose in Parliament during the passage of the Trade Marks Bill 1994, during which the Minister responsible, Patrick McLaughlin MP, responded in a written answer: 'the main characteristic of a lookalike product is that it does not copy a trade mark.'[37] Designers of parasitic copies are able to design around registered trade mark rights while still creating a similar overall impression for the consumer, complete with the visual cues that may be associated with the original branded product. In the case of Asda's Puffin biscuits, which were accused of copying McVitie's Penguin biscuits, no trade mark infringement was found.[38]

The *L'Oréal* v. *Bellure* case has been hailed as a move in favour of trade mark owners in relation to parasitic copying. However, this case involved the protection afforded to well-known marks against competitors who take unfair advantage. It is uncertain whether most packaging would

[34] Institute of Grocery Distribution, 'Dispute Resolution Procedure in Relation to Packaging and Trade Dress', November 1995.

[35] Hansard, House of Lords Official Report, vol. 747, no. 41, col. 1218.

[36] Gowers Review of Intellectual Property (2006), pp. 99–100, available at www.gov.uk/government/uploads/system/uploads/attachment_data/file/228849/0118404830.pdf (last accessed 1 August 2014).

[37] Hansard, House of Commons Debates, 16 May 1994, vol. 243 col. 299W, available at http://hansard.millbanksystems.com/written_answers/1994/may/16/trade-marks-bill#S6CV0243P0_19940516_CWA_45 (last accessed 26 February 2015).

[38] *United Biscuits (UK) Limited* v. *Asda Stores Limited* [1997], CH 1996 U 6471, p. 33.

be deemed to be sufficiently well known to warrant such protection. Certainly it would be no help for suppliers who found the packaging of their recently launched products copied.

As for copyright, the copy would have to involve substantial copying to infringe. A copy does not need to get so close in order to bring to the consumer's mind the heuristics associated with the brand.

Registered designs may give some protection for new brand designs, but they are of limited help to those whose designs are already well established both in the market and in the minds of shoppers. One difficulty with showing infringement of a registered design is the requirement for it to create a different overall impression on the informed user, which is taken to mean a designer. Even if the copy were sufficiently similar to confuse a typical consumer, a parasitic copy is likely to be considered sufficiently different by such an informed user so as not to infringe.

A more relevant basis for legal action, it could be argued, is the law of passing off. There is no statutory definition of passing off. Lord Oliver in the *Jif Lemon* case[39] devised a classic test whereby a claimant needed to demonstrate damage by reason of the erroneous belief engendered by the defendant's misrepresentation that the source of the defendant's goods or services is the same as the source of those offered by the claimant. To do so the claimant must demonstrate:

(1) there is goodwill or reputation attached to the goods or services;
(2) there has been a misrepresentation by the defendant to the public (whether or not intentional) leading or likely to lead the public to believe that the goods or services offered by him are the goods or services of the claimant;
(3) there has been damage to the claimant, by reason of the erroneous belief engendered by the defendant's misrepresentation, that the source of the defendant's goods or services is the same as the source of those offered by the claimant.

However, such an action is difficult and expensive to bring in cases involving similar packaging. Often the pack clearly gives the producer's name, reducing the likelihood of misrepresentation, and consumer confusion is hard to prove to a court's satisfaction. Consumers tend not to complain about low-priced items, evidence cannot be gathered in-store and the courts tend to be highly dismissive of survey evidence, considering it unreliable and artificial (which it is, when seeking to determine what

[39] *Reckitt & Colman Products Ltd* v. *Borden Inc* [1990] UKHL 12.

was in a consumer's mind in the midst of the weekly groceries shop in the supermarket).

The difficulty of providing evidence of confusion in both trade mark and passing off cases raises a significant question on the effectiveness of the tools available to courts. Currently much emphasis is placed on the opinion of the judiciary, albeit supported by witness statements and (to an extent) survey evidence. This contributes to great uncertainty when bringing such cases. There is clearly a need for a more quantifiable and predictable approach to evidence on confusion to supplement the existing tools.

In 2012 the European Commission published an extensive study into remedies against parasitic copying across Member States. Undertaken by Hogan Lovells, the study[40] found significant differences in legal regimes, no harmonised approach to dealing with such copies and a variety of approaches to the problem, some based on unfair competition law, some on trade mark law and some on unfair practices or consumer protection. Tellingly, the study took four examples and explored the likelihood of confusion of each across six Member States. There was no agreement that any one example was or was not actionable, resulting in the conclusion that the different requirements for taking action against parasitic copying across the European Union necessarily produce different results.

Turning to the UK specifically, the absence of an effective remedy has prompted scrutiny of the UK's compliance with its treaty obligations, notably Articles 10bis and 10ter of the Paris Convention and, by endorsement, TRIPS (Agreement on Trade-Related Aspects of Intellectual Property Rights 1994). Article 10bis binds countries 'to assure nationals ... effective protection against unfair competition' and goes on to define an act of unfair competition as 'any act of competition contrary to honest practices in industrial or commercial matters'. Acts that in particular are prohibited are those that 'create confusion by any means whatever with the establishment, the goods, or the industrial or commercial activities, of a competitor' and 'indications or allegations the use of which in the course of trade is liable to mislead the public as to the nature, the manufacturing process, the characteristics, the suitability for their purpose, or the quantity, of the goods'. The Gowers Review, in stating that brands are not effectively protected from misappropriation, adds further weight to the view that the UK is not compliant with this provision.

[40] Hogan Lovells, 'Study on Trade Secrets and Parasitic Copying (Look-alikes)', MARKT/2010/20/D, 2012, available at http://ec.europa.eu/internal_market/iprenforcement/docs/parasitic/201201-study_en.pdf (last accessed 1 August 2014).

That parasitic copying is against 'honest practices' is supported by the CAP Code, which includes measures against deception over origin and taking unfair advantage, and which applies across a wide range of marketing practices, though not packaging design. As such it represents the prevailing and accepted industry practice.

A Parliamentary Question was tabled in 2000 questioning the UK's compliance, in response to which the government listed a range of documents submitted to the World Trade Organization (WTO) that it claimed demonstrated compliance. These documents were subsequently scrutinised by Christopher Morcom QC and found not to support the view that the UK complies or that the TRIPS Council had found there to be such compliance.

The question of the UK's compliance remains open to this day. The government continues to maintain that it complies, as seen in recent years in the parliamentary debate on the IP Bill:[41]

> I can assure him that the UK is fully compliant in its obligations under TRIPS and other international agreements.
>
> Viscount Younger of Leckie, Parliamentary Under Secretary of State for Intellectual Property, Department for Business, Innovation & Skills

However, the government has yet to provide evidence to support the claim.

Remedies under consumer law

The UK's Consumer Protection from Unfair Trading Regulations (CPRs) implement the Unfair Commercial Practices (UCP) Directive.[42] This Directive imposes a duty on all consumer-facing businesses not to trade unfairly and came into force in the UK on 6 April 2008. It covers misleading packaging in its provisions. Such packaging constitutes a 'misleading action' as defined by Article 6 of the UCP Directive if it misleads consumers as to the commercial origins and/or characteristics of the product and/or creates confusion with products of a competitor, in either case causing the consumer to take a transactional decision that he or she

[41] Hansard, House of Lords, Grand Committee, 18 June 2013, col. GC65.

[42] The Consumer Protection From Unfair Trading Regulations 2008, Statutory Instrument no. 1277, available at www.legislation.gov.uk/uksi/2008/1277/made (last accessed 26 February 2015), implementing Directive 2005/29/EC concerning unfair business-to-consumer commercial practices in the internal market (unfair commercial practices directive) [2005] OJ L149/22, available at http://eur-lex.europa.eu/legal-content/en/ALL/;ELX_SESSIONID=N2pLTzvWX3vMdTTkr03Jv4y1gwT6Gp82jz22dJ5hsp8rdTl1HcXb!1976421071?uri=CELEX:32005L0029 (last accessed 26 February 2015).

would not otherwise take. Additionally, parasitic copying is covered by Clause 13 of the Annex to the Directive – 'Commercial Practices which are in all circumstances considered unfair'. It was this Directive that the Gowers Review wished to be given a chance to work.

The European Commission's guidelines on the Directive[43] clarify further that misleadingly similar packaging falls within its scope. It helpfully outlines the forms of deception covered, being outright confusion, deception over origin and deception over equivalence or quality. In this latter respect the Directive is understood to go further than IP remedies would allow.

This, one might think, would be cause for celebration for UK brand owners. That is not the case. The helpful words of the Directive, the UK's implementing regulations and the Commission's guidance were rendered ineffective by the UK government's decision to restrict enforcement to those organisations specified in Part 8 of the Enterprise Act 2013. In the case of parasitic copies this means the Office of Fair Trading (OFT), which merged with the Competition Commission in 2014 to become the Competition and Markets Authority (CMA) and Trading Standards (parasitic copies are irrelevant to sector regulators and not a 'market practice' open to a super complaint). The government brushed aside concerns that such an enforcement regime was ineffective by stating that the OFT and Trading Standards had a duty to enforce.

Both the OFT and Trading Standards have been called upon to enforce on several occasions with only one case being challenged in six years. Both organisations have limited resources and it is understood they must prioritise their activities. Parasitic copies do not feature in such priorities as they tend not to put public health or safety at risk. The OFT determines its priorities by assessing 'consumer detriment' and has judged that such detriment is not sufficient in this area, although the basis for this was not transparent.

A further hurdle to public enforcement is that shoppers tend not to complain, and without complaints Trading Standards and the CMA are unlikely to act. This does not mean that shoppers do not mind being misled. They indicate in research[44] that they do mind. In most cases they just

[43] Commission Staff Working Document, 'Guidance on the Implementation/Application of Directive 2005/29/EC on Unfair Commercial Practices', pp. 36–7, available at http://ec.europa.eu/justice/consumer-marketing/files/ucp_guidance_en.pdf (last accessed 1 August 2014).

[44] Don Edwards & Associates Ltd, 'A Study into the Impact of Similar Packaging on Consumer Behaviour', 2009, pp. 13–15, available at www.britishbrandsgroup.org.uk/upload/File/BBG%20packaging%20study%20Feb%2009.pdf (last accessed 26 February 2015).

do not realise they have been duped. If a shopper buys a product believing it to be made by a particular manufacturer when it is not (the test in the Directive), who is going to inform them of their error? If shoppers do realise that they have purchased the wrong product, they tend to blame themselves or, because the unit value is relatively low, will put the mistake down to experience and not complain. Consumer complaints in this instance are a poor indicator of misleading practice.

While the limited enforcement of the CPRs is of considerable frustration, most brand owners would accept that, given the limited resources of enforcement organisations, their time is most effectively spent focusing on widespread scams, rogue traders, practices that risk public health or safety and counterfeit goods.

Nevertheless, placing all the emphasis for enforcement on the CMA and Trading Standards represents a flaw in the UK's implementation of the Directive, a flaw that is evidenced by the paucity of enforcement action. Article 11 requires states to:

> ensure that adequate and effective means exist to combat unfair commercial practices in order to enforce compliance with the provisions of this Directive in the interest of consumers.

There is no additional consumer detriment test to be satisfied. Inadequate and ineffective enforcement in the UK has wider implications: the 'high level of consumer protection' is not achieved (Recital 1 of the Directive); a uniform regime across Europe that removes trade distortions resulting from divergent consumer protection regimes is unfulfilled (Recitals 3–6); the intention to allow all persons having a legitimate interest in the matter to initiate legal or administrative proceedings is not realised (Recital 21); and finally the protection of legitimate businesses from competitors who do not play by the rules, and the intended guarantee of fair competition in fields coordinated by the Directive, is not provided (Recital 8).

The straightforward solution is for companies with a legitimate interest to be granted the right to bring civil actions against those who infringe the Directive, an approach adopted in the majority of European countries including Ireland and specifically permitted in the Directive. Such an approach would relieve pressure on the public purse, would deliver higher levels of consumer protection and would promote fair competition in those areas coordinated by the Directive. It can also be expected to bring the UK closer into line with its treaty obligations. In February 2014 the government announced a consultation into the enforcement of the CPRs, specifically exploring this approach.[45]

Such a move would be consistent with government enforcement policy in competition matters. Vincent Smith, former Director of the OFT's Competition Enforcement Division, said of the Directive in July 2006:

> This [implementation of the UCP Directive] means that we have an opportunity here to develop, through guidance, a coherent consumer enforcement policy which is consistent with our processes for competition enforcement.[46]

A year later Philip Collins, Chairman of the OFT, in a speech to the Law Society made two particularly relevant observations:

> I firmly believe that private enforcement has a vital role to play in contributing to effective enforcement of the law and to encouraging a culture of compliance throughout the UK to the benefit of consumers.[47]

He went on to say:

> We regard private enforcement as an essential complement to public enforcement. At the OFT we strongly support the development of private enforcement – both follow-on and direct actions. And we are considering the ways in which we may be able to facilitate an increase in private actions.[48]

There are those who will argue, with justification, that however effective the legislation, brand owners will not bring civil actions where parasitic copies have been produced by major retail customers. Nevertheless, strong legislation with companies *and* public authorities as enforcers represents a far more comprehensive deterrent than the same legislation enforced by overstretched and constrained public authorities alone. It should also not be forgotten that suppliers of misleadingly packaged private label products, as well as the retailer, may be deemed to breach the Directive.

Conclusion

Any discourse on brands is inhibited by the lack of a common, widely understood and accepted definition of what a brand is. Reaching

[45] Hansard, Public Bill Committee, 30 January 2014, col. 103.

[46] Speech on protecting consumers by Vincent Smith, Director, Competition Enforcement at the Office of Fair Trading to the Law Society's European Group, 11 July 2006.

[47] Speech by Philip Collins, Chairman of the Office of Fair Trading to the European Group of the Law Society, 6 June 2007.

[48] *Ibid.*

consensus on this, however, is likely to be challenging and faces a number of obstacles, not least the very nature of brands themselves. Jeremy Bullmore in his Brands Lecture, for example, describes them as 'fiendishly complicated, elusive, slippery, half-real/half-virtual things'.[49] Resting in the minds of individuals, brands shift and change and vary from one person to another.

While defining brands is not straightforward, the activity of branding (the initiatives that companies undertake to build reputation and connections with individuals) provides a basis to explore inter-relationships with innovation, productivity, employment and growth. Positive correlations with brands have been found in each of these areas, underlining their wider contribution and importance, over and above what they deliver to individual consumers and the companies behind them. However, scope remains for further research to assess more precisely their economic contribution.

The interface between brands and regulation is equally complex, involving a matrix that includes IP, competition law, consumer law, marketing regulation and the many sectoral regulations that would apply to a specific product or service. Despite these diverse and sometimes overlapping areas of regulation, gaps still arise that leave consumers and those companies that seek to invest in innovation, strong reputations, quality and differentiation poorly served. The mimicking of the packaging designs of familiar brands, which shoppers use to identify and understand the products they wish to buy, is a case in point.

The evidence on the effect of such packaging on consumers is now overwhelming. The practice results in substantial numbers buying a product they did not intend to buy, misleads many shoppers over the origin of products and increases perceptions of quality and propensity to buy to a material degree.

Evidence on the impact on companies has so far proved less straightforward to quantify, partly because of the difficulty in isolating packaging design from other effects on consumer behaviour and the difficulty in accessing relevant sales data that is only available via retailers or with their permission.

In seeking a remedy, a number of routes have been explored covering intellectual property (including passing off/unfair competition), misleading and comparative advertising provisions and consumer protection law.

[49] Bullmore, 'Posh Spice and Persil', p. 3.

In all three areas, states are under either a treaty obligation or a requirement in a directive to provide effective remedies.

Brand owners in the UK are alert to the care needed in determining the most appropriate remedy. An extension of IP rights risks restricting competition, while the harmonisation of unfair competition rules across Europe might well represent a solution that goes much wider than is required. In the absence of a specific, narrowly drawn legislative solution, for which there may be limited parliamentary appetite, the effective application of consumer law, adequately enforced as is required in the UCP Directive, seems the optimum approach. This places the consumer test first and foremost.

PART II

Brands and competition law

4

Brands, competition, and antitrust law

DEVEN R. DESAI AND SPENCER WEBER WALLER

1. Introduction

Brands and brand management have become a central feature of the modern economy and a staple of business theory and business practice. Coca-Cola, Nike, Google, Disney, Apple, Microsoft, BMW, Marlboro, IBM, Kellogg's, Gucci, and Virgin are all large companies. They are also brands that present powerful and valuable tools for business. Business is fully aware of that power and value.[1] Contrary to the law's conception of trademarks, brands are used to indicate far more than source and/or quality. Indeed, those functions are far down on the list of what most businesses want for their brands. Brands allow businesses to reach consumers directly with messages regarding emotion, identity, and self-worth, such that consumers are no longer buying a product but buying a brand. Businesses pursue this strategy to move beyond price, product, place, and position and create the idea that a consumer should buy a branded good or service at a higher price than the consumer might otherwise pay. Branding explicitly contemplates reducing or eliminating price competition, as the brand personality cannot be duplicated. In addition, this practice can be understood as a product differentiation tactic that allows a branded good to turn a commodity into a special category that sees higher margins compared to the others in that market space. In sum, brands have important effects on competition and the marketplace.

Price theory animates both trademark and antitrust doctrine; yet businesses and business literature explicitly acknowledge that brands are used

This chapter is adapted from D. R. Desai and S. Waller, 'Brands, Competition, and the Law', *Brigham Young University Law Review* (2010): 1425.

1 See, e.g., Bloomberg, *Top 100 Global Brands Scoreboard*, Businessweek.com (6 August 2007) (listing Coca-Cola as the number one brand with a $65 billion value and Hertz as the number one hundred brand with a value of $3 billion); Millward Brown Optimor, *Brandz Top 100 Most Valuable Global Brands* (2009). See www.rankingthebrands.com/The-Brand-Rankings.aspx?rankingID=30.

to compete on dimensions other than price.[2] From a business point of view, brands are levers that permit companies to differentiate their products and services, price discriminate, and increase customer loyalty. Price theory no longer explains well what brands (if any) consumers view as substitutes, when confusion does or does not arise in the marketplace, and how consumers choose between brands and between dealers in the same brands.[3] Antitrust doctrine's emphasis on neo-classical price theory interferes with the doctrine's ability to understand and respond to the rise of the brand as a tool for possible anti-competitive behaviors such as diminishing the role of price competition, segmenting market demand, facilitating price discrimination, and locking in consumers to a favored brand. Two critical questions remain underdeveloped. First, when do brands confer meaningful market power? And second, how should brand management be integrated into the calculus of existing antitrust analysis? Yet like trademark law, antitrust law either fails to ask the right questions, ignores the non-price aspects of how brands and branding affect market competition, or defers to trademark law to set the proper limits of the intellectual property rights in question.

In this chapter, we analyze the limited ways that antitrust has sought to come to grips with competition issues relating to brands. First, antitrust law has focused on narrow notions of trademark rather than the broader notion of the brand. Second, antitrust has relied on price theory in defining relevant markets and measuring potential competitive harms, thus again missing the significance of the role of the brand. Third, antitrust perversely has become the enabler of brands by simplistically using key concepts such as inter-brand competition and intra-brand competition that fly in the face of the realities of the business world and the current role of the brand. Finally, we address what would be required for a brand perspective to take hold in antitrust law and where such a perspective could lead. We conclude that branding is so central to the business world, the modern economy, and the law that legal discourse must understand brands or it will continue to reach incoherent results as it tries to navigate the realities of business competition in the twenty-first century.

[2] See, e.g., Millward Brown Optimor, *Brandz Top 100*, p. 8 (noting that brands are "among a company's most valuable assets" as they can "ensur[e] higher demand and market share," "[command] premium prices and better supplier terms," and "create differentiation that allows companies to overcome commoditization").

[3] *Ibid.*

2. Brands: what they are and what they do

Although there is voluminous literature that explores brand theories, brand strategies, brand meaning, brand components, and brand functions,[4] it is difficult to find a succinct definition of what a brand is. Marketing expert Sidney Levy's characterization of a brand as a complex symbol that incorporates consumers' motives, feelings, logic, and attitudes[5] captures some major functions of a brand. For our purposes, we will refer to brands as manufacturers' or service providers' coordinated use of design, packaging, graphics, logos, advertising, promotion, public relations, marketing, distribution, pricing, communications, and other strategies to create a durable identity and loyalty with their consumers. We believe this view fairly synthesizes the mainstream serious business literature on branding and provides a useful starting place for the topic that interests us the most – namely, how should the law account for the importance of brands in the business world?

Despite the rich business literature on brands and branding, the question of what is a brand or what makes a brand has received little attention in legal literature.[6] Part of the problem stems from historical accounts of the development of trademarks, which often look to early uses of markings on goods as examples, if not the seeds, of modern trademark usage and law.[7] Although many different ancient and medieval civilizations – from the Indus river valley to China to several Mediterranean cultures

[4] See, e.g., M. Batey, *Brand Meaning* (London: Routledge, 2008); S. J. Levy, *Brands, Consumers, Symbols, and Research: Sidney J. Levy on Marketing*, D. W. Rook (ed.) (Thousand Oaks, CA: Sage Publications, Inc., 1999); G. Franzen and S. Moriarty, *The Science and Art of Branding* (Armonk, NY: M.E. Sharpe, 2009). In addition to serious business scholarship, there are literally hundreds of more general books and articles on how to create a successful brand and case studies of successes and failures in the field.

[5] B. B. Gardner and S. J. Levy, "The Product and the Brand", *Harvard Business Review* 33 (1955), 33.

[6] M. P. McKenna, "Testing Modern Trademark Law's Theory of Harm", *Iowa Law Review*, 95 (2009), 67–8 (noting that trademark theory regarding confusion has not used "a growing body" of brand-related literature to inform trademark theory's views).

[7] See F. I. Schechter, *The Historical Foundations of the Law Relating to Trade-Mark Law* (New York: Columbia University Press, 1925); S. A. Diamond, "The Historical Development of Trademarks", *Trademark Reporter*, 65 (1975), 265–6; D. M. McClure, "Trademarks and Unfair Competition: A Critical History of Legal Thought", *Trademark Reporter*, 69 (1979), 305; B. G. Paster, "Trademarks – Their Early History", *Trademark Reporter*, 59 (1969), 551; E. S. Rogers, "Some Historical Matter Concerning Trade-Marks", *Michigan Law Review*, 9 (1911), 29.

to Nigeria to the Arab Empire to medieval England – used brands and a variety of other commercial symbols to indicate ownership[8] and facilitate commerce, none of those uses corresponds to modern brands.[9] As economies grew and centralized under the auspices of a royal, religious, and/or guild authority, marks were used to regulate industry.[10] Unlike modern trademark systems, where the company decides whether and what trademark to use, ancient and medieval industries did not choose to use marks. Instead, the government required these industries to use marks to allow the government to trace a good to a specific manufacturer so it could be held accountable for products that did not meet government-established standards.[11]

Even in such limited market systems, as trade expanded beyond local environs and reached far-flung areas, marks came to indicate source and quality. In some specific industry sectors leading up to the mid-nineteenth century, British law began to recognize the goodwill value and property-like interests that grew with the use of liability marks.[12] Once an economy moves towards a purer private market system and away from face-to-face transactions, marks seem, of necessity, to become predominantly symbols of origin and quality, with modern trademark systems using voluntary mechanisms to fuel the system.[13]

Nonetheless, using marks for the "utilitarian provision of information regarding origin and quality in order to reduce risk and uncertainty"[14]

[8] See Diamond, "The Historical Development of Trademarks", 266–7, 273, 283–5.

[9] K. Moore and S. Reid, "The Birth of the Brand: 4,000 Years of Branding History", (MPRA, Working Paper No. 10169, 2008, available at http://mpra.ub.uni-muenchen.de/10169/ (studying the transition from proto-brands to brands and the features of these two categories across the Indus River Valley, Shang Chinese, Cyprian, Tyrian, Greek, and modern civilization).

[10] See, e.g., Moore and Reid, "The Birth of the Brand", 7–10, 14–18 (explaining the connection between religious/state authority symbols and long-distance trade in the Indian and Tyrian civilizations); Schechter, *The Historical Foundations of the Law*, p. 129 ("The slight degree of national economic significance acquired by trade-marks prior to the middle of the nineteenth century accounts for much of the tardiness in the growth of modern trade-mark law both in England and in the United States").

[11] See, e.g., Schechter, *The Historical Foundations of the Law*, pp. 26, 38–121; Rogers, "Some Historical Matter Concerning Trade-Marks", 29 (use of symbols as quality control for bricks in Roman Empire).

[12] See Schechter, *The Historical Foundations of the Law*, pp. 26, 38–121.

[13] See D. Higgins, "The Making of Modern Trade Mark Law: The UK, 1860–1914", in L. Bentley, J. Davis and J. Ginsburg (eds.), *Trademarks and Brands: An Interdisciplinary Critique* (Cambridge University Press, 2008), pp. 42–3.

[14] Moore and Reid, "The Birth of the Brand", 122–3.

is only a part of what brands encompass.[15] Brands have "more complex ... characteristics ... which are related to image building and include status/power, inherent value and finally, the development of brand personality (transformational)."[16] As one study has put it, marks that only convey information and/or offer only one part of image-building are proto-brands.[17] Not until the late nineteenth century did the birth of modern brands occur, where a private mark provided information regarding source and quality and simultaneously had image components regarding power, value, and personality.[18]

Unlike trademark law, the business literature has moved quickly to keep pace with the realities of modern branding. Writers in the early 1980s, such as Kotler, defined the brand in terms roughly coextensive with the legal definition of a trademark: a "name, term, symbol, or design, or a combination of them, which is intended to signify the goods or services of competitors."[19] Even at the start of the 1990s, marketing theorist David Aaker argued that a brand is "a distinguishing name and/or symbol (such as a logo, trademark, or package design) intended to identify the goods or services of either one seller or a group of sellers, and to differentiate those goods or services from those of competitors."[20] By the end of the 1990s, brand theorists had moved well beyond considering brands as only indicating source and/or guaranteeing quality, and instead explicitly saw them as encompassing a broader array of functions.

Moore and Reid document the growth of the brand, which entails a company creating a personality for a brand that a consumer then incorporates into how he or she "express[es] his or her own self, an ideal self, or specific dimensions of the self."[21] Other marketing literature emphasizes the way a brand allows product differentiation, impacts consumer preferences, and enables cross-cultural marketing.[22] Recent work has described a

[15] See, e.g., S. Fournier, "Consumers and their Brands: Developing Relationship Theory in Consumer Research", *Journal of Consumer Research*, 24 (1998), 343–4 (challenging the way in which brand theory often reduces to utilitarian views); A. Katz, "Beyond Search Costs: The Linguistic and Trust Functions of Trademarks", *Brigham Young University Law Review*, (2010), 1564 (noting that pure utilitarian views of trademark functions are "naïve" and fail to capture the persuasive branding aspect of trademarks).

[16] Moore and Reid, "The Birth of the Brand", 25.

[17] *Ibid.*, 26. [18] *Ibid.*, 24–6.

[19] P. Kotler, *Marketing Management, Analysis, Planning, Implementation, and Control*, 5th edn (Englewood Cliffs, NJ: Prentice Hall, 1984), p. 482.

[20] D. A. Aaker, *Managing Brand Equity* (New York: Free Press, 1991), p. 7.

[21] Moore and Reid, "The Birth of the Brand", 24 (citations and internal quotations omitted).

[22] D. Arnold, *The Handbook of Brand Management* (Reading, MA: 1993), p. 2 ("Today's great brands are personalities ... branding, therefore, has to do with the way

brand as a promise,[23] a relationship between company and consumer,[24] and even as having a soul.[25]

From the end of the nineteenth century to the middle of the twentieth century to today, companies have had to find ways to compete over selling essentially the same goods and manage excess production capacity.[26] Product design became a key factor in developing and marketing a good because "the lack of obvious differences between products made good appearance a 'necessity.'"[27] By the 1960s and 1970s, this new emphasis on design connected to the larger aim of creating a brand that projected a singular corporate identity with integrated design coordination and a more scientific approach to marketing.[28] A key insight was that brands allowed

customers perceive and buy things; it is not simply a characteristic of certain industries"); M. Fioroni and G. Titterton, *Brand Storming: Managing Brands in the Era of Complexity* (New York: Palgrave Macmillan, 2009), p. 32 ("[A] brand today can really be thought of as being like a living organism, with an identity and a personality which the consumers themselves have asked it to take on – perhaps in order to re-appropriate them later").

[23] A. P. Adamson, *BrandSimple: How the Best Brands Keep it Simple and Succeed* (New York: Palgrave Macmillan, 2006), p. 3 ("[A] brand is something that lives in your head. It's a promise that links a product or service to a consumer"); S. M. Davis, *Brand Asset Management: Driving Profitable Growth through your Brands* (San Francisco: Jossey-Bass, 2002), p. 3 ("[A] brand is a set of promises. It implies trust, consistency, and a defined set of expectations").

[24] S. Davis, "Building a Brand-Driven Organization", in A. M. Tybout and T. Calkins (eds.), *Kellogg on Branding: The Marketing Faculty of The Kellogg School of Management* (Hoboken, NJ: Wiley, 2005), p. 226 ("[A brand is] about the relationship forged between an entity and its products and services – represented by the brand – and consumers"); L. Moor, *The Rise of Brands* (New York: Berg Publishers, 2007), p. 6 (internal quotations omitted) (describing brands as an "ongoing relationship between consumers and businesses"); J. F. Sherry, Jr., "Brand Meaning", in A. M. Tybout and T. Calkins (eds.), *Kellogg on Branding: The Marketing Faculty of the Kellogg School of Management* (Hoboken, NJ: Wiley, 2005), p. 41 ("A brand is a contract, a relationship, a guarantee; an elastic covenant with loose rules of engagement").

[25] A. Rothacher (ed.), *Corporate Cultures and Global Brands* (Singapore: World Scientific Pub., 2004), p. 2 ("Simply put, a brand is the soul of a product. It facilitates consumer choice as it represents reliable qualities, images and pricing"); Sherry, "Brand Meaning", p. 41 ("A brand is a mental shortcut that discourages rational thought, an infusing with the spirit of the maker, a gathering, an inspiration. A brand is a semiotic enterprise of the firm, the companion spirit of the firm, a hologram of the firm").

[26] Moor, *The Rise of Brands*, pp. 26–7.

[27] *Ibid.*, p. 27 (citation omitted); M. Danesi, *Brands* (London: Routledge, 2006), pp. 60–7 (detailing the importance of product and package design through the examples of the automobile, perfume, and tobacco industries).

[28] See Moor, *The Rise of Brands*, pp. 30–1; C. Lury, *Brands: The Logos of the Global Economy* (London: Routledge, 2004), pp. 20–2; cf. Moore and Reid, "The Birth of the Brand", 3 (noting that branding had been a topic in marketing studies prior to the 1970s but was only "a major topic of study" from 1970 onward).

companies to move beyond the 4 "P"s – product, price, place, and promotion – which a competitor could duplicate, to include a fifth P – personality of a company – which competitors could not copy.[29] Although manufacturers used brands and marketing strategy to provide information about why a new or branded good should be purchased, advertising and even a good's packaging could communicate values to encourage consumers to purchase one company's product over a competitor's for reasons other than the price or the quality of the good.[30]

In both the United States and Britain one sees "the emergence of a system that could link brand names to broader values and meanings."[31] As Lury explains, in the 150 years of modern brand history, companies used marketing, messaging, special events, and more to offer the consumer the perception that the product carried more than its functional qualities.[32] Products had "essence[s]" that met consumers' psychological needs and lifestyle goals.[33] Furthermore, this broad conception of the brand can be seen right from the birth of the modern brand.

Brands allow companies to create a type of product differentiation that might turn a commodity into a special category that attains higher margins compared to other products in that market space.[34] One modern case study shows how in several industries companies used brands and brand identity to demand higher prices in what had been a commodity market or isolated market. For example, The Body Shop offers a "profits-with-a-principle" philosophy that has linked its business to social causes in a market where most product "lines are indistinguishable."[35] The Body Shop has differentiated its cosmetics line by turning it "into something more than it has ever been."[36] Once it was suggested that The Body Shop might be more talk than action, some questioned whether the brand identity was

29 Lury, *Brands: Logos of the Global Economy*, pp. 24, 33–4; cf. Danesi, *Brands*, p. 33 (explaining brands as personalities with identities).

30 See Moor, *The Rise of Brands*, pp. 18–20; cf. E. Joachimsthaler and D. A. Aaker, "Building Brands without Mass Media", *Harvard Business Review*, 75 (1999), 39 ("[M]ass-media advertising has long been the cornerstone of most brand-building efforts").

31 Moor, *The Rise of Brands*, p. 23; Danesi, *Brands*, p. 8.

32 Lury, *Brands: Logos of the Global Economy*, p. 24.

33 *Ibid.*, pp. 24–5; cf. Danesi, *Brands*, pp. 8, 16 (describing how advertising aims to persuade a consumer that a product will fulfill "emotional, social, and other kinds of human needs").

34 D. A. Aaker, "Should You Take Your Brand to Where the Action Is?", *Harvard Business Review*, 75 (1997), 141.

35 Joachimsthaler and Aaker, "Building Brands without Mass Media", 40–1.

36 *Ibid.*, 41.

bogus and how divergence from its stated identity posed problems.[37] The company was nonetheless acquired by L'Oréal for £652.3 million in 2006 because of the way The Body Shop's brand complemented L'Oréal's brand,[38] thus proving that the talk may matter more than the action.

Likewise, Häagen-Dazs used branding so that its brand came to mean "thicker, creamier, and pricier than any other ice cream on the market; a sensual, self-indulgent, pleasurable treat targeted at sophisticated, affluent adult consumers," which allowed it to enter the ice cream market at "a price 30 percent to 40 percent higher than its closest competitors and many times higher than the lower-priced products."[39] Hugo Boss went from a DM4 million-a-year company to one with sales of "100 million in 1980 [that] increased tenfold during the 1980s" because of its sponsorship strategy that raised the brand's visibility by affiliating with elite, exclusive events such as Formula One racing and its placement on stylish television shows.[40] SMH's Swatch transformed the watch market from "either low-cost time-measurement instruments or a high-cost combination of heirloom and investment" to one where Swatch became the symbol for Swiss watches that had a "stylish, fun, youthful, provocative, and joyful brand personality."[41] In so doing, SMH created the fashion watch market.[42]

These strategies arguably satisfy unmet demand or create demand. In either case, the brand is used as a way to move beyond product, price, place, and promotion, so that companies face less, or ideally no competition as consumers remain loyal to the brand, even if a competitor offers an arguably interchangeable good or service for the same or less cost.[43]

Brands have become complex strategic tools that perform a variety of functions including creating demand, circumventing middlemen so that a company can reach consumers directly, controlling prices, managing quality, providing a platform for trademark enforcement, defining national identities, and satisfying a consumer's emotional and

[37] T. Heding, C. F. Knudtzen and M. Bjerre, *Brand Management Research, Theory and Practice* (London: Routledge, 2009), p. 63 (noting the problem of "misaligned identities" that The Body Shop faced); J. Entine, "High St Chain's Idealism Masks a Harsh Reality", *UK Mail*, 29 August 2001, available at www.jonentine.com/reviews/mail_on_Sunday_roddick.htm (reporting on claims of environmental harms and poor treatment of developing countries' industries as trading partners).

[38] "L'Oreal Buys Body Shop for £652m", *The Independent*, 17 March 2006, available at www.independent.co.uk/news/business/news/loreal-buys-body-shop-forpound652m-470244.html.

[39] Joachimsthaler and Aaker, "Building Brands without Mass Media", 41.

[40] *Ibid.*, 44. [41] *Ibid.* [42] *Ibid.*

[43] Davis, "Building a Brand-Driven Organization", p. 5.

psychological needs. These functions, separately and in combination, allow a company to differentiate products, avoid commoditization of its products or services, and distinguish the company and its goods or services from its competition, thus building loyal customer bases for whom no other brand or item will suffice. Regardless of what dimension or dimensions of a brand a company pursues to build its brand, commentators recognize the power of a strong brand. A strong brand creates the ability to attain "real and sustainable competitive advantage … [because] the resulting effectiveness and efficiency of the program can represent significant barriers to competitors."[44]

Brands affect both price and competition in ways that the law may not wish to foster. The law, however, has ignored the full role of brands and focused solely on the trademark, source/quality dimension of brands. The law has failed to capture the way companies use brands as a competitive advantage and the possible harm brands can pose for markets and consumers. The current permissive trademark and antitrust system effectively grants brand protection and generates sub-optimal outcomes but does not acknowledge this reality.

3. Antitrust law's failure to grasp the power of brands

Antitrust law has never developed an appropriate set of tools designed to measure brand power, distinguish lawful branding techniques from unlawful exclusionary conduct, or design functional remedies to deal with these issues. In this section, we focus on the missed opportunities to incorporate the key aspects of brand management into competition policy. We show how an understanding of modern branding can provide a tool to address issues such as market power, market definition, merger enforcement, and vertical restraints as exemplified by resale price maintenance doctrine.

A. *Missed opportunities: antitrust's view of product differentiation and struggle to understand brands*

Antitrust law and economics in the early decades of the twentieth century missed an early opportunity to take advantage of the growing importance of brands and, more generally, product differentiation. Edward Chamberlin, one of antitrust's pioneering economists, was deeply

[44] Joachimsthaler and Aaker, "Building Brands without Mass Media", 50.

interested in this topic and made it the focus of his principal work, *The Theory of Monopolistic Competition*.[45]

In *The Theory of Monopolistic Competition*, he investigated the vast middle ground between perfect or pure competition and monopoly. At the time, the only middle ground had been the exploration of duopoly by Cournot and others.[46] Chamberlin instead focused on product differentiation, the critical real-world phenomenon that rendered useless the prevailing models of pure monopoly and perfect competition.

As he noted:

> Where there is any degree of differentiation whatever, each seller has an absolute monopoly of his own product, but is subject to the competition of more or less imperfect substitutes. Since each is a monopolist and yet has competitors, we may speak of them as "competing monopolists," and, with peculiar appropriateness, of the forces at work as those of "monopolistic competition."[47]

Chamberlin defined product differentiation broadly. He viewed patents, trademarks, and copyrights as critical for product differentiation and considered them monopolies, though normally in competition with other more or less imperfect substitutes.[48] He was uncertain whether patents or trademarks had the greater potential for monopoly power and pointed to the example of the prestige value of such 1930s brand names as Coca-Cola, Ivory, and Kodak.[49] Regardless of which was more important – patents or trademarks – all types of intellectual property were critical in preventing the erosion of high returns. Intellectual property rights rendered competitors unable to create effective substitutes because of strong consumer preferences for the IP-protected products.[50]

Chamberlin conceived of competition as a spectrum where perfect competition and monopoly were limits, not equilibriums.[51] He noted: "As long as the substitutes are to any degree imperfect, [the producer] still has a monopoly of his own product and control over its price within the limits imposed upon any monopolist – those of the demand."[52] The closeness of the available

[45] E. H. Chamberlin, *The Theory of Monopolistic Competition: A Re-orientation of the Theory of Value*, 8th edn (Cambridge, MA: Harvard University Press, 1962).

[46] A. A. Cournot, *Recherches sur les principes mathématiques de la théorie des richesses* (Paris: Hachette, 1838); F. Y. Edgeworth, *Mathematical Physics* (London: C. Kegan Paul & Co. 1881).

[47] Chamberlin, *The Theory of Monopolistic Competition*, p. 9.

[48] *Ibid*., pp. 60–1. [49] *Ibid*., p. 62. [50] *Ibid*., pp. 111–12.

[51] *Ibid*., p. 63. [52] *Ibid*., p. 67.

substitutes determined the extent that price would exceed and quantity would fall short of the predictions of a competitive model.[53]

For Chamberlin, product differentiation changes one's world view.[54] However, product differentiation does not automatically produce classical monopoly. Even if every producer has a monopoly of their own variety of product, they still face the competition of imperfect substitutes.[55] Because the competitive ideal was no longer possible in a world of differentiated products: "[h]ow much and what kinds of monopoly, and with what measure of social control, become the questions."[56]

As Rudolph Peritz notes, Chamberlin's theory of monopolistic competition transformed traditional notions of a market for goods and services "into a commercial marketplace of ideas and images."[57] Unfortunately, Chamberlin's insights regarding product differentiation and brands as they existed in his time were never deeply integrated into antitrust policy. He is cited in only a limited number of places, but never relied upon, in the contemporary legal or economic treatises, textbooks, and court opinions.[58]

Other commentators have glimpsed the importance of brands, but similarly had little effect on modern antitrust law and policy on this issue. For example, Joe Bain had important insights into the importance of advertising for competition policy.[59] Bain, however, did not move beyond advertising into the broader concept of the brand, and much of his work on advertising and his broader interest in the structure of markets has

[53] *Ibid.*, pp. 103–4, 112, 117. [54] *Ibid.*, pp. 204–5.

[55] *Ibid.*, pp. 205–6. [56] *Ibid.*, pp. 214–15.

[57] R. J. R. Peritz, *Competition Policy in America, 1888–1992: History, Rhetoric, Law* (New York: Oxford University Press, 1996), p. 109.

[58] See, e.g., *Baltimore and Ohio R. Co.* v. *United States*, 386 U.S. 372, 448 n.9 (1967); *F.T.C.* v. *H.J. Heinz Co.*, 246 F.3d 708, 724 n.23 (D.C. Cir. 2001); *International Detective Service, Inc.* v. *Interstate Commerce Commission*, 613 F.2d 1067, 1075 n.18 (D.C. Cir. 1979); *Northern Natural Gas Co.* v. *Federal Power Commission*, 399 F.2d 953, 965 n.21 (D.C. Cir. 1968); *Pevely Dairy Co.* v. *United States*, 178 F.2d 363, 368 (8th Cir. 1950); *Durable, Inc.* v. *Twin County Grocers Corp.*, 839 F. Supp. 257, 261 n.3 (S.D.N.Y. 1993); *United States* v. *Twentieth-Century Fox Film Corp.*, 137 F. Supp. 78, 93 nn.22–3 (S.D. Cal. 1956); D. W. Carlton and J. M. Perloff, *Modern Industrial Organization*, 4th edn (Boston, MA: Pearson/ Addison Wesley, 1990), pp. 318, 344; W. K. Viscusi, J. E. Harrington, Jr. and J. M. Vernon, *Economics of Regulation and Antitrust*, 4th edn (Cambridge, MA: MIT Press, 2005), pp. 87–8, 119. But see F. M. Scherer and D. Ross, *Industrial Market Structure and Economic Performance*, 3rd edn (Dallas: Houghton Mifflin, 1990) in which Chamberlin's work is more central.

[59] J. S. Bain and P. D. Qualls, *Industrial Organization: A Treatise* (Greenwich, CT: JAI Press, 1987), pp. 310–11, 395–6; J. S. Bain, *Barriers to New Competition: Their Character and Consequences in Manufacturing Industries* (Cambridge, MA: Harvard University Press, 1956), pp. 115, 217.

been rejected by price theory and other "Chicago School" approaches to competition policy.[60]

Lester Telser, a figure more associated with the Chicago School, provides an unexpected example of where antitrust literature understood why brands matter. In his 1972 book, Telser recognized the price premium aspect of successful branding and called for its recognition in market definition and the measurement of market power.[61] Unfortunately, as with Chamberlin, most recent commentators and courts have not engaged Bain or Telser on these points or have too reflexively come to the opposite conclusion.[62]

Despite these apparent blind spots, there has been a somewhat greater willingness to recognize the importance of premium brands as opposed to value brands and branded products as a separate market segment from the unbranded and private label segments of the same industry. For example, the 2006 Commentary to the Merger Guidelines discusses several enforcement actions in the butter, flour, tissue, and bread industries where branded products were recognized as distinct markets for merger analysis, despite the presence of important producers of generic and private label goods.[63] In addition, there is an older Federal Trade Commission (FTC) challenge to a merger in the soft drink industry that focused on the major branded segment of the industry as the relevant market for merger analysis.[64] Most recently, the Antitrust Division of the Justice Department challenged a merger in the value segment of the shampoo and

[60] T. J. Muris, "Improving the Economic Foundations of Competition Policy", *George Mason Law Review*, 12 (2003), 8–9.

[61] L. G. Telser, *Competition, Collusion and Game Theory* (Chicago: Aldine-Atherton, 1972).

[62] W. M. Landes and R. A. Posner, "Market Power in Antitrust Cases", *Harvard Law Review*, 94 (1981), 956–7.

[63] US Department of Justice and Federal Trade Commission, Commentary on the Horizontal Merger Guidelines (2006), available at www.justice.gov/atr/public/guidelines/215247.pdf [hereinafter Commentary to the Merger Guidelines] (citing *United States* v. *Dairy Farmers of America*, 2001-1 Trade Cas. (CCH) P 73,136 (E.D. Pa. 2000); *United States* v. *Kimberly-Clark Corp. and Scott Paper Co.*, 1996-1 Trade Cas. (CCH) P 71,405 (N.D. Tex. 1995); *United States* v. *Interstate Bakeries Corp.*, 1996-1 Trade Cas. (CCH) P 71,271 (N.D. Ill. 1995); cf., *Commission Decision 2002/156/EC in Case COMP/M.2097- SCA/Metsa Tissue*, 2002 OJ (L 57) 1 at pp. 84, 94 (barring merger under EU merger regulation combining four major brands where minor brands are not effective substitutes).

[64] *Coca-Cola Bottling Co. of the Southwest* v. *F.T.C.*, 85 F.3d 1139 (5th Cir. 1996); cf. *Commission Decision 98/327/EC in Case IV/M.833 The Coca-Cola Company/Carlsberg A/S*, 1998 OJ (L 145) 41 at pp. 72–3, 110, 118 (permitting soft drink merger reducing international brands from four to three upon condition of divestiture of brand and assets).

conditioner market that incorporated a realistic understanding of brand competition.[65]

There is a growing scholarly engagement with the broader effects of branding on market definition, such as the second edition of the Sullivan and Grimes treatise, which states:

> When market power is properly defined as power over price, it is clear that sellers of branded products often exercise market power. Just as a pure monopolist, the seller of a branded good may face an inelastic demand curve, allowing it to raise price without losing offsetting sales revenues … A seller with a powerful brand, for example, may have brand-loyal consumers who will absorb price increases rather than switch to a different brand. The basis for this brand loyalty may be accurate information about the characteristics of the favored brand and all rival offerings. But brand loyalty may also be based on inaccurate, out-of-date or incomplete information. Brand loyalty will be reinforced by "satisficing" conduct – where market actors are not constantly reevaluating their alternatives and patterns tend to stabilize and be repeated until something disorienting occurs.[66]

From the time of Edward Chamberlin to the present, two crucial questions remain: When do brands confer meaningful market power, and how to integrate brand management into the calculus of existing antitrust analysis? Even critics of Chamberlin acknowledge that the key issue is identifying the "noticeable 'gap[s] in the chain of substitutes.' "[67]

Despite robust economic theories about product differentiation, antitrust law and policy have not done a good job of incorporating these insights. The brand and business literature is quite clear about the way brands are used to achieve product differentiation and control price. As one business school professor noted in a recent hearing before the FTC and the Antitrust Division about the importance of brands:

[65] *United States* v. *Unilever N.V.*, Case No: 1:11-cv-00858 (July 19, 2011) (final judgment), available at www.justice.gov/atr/cases/f276300/276306.pdf.

[66] L. A. Sullivan and W. S. Grimes, *The Law of Antitrust: An Integrated Handbook*, § 2.4e, 2nd edn (St Paul, MN: West Group, 2000), p. 43 (footnote omitted); see also W. S. Grimes, "Brand Marketing, Intrabrand Competition, and the Multibrand Retailer: The Antitrust Law of Vertical Restraints", *Antitrust Law Journal*, 64 (1995), 83; M. A. Lemley and M. P. McKenna, "Is Pepsi Really a Substitute for Coke? Market Definition in Antitrust and IP", *Georgetown Law Review*, 100 (2012), 2055.

[67] R. Schmalensee, "On the Use of Economic Models in Antitrust: The Realemon Case", *University of Pennsylvania Law Review*, 127 (1979), 1010 (quoting J. Robinson, *Economics of Imperfect Competition*, 2nd edn (New York: Macmillan, 1969), p. 5).

> [W]hat's missing from all that is the search for and the attempt to maximize scarcity rents. And that's kind of what brands are about. In brands you are trying to create a scarce asset and try to extract as much profit as you can from that scarce asset that you're creating.
>
> And that's an awful lot about what business is trying to do left and right. And I think, to a large extent, the way we think about antitrust, both economists and lawyers often kind of misses [*sic*] that. And I think that perspective is enormously useful.[68]

Put differently, cultivating powerful brands is the principal competitive strategy of many actors whom antitrust purports to regulate. Rather than embrace these perspectives, the antitrust world heavily discounts what is obvious to the business world – that brands matter and can be the source of durable competitive advantage and the ability to sell at a premium without significant constraint from potentially competing substitutes.

The rise of the Chicago School as the prevailing economic discourse for antitrust reinforced the focus on price theory to the exclusion of most other factors.[69] It relegated business discourse to the fringes of the profession of antitrust, whether practiced by the liberal or conservative wings of the discipline. Consider this quote by Judge Easterbrook about predatory pricing as an example of the prevailing ethos in antitrust law:

> Firms "intend" to do all the business they can, to crush their rivals if they can … Rivalry is harsh, and consumers gain the most when firms slash costs to the bone and pare price down to cost, all in pursuit of more business. Few firms cut price unaware of what they are doing; price reductions are carried out in pursuit of sales, at others' expense. Entrepreneurs who work hardest to cut their prices will do the most damage to their rivals, and they will see good in it. You cannot be a sensible business executive without understanding the link among prices, your firm's success and other firms' distress. If courts use the vigorous, nasty pursuit of sales as evidence of forbidden "intent," they run the risk of penalizing the motive forces of competition.[70]

Compare Judge Easterbrook's rhetoric to that used by Michael Porter, an economist by training, who established a preeminent reputation as

[68] R. Gertner, Testimony before Horizontal Merger Guidelines Review Project: A Series of Five Workshops (10 December 2009), p. 46, available at www.ftc.gov/sites/default/files/documents/public_events/horizontal-merger-guidelines-review-project/091210transcriptchicago.pdf.

[69] S. W. Waller, "The Language of Law and the Language of Business", *Case Western Reserve Law Review*, 52 (2001), 283–4; S. W. Waller, "The Use of Business Theory in Antitrust Litigation", *New York Law School Law Review*, 47 (2003), 120.

[70] *A.A. Poultry Farms, Inc.* v. *Rose Acre Farms, Inc.*, 881 F.2d 1396, 1401–2 (7th Cir. 1989). See also F. H. Easterbrook, "The Limits of Antitrust", *Texas Law Review*, 63 (1984), 6.

a business strategist. In his classic treatise *Competitive Strategy*, Porter lays out a roadmap of how to build and increase entry barriers, mobility barriers, and switching costs to maintain competitive advantage in the face of a strategic challenge from another firm.[71] In his catalog of strategies for raising structural barriers, increasing expected retaliation, and lowering the inducement for attack, he continues to emphasize product differentiation as the most effective strategy for obtaining a sustainable competitive advantage, while downplaying price competition.[72] He tellingly states: "Any fool can cut the price, goes the old maxim, and a firm often hurts itself more than the challenger in defending in this way."[73]

As a result of this cognitive dissonance, there has been a limited incorporation of brand management in antitrust.[74] This incoherence has allowed the continued and virtually unchecked growth of brand power. Strategic brand management has grown with little or no IP or antitrust consequences even where branding is a basis for meaningful market power, as traditionally defined in antitrust law. In other cases, a brand perspective may show that there is less, not more, cause for antitrust concern. Yet given that antitrust does not understand branding, antitrust cannot coherently navigate when brands have, or do not have, negative effects. Applying a knowledge of brands to antitrust law provides at least two benefits. First, understanding brands is necessary if antitrust law is to make coherent decisions about the businesses it regulates. Second, brands offer a powerful way to understand and improve specific aspects of antitrust doctrine and analysis.

4. Brand issues in antitrust doctrine

Although there are numerous antitrust cases that involve trademarks in some way, most of these contain no discussion, let alone analysis, of the

71 M. E. Porter, *Competitive Strategy: Techniques for Analyzing Industries and Competitors* (New York: Free Press, 1980).

72 *Ibid.*, pp. 21–2, 170–1. As one business commentator more succinctly noted, "Differentiate or die": J. Griffin, *Taming the Search-and-Switch Consumer: Earning Customer Loyalty in a Compulsion-to-Compare World* (San Francisco: Jossey-Bass, 2009), p. 119.

73 M. E. Porter, *Competitive Advantage: Creating and Sustaining Superior Performance* (New York: Free Press, 1985), p. 501.

74 M. D. Whitener, "Business Strategy and Antitrust: Editor's Note", *Antitrust*, 21 (Fall 2006), 5 (stating that business school perspective is "probably the least understood by most antitrust practitioners"); J. P. Guiltinan, "Choice and Variety in Antitrust Law: A Marketing Perspective", *Journal of Public Policy and Marketing*, 21 (2002), 260 (observing that, because of an emphasis on price, antitrust has tended to ignore non-price aspects that a marketing theory can illuminate).

role of brands more generally. Several reasons account for this peculiarity. First, most courts do not distinguish between the general issue of brands and the specific, but lesser, role of trademarks in supporting the larger branding effort. Second, most of the leading trademark-antitrust cases have been relatively easy cases where the use or licensing of a trademark has been a sham designed to implement a typical per se unlawful price-fixing or market division conspiracy.[75] Thus trademarks (and sometimes brands) were important factually, but not analytically, in deciding these cases.

What is more troubling is that antitrust law does not take its own methods seriously when applied to brands. As a result, antitrust law has tilted toward a laissez-faire, hands-off approach in a number of areas where the questions are much more difficult and complex than normally acknowledged. This section examines issues of market definition, all the different stages of merger analysis, and vertical distribution issues as areas where a more significant analysis of the power of brands leads to a richer analysis, even if it does not always change the outcome. The section also briefly analyzes the area of after-market restrictions where the brand issue has been discussed but ironically has served as a red herring to obscure the real issues at stake.

A. *Brands and the curious case of market definition*

Antitrust law depends heavily on market definition in almost every case and investigation except for hard-core price fixing and other cartel activity. Antitrust law has used a number of related methods to define the group of products and services that are viewed as effectively competing with each other. None have properly taken account of the power of brands.

The modern law of market definition began with the Supreme Court's 1956 decision in a monopolization case involving DuPont, the company that invented cellophane. Market definition was crucial to the case because monopolization law requires both proof of market power (the power to raise price or exclude competition) and an exclusionary act that injures competition.[76] While DuPont dominated sales of cellophane, it argued that the

[75] See *Palmer* v. *BRG of Georgia, Inc.*, 498 U.S. 46 (1990); *United States* v. *Sealy, Inc.*, 388 U.S. 350 (1967); *Timken Roller Bearing Co.* v. *United States*, 341 U.S. 593 (1951); see generally W. C. Holmes, *Intellectual Property and Antitrust Law* (New York: C. Boardman 2012), §§ 30.5, 31.1 n.8 (collecting cases).

[76] *United States* v. *E. I. du Pont de Nemours and Co.*, 351 U.S. 377, 389 (1956) (citing *Standard Oil Co. of New Jersey* v. *United States*, 221 U.S. 1, 85 (1911)).

relevant market was a much broader market for flexible wrapping materials in which it lacked any significant market share or power.[77]

The Court held that the relevant market for antitrust purposes consisted of those products and services that were reasonably interchangeable.[78] The opinion also identified cross-elasticity of demand, whether a decrease in price for one product would substantially reduce demand for potentially competing products, as a critical element in defining the contours of the market.[79]

The Court specifically rejected an important role for brands in this analysis, stating the "power that ... automobile or soft-drink manufacturers have over their trademarked products is not the power that makes an illegal monopoly."[80] The majority concluded that, except for some niche aspects of the industry, cellophane did in fact compete with such alternatives as glassine and greaseproof papers and that any attempted price increase for cellophane would cause substantial defection to these other wrapping materials for most foods and other pre-packaged consumer products.[81] As a result, DuPont could not be liable for monopolization because it lacked any significant market power in the properly defined market, despite the possibility that the DuPont cellophane brand conferred substantial real-world power.

The Supreme Court returned to the question of market definition in its 1962 Brown Shoe merger decision.[82] As in DuPont, the Court held that the outer boundary of a relevant market for antitrust purposes is set by reasonable interchangeability and cross-elasticity of demand.[83] The Court likewise indicated that "practical indicia" of how the products or services were sold and perceived by consumers were also relevant parts of the analysis and that "submarkets" may be relevant for antitrust purposes.[84]

The 1982 Merger Guidelines and its subsequent iterations introduced a somewhat more technical version of the same type of analysis to guide the Antitrust Division and the FTC in deciding whether to challenge proposed mergers and acquisitions between horizontal competitors.[85] These

[77] *Ibid.*, 381. [78] *Ibid.*, 395. [79] *Ibid.*, 400. [80] *Ibid.*, 393.

[81] *Ibid.*, 401, 403 nn.29 and 31. While many commentators have pointed out the so-called "Cellophane Fallacy," that relying on cross-elasticity of demand under these circumstances produced an unnecessarily broad relevant market (and hence no finding of market power), few have done so by considering brand issues.

[82] *Brown Shoe Co.* v. *United States*, 370 U.S. 294 (1962).

[83] *Ibid.*, 325. [84] *Ibid.*

[85] The current version of the guidelines is set forth in U.S. Department of Justice and Federal Trade Commission, Horizontal Merger Guidelines (August 2010), available at http://ftc.gov/os/2010/08/100819hmg.pdf [hereinafter Horizontal Merger Guidelines].

guidelines, as revised, have been adopted by numerous lower courts as the appropriate methodology for market definition in merger cases.[86]

The current version of the guidelines state:

> The hypothetical monopolist test requires that a product market contain enough substitute products so that it could be subject to post-merger exercise of market power significantly exceeding that existing absent the merger. Specifically, the test requires that a hypothetical profit-maximizing firm, not subject to price regulation, that was the only present and future seller of those products ("hypothetical monopolist") likely would impose at least a small but significant and non-transitory increase in price ("SSNIP") on at least one product in the market, including at least one product sold by one of the merging firms. For the purpose of analyzing this issue, the terms of sale of products outside the candidate market are held constant. The SSNIP is employed solely as a methodological tool for performing the hypothetical monopolist test; it is not a tolerance level for price increases resulting from a merger.[87]

The "small but significant and non-transitory" increase in price in the Guidelines is generally referred to as the SSNIP test and normally utilizes a hypothetical 5 percent price increase to determine the parameters of the relevant product and geographic market.[88] It has been widely adopted by other leading competition regimes for their own merger analysis processes.[89] Smaller market definitions are used when the agencies can show that the merging firms will effectively be able to price-discriminate and raise price against a subset of its customers within the relevant market.[90]

The economics literature suggests another test for market power. The Lerner index relies on the ratio of price over price minus marginal cost.[91]

See also Federal Trade Commission, Horizontal Merger Investigation Data, Fiscal Years 1996–2007 (2008), available at www.ftc.gov/os/2008/12/081201hsrmergerdata.pdf.

86 See, e.g., *F.T.C.* v. *Whole Foods Market, Inc.*, 548 F.3d 1028 (D.C. Cir. 2008); *F.T.C.* v. *H.J. Heinz Co.*, 246 F.3d 708 (D.C. Cir. 2001); *F.T.C.* v. *Tenet Health Care Corp.*, 186 F.3d 1045 (8th Cir. 1999); *United States* v. *Oracle Corp.*, 331 F. Supp. 2d 1098 (N.D. Cal. 2004); *F.T.C.* v. *Swedish Match*, 131 F. Supp. 2d 151 (D.D.C. 2000).

87 Horizontal Merger Guidelines, § 4.1.1 (footnote omitted).

88 *Ibid.*, § 4.1.2.

89 Commission, Guidelines on the Assessment of Horizontal Mergers Under the Council Regulation on the Control of Concentrations Between Undertakings, 2004 OJ (C31) 5, 6 at p. 10 [hereinafter EC Merger Guidelines] (incorporating by reference the Commission's separate 1997 Market Definition Notice (1997 OJ (C372) 5); Competition Bureau, Merger Enforcement Guidelines (2011) (Can.) Part 4, available at www.competitionbureau.gc.ca/eic/site/cb-bc.nsf/vwapj/cb-meg-2011-e.pdf/$FILE/cb-meg-2011-e.pdf. [hereinafter Canadian Guidelines].

90 Horizontal Merger Guidelines, § 4.1.4.

91 A. P. Lerner, "The Concept of Monopoly and the Measurement of Monopoly Power", *Review of Economic Studies*, 1 (1934), 169.

The Lerner index reflects the notion that the higher the ratio, the greater degree of monopoly power, reflecting the ability of the monopolist to increase price above the limits in a perfectly competitive market.[92] The Lerner curve is thus a measure of the firm's own price elasticity rather than the cross-elasticity of demand with other products.

An excellent hypothetical from Professor Glynn Lunney shows how none of these approaches to market definition, particularly the SSNIP test, work in a world of brands.[93] Professor Lunney posits a student lounge with a vending machine selling Coke soft drinks and one immediately next to it selling the equivalent Pepsi products. As one might expect, raising or lowering the price of soda even more than the 5 percent used in the standard version of the SSNIP test is unlikely to move a substantial proportion of loyal Coke drinkers over to the Pepsi machine or vice versa.[94]

As Professor Lunney concludes:

> If we were to extend this type of pricing analysis to other products, we would almost certainly find that many popular brands do possess sufficient brand loyalty to constitute distinct product markets. To the extent a protected trademark serves as the device for capturing such brand loyalty, even narrow trademark protection will quite often prohibit competitors from marketing a product that consumers will recognize and accept as a perfect or even reasonable substitute for the popular brand.[95]

This common-sense proposition is borne out by the very existence of brands. If cigarette smokers of a particular brand would "rather fight than switch," then there is no reasonably effective substitute for that brand and the relevant market is that brand of cigarettes.[96] If it is true (as opposed to just being a catchy slogan) that "nothing Runs like a Deere," then your market definition exercise is complete for the type of farm equipment you are examining for antitrust purposes.[97] At a more technical level, scholars have analyzed the effect of branding on internet price comparison sites and have shown that successful retail branding can maintain price disparities on identical electronic goods even though lower prices for the same item are at most one mouse click away.[98]

Once one considers the role of price discrimination, the need to consider brands increases. The Merger Guidelines also state that the ability to

[92] *Ibid.*
[93] G. Lunney, "Trademark Monopolies", *Emory Law Review*, 49 (1999), 424–5.
[94] *Ibid.* [95] *Ibid.*, 426–7 (citation omitted).
[96] *Ibid.*, 427–9. [97] *Ibid.*, 409 n.161.
[98] M. R. Baye and J. Morgan, "Advertising in Online Markets", *Management Science*, 55 (2009), 1139.

price-discriminate may be evidence of a smaller market definition than might otherwise be the case.[99] The 2006 Commentary to the Merger Guidelines points out several instances where the ability to price-discriminate has been the basis for government enforcement action.[100] The former chief economists for both United States antitrust agencies also have noted the importance of this concept in their scholarly writings and rely on price discrimination to establish relatively narrow market definitions when courts are reluctant to accept direct proof of anticompetitive unilateral effects.[101]

What is noticeably missing is the role of brand management in establishing the ability to price discriminate. As discussed above, brand management can be a critical element in facilitating price discrimination in important, but underappreciated, ways for market definition purposes. The very purpose of branding is to allow a company to charge higher prices compared to unbranded or commodity goods. The same producer may thus manufacture a branded item for a significant premium, a house (or private label) brand of the same item at a lesser price, and where necessary the bulk form of the item at prevailing market prices.[102] More generally, the branded segment of a market will typically enjoy a substantial premium over the unbranded segment even when produced by different manufacturers. This can even be the case for agricultural goods, the ultimate commodity goods for most purposes.[103]

Even when market power is recognized as a function of brands, courts and commentators misunderstand how the brands and market definition interact. For example, when an accepted market definition test is applied and shows the market power of a successful brand, the market power is often dismissed as either trivial or irrelevant for antitrust purposes.[104] As the Seventh Circuit noted in a recent case:

[99] Horizontal Merger Guidelines, § 4.14.

[100] US Department of Justice and Federal Trade Commission, Commentary on the Horizontal Merger Guidelines (2006), pp. 7–9.

[101] G. K. Leonard and M. A. Lopez, "Farrell and Shapiro: The Sequel", *Antitrust*, 14 (Summer 2009), 17.

[102] See generally A. Ezrachi and U. Bernitz (eds.), *Private Labels, Brands, and Competition Policy: The Changing Landscape of Retail Competition* (New York: Oxford University Press, 2009) (providing a detailed overview of the competitive and intellectual property issues raised by private brands in Europe and the US); J. A. Quelch and D. Harding, "Brands versus Private Labels: Fighting to Win", in *Harvard Business Review on Brand Management* (Boston, MA: Harvard Business School Press, 1999), p. 23.

[103] D. J. Hayes, S. H. Lence and A. Stoppa, "Farmer-Owned Brands?", *Agribusiness*, 20 (2004), 269, 270.

[104] D. J. Gifford, "Farewell to the Robinson-Patman Act? The Antitrust Modernization Commission's Report and Recommendation", *Antitrust Bulletin*, 53 (2008), 481, 485

> What is true is that a firm selling under conditions of "monopolistic competition" – the situation in which minor product differences (or the kind of locational advantage that a local store, such as a barber shop, might enjoy in competing for some customers) limit the substitutability of otherwise very similar products – will want to trademark its brand in order to distinguish it from its competitors' brands. But the exploitation of the slight monopoly power thereby enabled does not do enough harm to the economy to warrant trundling out the heavy artillery of federal antitrust law.[105]

The "slight" market power conferred by a location advantage in a particular neighborhood that the Court mocks says nothing, however, about the more real market power that a successful brand can confer.

Sometimes the criticism of markets defined by significant brand power is simply contradictory. As one commentator states:

> [W]here differentiation is significant among an array of products, many products that are interchangeable will not have a high degree of cross-elasticity of demand with other substitutes or may have none at all.[106]

The problem with this line of analysis is that if the products do not have a significant degree of cross-elasticity, then they should not be considered substitutes in the first place, despite physical or functional similarities. This line of reasoning trivializes a sophisticated branding industry whose entire purpose is to reduce or eliminate the substitutability of intuitively competing products or services. In simplest terms, when branding

(classifying the "'power' possessed by the seller of a product differentiated by brand name" as "often trivial"); B. Klein, "Market Power in Antitrust: Economic Analysis After Kodak", *Supreme Court Economic Review*, 3 (1993), 43, 72 (arguing that "no court would conclude that the manufacturers of [branded products possess] market power" based on the existence of "significant pricing discretion"); Landes and Posner, "Market Power in Antitrust Cases", 956–7 (rejecting Telser's analysis of own elasticity of branded consumer goods as irrelevant to market power for antitrust analysis); W. M. Landes and R. A. Posner, "Trademark Law: An Economic Perspective", *Journal of Law and Economics*, 30 (1987), 274–5; E. Elhauge, "Defining Better Monopolization Standards", *Stanford Law Review*, 56 (2003), 260 (noting that Landes and Posner would "recoil" from the suggestion that price discrimination due to branding indicates monopoly power); Schmalensee, "On the Use of Economic Models in Antitrust", pp. 1015–16 (arguing that ReaLemon, other brands of reconstituted lemon juice, and fresh lemon juice are all imperfect substitutes, but rejecting meaningful long-term market power for ReaLemon in any of the potential relevant markets).

105 *Sheridan* v. *Marathon Petroleum Co.*, 530 F. 3d 590, 595 (7th Cir. 2008).

106 J. A. Keyte, "Market Definition and Differentiated Products: The Need for a Workable Standard", *Antitrust Law Journal*, 63 (1995), 702 (ultimately arguing for a 20 percent or more version of the SSNP test for differentiated products).

strategies are successful, that success should be recognized rather than ignored, or assumed away.

Those proceeding from a trademark perspective err as well. Too often, those who do take the power of trademarks seriously err in the other direction and often assert that trademarks frequently or inevitably constitute monopolies. Even the work in this field that is more sophisticated is rarely being done by antitrust specialists and has not had a major impact in the competition law field.[107] Much of this work is also focused more narrowly on trademark law and not on the broader concept of the brand.[108]

Engaging with brands as part of market definition analysis does not mean that each brand is its own market for antitrust purposes or that the existence of a successful brand automatically constitutes proof of monopoly power. But taking brands seriously calls into question whether antitrust is ignoring the central reality of modern business practice in judging the competitive impact of those practices.

Nor is this an excuse for lazy lawyering. Courts are correct to reject facile shortcuts where market power based on the presence of brands is asserted but not proved. For example, it is hard to argue with a decision that declines to take judicial notice of the "fact" that Splenda-brand artificial sweetener is a separate market unto itself.[109] An attempt to prove that Marathon-brand gasoline had market power in the gasoline or credit card market based solely on submission of volume of sales and number of dealers also seems appropriately doomed to failure.[110] Similarly, most attempts to prove that franchise systems are their own markets will be problematic, particularly if viewed *ex ante* in a broader market of similarly branded franchise opportunities.[111] Mere invocation of the existence of brand power without rigorous proof is insufficient and not what we advocate.

[107] See C. J. Doellinger, "A New Theory of Trademarks", *Pennsylvania State Law Review*, 111 (2007), 823 (arguing that "trademark law provides a normative code of proper business conduct"); Lunney, "Trademark Monopolies"; D. E. Long, "Is Fame All There Is? Beating Global Monopolists at their Own Marketing Game", *George Washington International Law Review*, 40 (2008), 123.

[108] See Long, "Is Fame All There Is?"

[109] *Diamond Crystal Brands, Inc.* v. *Food Movers International, Inc.*, No. CV407-42, 2008 WL 2811940, at *3 (S.D. Ga. July 21, 2008).

[110] *Sheridan* v. *Marathon Petroleum Co.*, 530 F.3d 590, 595 (7th Cir. 2008), at 594–5.

[111] *Domed Stadium Hotel, Inc.* v. *Holiday Inns, Inc.*, 732 F.2d 480, 487–8 (5th Cir. 1984) (rejecting market of Holiday Inn franchises); *Midwestern Waffles, Inc.* v. *Waffle House, Inc.*, 734 F.2d 705, 713 (11th Cir. 1984) (no market for Waffle House franchise system). See generally Keyte, "Market Definition and Differentiated Products", 697 n.3 (collecting cases).

If one takes the notion of brands and branding seriously, however, there will be instances where a single brand of a product or service is the relevant market, even if there are physically identical or similar alternatives. The so-called cellophane fallacy may be an indirect recognition of just this reality.[112] The courts and agencies must look beyond the physical similarities and focus on whether the branding campaign has been successful enough so that consumers do not view the possible alternatives as reasonably effective substitutes.[113] This can also be true even when the brand is not accompanied by a registered trademark.[114]

B. *Brands and proof of anticompetitive harm*

The prediction of anticompetitive harm in merger cases is the closest that antitrust comes to the effective recognition of the unique role of brands. Following the definition of the relevant market and the measurement of the market share of the merging firms, the government or private plaintiff must show that the transaction is likely to produce a "substantial lessening of competition" or a tendency to create a monopoly.[115]

There are two theories of competitive harm in merger cases. The first – coordinated effects theory – is only rarely relevant to brand issues.[116] Coordinated effects theories of harm focus on whether the merger will raise the likelihood of collusion or oligopolistic interdependency as a result of changes in the structure of the market.[117] It is the most traditional of merger theories and focuses on the change in the market share of the merging firm, the increase in the concentration of the industry, and whether these changes will make it more likely that the merging firms will take the behavior of the remaining firms into account and limit their competitive zeal.[118]

112 See notes 76–84 and accompanying text.

113 *U.S. Anchor Mfg., Inc.* v. *Rule Industries, Inc.*, 7 F.3d 986, 997–8 (11th Cir. 1993), (explaining the dominant brand of anchors is the relevant product market because of consumer perception and behavior that competing makes and models of anchors are not effective substitutes).

114 *Vitale* v. *Marlborough Gallery*, No. 93 Civ. (PKL) 6276, 1994 WL 654494, at *3–4 (S.D.N.Y. July 5, 1994) (showing Jackson Pollack sub-market as example of powerful brand without trademark).

115 15 U.S.C. § 18 (2014).

116 Council Regulation 31/03, Guidelines on the Assessment of Horizontal Mergers Under the Council Regulation on the Control of Concentrations Between Undertakings, 2004 OJ (C 31/5) § IV.22 [hereinafter EU Merger Guidelines].

117 *Ibid.*, § IV.39.

118 Horizontal Merger Guidelines, § 7. The FTC did challenge the Diageo–Vivendi merger in the liquor industry on the grounds that the consolidation of the brands of

In contrast, unilateral effects (or non-coordinated effects) theories of harm focus on the effect of the merger regardless of the behavior of other firms.[119] Harm from unilateral effects can be shown at far less than near-monopoly market shares in markets with more differentiated products – precisely the type of markets where brands are likely to be involved.[120]

Mergers at relatively low market share levels can be barred on this theory when the government or private plaintiff can prove that customers view the merging firms as the closest substitutes to each other.[121] If no other firm is viewed as a close substitute, this would allow the merging firms to raise price or limit output and capture more profits than they would lose through customers migrating to weak substitutes.[122] In its strongest form, proponents of the unilateral effects theory suggest that proof of likely anticompetitive harm can be shown directly through proof of low customer loss without the indirect proxy of proof of market definition and market share.[123]

The older General Mills–Pillsbury merger involving flour is of importance because of the commodity nature of business.[124] The key to understanding the competitive harm alleged by the government lies in the success of these two firms in creating effective brands for what was otherwise a functionally equivalent baking product. Because of the branding,

rum caused by the merger would make coordination more likely with Seagrams, the remaining important player in the market. Diageo plc, 66 Fed. Reg. 66,896 (F.T.C. 27 December 2001).

[119] Horizontal Merger Guidelines, § 6. See also EU Merger Guidelines, at 36 (discussing role of brands in EU version of unilateral effects theory of competitive harm). See generally H. J. Hovenkamp, "Analyzing Horizontal Mergers: Unilateral Effects in Product-Differentiated Markets", University of Iowa Legal Studies Research Paper No. 09-12 (March 2009), available at http://ssrn.com/abstract=1359288.

[120] Horizontal Merger Guidelines, § 6.

[121] *Ibid.* [122] *Ibid.*

[123] J. B. Baker and C. Shapiro, "Reinvigorating Horizontal Merger Enforcement", in R. Pitofsky (ed.), *How the Chicago School Overshot the Mark: The Effect of Conservative Economic Analysis on U.S. Antitrust* (New York: Oxford University Press, 2008), p. 235; J. B. Baker and D. Reitman, "Research Topics in Unilateral Effects Analysis", American University Washington College of Law Research Paper No. 2009–37, available at http://papers.ssrn.com/sol3/papers.cfm?abstract_id=1504863. However, courts have been suspicious when the government's proof of harm under any theory has not also been accompanied by traditional market definition. *F.T.C.* v. *Whole Foods Market, Inc.*, 548 F.3d 1028, 1036 (D.C. Cir 2008); *United States* v. *Oracle Corp.*, 331 F. Supp. 2d 1098, 1110 (N.D. Cal. 2004).

[124] *General Mills Inc./Diageo PLC/Pillsbury Co.*, F.T.C. file No. 001-0213, available at www.ftc.gov/enforcement/cases-proceedings/001-0213/general-mills-incdiageo-plcpillsburyco-matter.

neither unbranded flour nor the imperfect substitute of certain regional brands were predicted to be an effective constraint on the merged companies' ability to raise prices and the merger was permitted subject to divestiture of Pillsbury's baking products line.[125]

The Merger Commentary also discusses the 1996 merger between Kimberly Clark and Scott as likely to produce anticompetitive harm for consumers of tissue paper and baby wipes on a similar unilateral conduct theory.[126] In another example, the Federal Trade Commission challenged a merger between Dreyer and Nestlé in a market they defined as "superpremium ice cream."[127] In these cases, there were a large number of potential suppliers of functionally interchangeable, and often physically identical, substitutes. That fact would indicate that courts would not be concerned with such mergers. Yet when the FTC considered the power of successful branding, they had a meaningful, accurate basis for being concerned about the transaction.

Nonetheless, the unilateral effects theory has not proved to be a fully viable entry point for brand management into antitrust theory and practice.[128] It remains the more controversial of two different theories in merger law, which is merely one of the important segments of antitrust practice. In addition, it has become highly technical and has lost sight of the importance of product differentiation and branding that gave birth to the theory in the first place.[129]

Despite these limitations, unilateral effects analysis is not always blind to the power of brand in market definition and does focus directly on the likely harms of product differentiation.[130] It addresses the vital question of the closeness of the available substitutes and avoids the artificial line-drawing common to traditional market definition.[131] It also suggests that harm to competition may occur at market shares not normally defined as potentially anticompetitive.[132] Here antitrust begins to

[125] *Ibid.*

[126] Commentary on the Merger Guidelines, pp. 29–30.

[127] *Ibid.*, pp. 28–9. *Nestlé Holdings, Inc.*, 68 Fed. Reg. 39,564, 39,565 (2 July 2003). But see *In re Super Premium Ice Cream Distribution Antitrust Litigation*, 691 F. Supp. 1262, 1268 (N.D. Cal. 1988) (indicating no separate market for superpremium ice cream, just a continuum of price and quality).

[128] See, e.g., *Oracle Corp.*, 331 F. Supp. 2d 1098; *State* v. *Kraft General Foods*, 926 F. Supp. 321 (S.D.N.Y. 1995). But see Horizontal Merger Guidelines, § 6 (expanding treatment of unilateral effects).

[129] Hovenkamp, "Analyzing Horizontal Mergers", pp. 16, 27–30.

[130] *Ibid.*, pp. 19–20. [131] *Ibid.*, pp. 23–4.

[132] *Ibid.*, pp. 18–20.

appreciate the central insight of brand management. When successful branding generates sufficient customer loyalty, customers simply do not regard other products as reasonably effective substitutes and are unwilling to switch.[133]

C. *Brands, entry barriers, and remedies*

Brands are quite important at a later stage in antitrust analysis. Once the relevant markets are defined, power within those markets is measured, and anticompetitive harm is shown to be likely, the agency or court will normally proceed with an analysis of barriers to entry.[134] If barriers to entry are low, then the firms are presumed to lack the ability to raise price or restrict entry and the merger is normally allowed.[135]

It has long been recognized that the possession of a strong brand or brands by the merging firms can constitute a barrier to entry.[136] If the presence of strong branding (or any other factor) would prevent timely and effective entry at pre-merger prices, then the Merger Guidelines and the Commentary will deem there to be substantial barriers to entry and continue on to later steps in the merger analysis.[137]

The EU Merger Guidelines also state that brands and patents may create entry barriers:

> [I]ncumbents may … enjoy technical advantages, such as preferential access to essential facilities, natural resources, innovation and R and D, or intellectual property rights … In particular, it may be difficult to enter a particular industry because experience or reputation is necessary to compete effectively, both of which may be difficult to obtain as an entrant. Factors such as consumer loyalty to a particular brand, the closeness of relationships between suppliers and customers, the importance of promotion or advertising, or other advantages relating to reputation will be taken into account in this context.[138]

[133] *Ibid.*, p. 22 (citations omitted).

[134] Horizontal Merger Guidelines, §9.

[135] *Ibid.*

[136] Commentary on the Horizontal Merger Guidelines, pp. 38–9 (addressing the likelihood of entry). See generally Scherer and Ross, *Industrial Market Structure and Economic Performance*, p. 600; Carlton and Perloff, *Modern Industrial Organization*, p. 609.

[137] Horizontal Merger Guidelines, §§ 3.0–3.3. Commentary on the Horizontal Merger Guidelines, pp. 38, 45. In addition, the presence or absence of strong brands can be a factor in determining whether a firm is deemed a rapid entrant, one whose ability to enter is so timely and effective that it should be considered a current participant in the relevant market. Horizontal Merger Guidelines, § 5.1.

[138] EU Merger Guidelines, § VI.71.

The United States Merger Commentary suggests that if competing producers can reposition their existing brands, then this will also be considered as an alternative to entry, determining whether the merger is likely to pose a threat to competition.[139] The reference to repositioning brands is one small example of the need to better understand the brand literature. The business literature on branding discusses in considerable detail why brand repositioning in the sense used by the Merger Guidelines is virtually impossible.[140] Brand repositioning normally refers to moving a brand either upwards or downwards in the minds of consumer. Both are difficult and problematic for different reasons. David Aaker notes:

> Straightforward repositioning from a mainstream or value market into an upscale one is nearly impossible. A mainstream brand simply lacks the upscale associations – such as user image, brand personality, and perceived quality – that are necessary to convince customers that the product or service should command a premium price.[141]

Moving a brand from a premium position to a mainstream or value brand is easier, but creates such significant risks that it is rarely worth doing.[142] The principal risk is forfeiting the price premium that having a premium brand allows in the first place.[143] The price reductions normally involved in such a move are extremely costly in both the short term and the long term and risk turning a branded, differentiated product or service back into a commodity.[144] Price reductions are normally a signal that the product has become an entirely different kind of brand.[145] Taken to an extreme, this is referred to as the "branding doom loop."[146]

As a result, most brand strategists suggest creating sub-brands where a new product or service is offered, rather than changing the core

[139] Commentary on the Horizontal Merger Guidelines, p. 31.

[140] Aaker, "Should You Take Your Brand to Where the Action Is?", 136.

[141] *Ibid.*, 142. See also D. Travis, *Emotional Branding: How Successful Brands Gain the Irrational Edge* (Roseville, CA: Prima Venture, 2000), p. 18 ("When a brand is first being introduced, there is a short period of time when marketers can influence its positioning. But after that, consumers decide what it means, and once they've decided, they don't like to change it."); Aaker, *Managing Brand Equity*, p. 122 ("upgrading a brand can be tricky").

[142] Aaker, "Should You Take Your Brand to Where the Action Is?", 137.

[143] *Ibid.* [144] *Ibid.*

[145] D. A. Aaker, *Building Strong Brands* (New York: Free Press, 1996), pp. 281–2 (citing Marlboro and Schlitz price-cutting strategies as examples).

[146] T. Calkins, "The Challenge of Branding", in A. M. Tybout and T. Calkins (eds.), *Kellogg on Branding: The Marketing Faculty of The Kellogg School of Management* (Hoboken, NJ: Wiley, 2005), pp. 1, 5.

brand products or services themselves.[147] A frequent example given is Courtyards by Marriott, which allowed Marriott to enter a lower-priced segment of the hotel industry, draw on the positive aspects of the Marriott brand, without damaging the core portion of Marriott's more upscale hotels. These strategies can be successful if done correctly, but to call this repositioning in the sense used by the Guidelines is a misnomer. Rather than repositioning an existing brand, companies normally create a new sub-brand to enter a different slice of the market.[148] This is simply a new entry, rather than brand repositioning, and is already adequately covered by the existing Guidelines.[149]

On the remedy side, brands have played an important role in deciding what to do about a transaction once the Agencies conclude that it represents a substantial risk to competition. The Agencies will work with the parties before proceeding to court to address areas of concern if the threat to competition can be remedied through partial divestitures, rather than a challenge to the entire transaction.[150] Numerous challenges to mergers have been resolved through the divestiture of assets that have consisted of, or included, competing brands, so that the post-merger market will consist of the same number of viable competitors as before.[151]

D. *Antitrust as enabler of brands: vertical restraints and resale maintenance*

Manufacturers' use of brands to control price and extract value that may otherwise go to a wholesaler or retailer or be retained by the consumer relates to the issue of vertical restraints, which addresses the relationship among manufacturers, wholesalers, and retailers. Vertical restraints are

[147] See Aaker, "Should You Take Your Brand to Where the Action Is?", 140–1; R. F. Maruca, "How Do You Grow a Premium Brand?", *Harvard Business Review*, 73 (Mar.–Apr. 1995), 22, 26.

[148] Aaker, "Should You Take Your Brand to where the Action Is?"

[149] Horizontal Merger Guidelines, § 9.

[150] US Department of Justice, Antitrust Division, Policy Guide to Merger Remedies (2004), pp. 30–1, available at www.usdoj.gov/atr/public/guidelines/205108.pdf.

[151] Commentary on the Horizontal Merger Guidelines, p. 38. Similarly, the divestiture or licensing of brands has been a condition of EU approval of a number of mergers. See, e.g., Case T-114/02, *Babyliss* v. *Commission*, 2003 ECR II-000, p. 176 (stating approval of merger of small kitchen appliance makers on condition of five-year exclusive trademark license); *Coca-Cola Bottling Co.* v. *F.T.C.*, 85 F.3d 1139 (5th Cir. 1996); cf. *Commission Decision (EC) 98/327 in Case IV/M.833, The Coca-Cola Company/Carlsberg A/S*, 1998 OJ (L 145), pp. 72–3, 110, 118 (permitting soft drink merger reducing international brands from four to three upon condition of divestiture of brand and assets).

imposed by a manufacturer on someone "down" the distribution chain such as a wholesaler or distributor, or between a wholesaler/distributor and a retailer. The restraints can involve price terms, which are referred to as resale price maintenance, or non-price terms such as the location, territories, or customers that a wholesaler, distributor, or retailer can serve. Antitrust has trended toward a permissive case-by-case rule of reason review of such restraints and away from per se rules barring such practices. A largely unobserved result of this trend has been that antitrust law has become the ultimate enabler of the growth of brands as a marketing strategy.

The seminal case in this regard, *Sylvania*, was premised on the importance of inter-brand competition, which is arguably an oxymoron, for any powerful successful brand by definition seeks to be its own category and face no competition.[152] *Sylvania* was decided against a complicated and rapidly evolving antitrust landscape for vertical non-price restraints.[153] In 1963 the Supreme Court declined to impose a per se rule against such restraints in *White Motors*.[154] Yet four years later, in *Schwinn*, the court held that non-price vertical restraints, which forbade the retailer to sell bicycles outside a certain geographic territory, were per se illegal if title had passed from the manufacturer to the bicycle dealer.[155] If title had not passed and the dealer was acting as the agent or consignee of the manufacturer, the restraints were subject to the rule of reason.[156]

Ten years later, the Court reversed itself and established a broad rule of reason analysis for all vertical non-price restraints. *Sylvania* itself concerned the efforts of a small market share television manufacturer to restructure its distribution system to stay alive and attempt to regain market share. To do so, the defendant established location and territorial restraints for its dealers and terminated its contract with a Northern California dealer who did not abide by those restrictions.[157]

The *Sylvania* Court began with the unsupported proposition that inter-brand competition was "the primary concern of antitrust law."[158] It then reasoned that certain restrictions on intra-brand competition (consumers' ability to shop at different dealers in the same brand) were necessary

152 *Continental T.V., Inc.* v. *G.T.E. Sylvania, Inc.*, 433 U.S. 36, 51–2 (1977).

153 *Ibid.*, 53 n.21.

154 *White Motor Co.* v. *U.S.*, 372 U.S. 253, 261–2 (1963).

155 *U. S.* v. *Arnold, Schwinn and Co.*, 388 U.S. 365, 373–5 (1967).

156 *Ibid.*, 380–2.

157 *Continental T.V.* v. *G.T.E. Sylvania*. at 38–40.

158 *Ibid.*, 52 n.19.

to promote inter-brand competition.[159] The Court noted that restrictions on intra-brand competition might also create incentives for dealers to promote a given brand and would prevent one dealer from free-riding off the promotional efforts of another.[160] In the Court's view, non-price vertical restraints could promote inter-brand competition more than it restricted intra-brand competition.[161] Such restraints were unlikely to harm consumers if the manufacturer imposing the restriction lacked significant market power.[162] The Court concluded that a broad rule of reason was the appropriate standard against which to weigh the antitrust consequences of such restrictions, regardless of the common law property concepts of title ownership and risk of loss.[163]

Missing from this analysis is any assessment of brand strength and product differentiation. We are not the first to note that the relationship between inter-brand and intra-brand is far more complex than the court acknowledges in *Sylvania* and its progeny. As Professor Grimes notes:

> The Court was on solid ground when it found that vertical restraints can provide an effective tool for promoting a producer brand. But the Court's assertion that interbrand competition provides "a significant check on the exploitation of intrabrand market power" fails to recognize that the brand promotion associated with vertical restraints tends to increase brand differentiation and that increased brand differentiation means lower demand elasticity, and hence greater market power. To put it another way, the more effective a vertical restraint is in differentiating a brand, the greater the reduction in interbrand competition.[164]

There are numerous examples of the concerns raised by Professor Grimes. Products like the Apple computer, the iPod, high-end bicycles, golf clubs, luggage, electronics, and a number of luxury and status goods have been subject to an increasing array of vertical price and non-price restraints.[165] While free-riding and other traditional justifications for resale price maintenance (RPM) and non-price vertical restraints may be present to varying degrees for some of these items, such concerns are not uniformly applicable or necessarily significant.[166] What is present across the board is

159 *Ibid.*, 54–5. 160 *Ibid.*, 55.

161 *Ibid.*, 65 (White, J., concurring).

162 *Ibid.*, 52 n.19. (majority opinion). 163 *Ibid.*, 57–8.

164 Grimes, *Brand Marketing*, 96 (citations omitted); see also R. L. Steiner, "The Inverse Association Between the Margins of Manufacturers and Retailers", *Review of Industrial Organization*, 8 (1993), 717 (arguing that strong advertised brands increase manufacturer's margins and prices and decrease retailer's gross margin).

165 Grimes, "Brand Marketing", 100–6.

166 *Ibid.*, 100–6.

the perceived need to build an effective branding strategy with the goal of creating consumers who no longer recognize other potential functional substitutes as effective substitutes.[167] As Professor Grimes notes, at some point the vertical restraints reduce both intra- and inter-brand competition.[168] Equally importantly, they increase the power and value of the brand in question.[169]

The most recent example of this line of simplistic thinking is the 2007 *Leegin* decision where the Supreme Court held 5–4 that even minimum resale price maintenance should be subject to the rule of reason.[170] The Court's decision was based on the same inter-brand competition and free-rider rationale used in *Sylvania*.[171] While the history of resale price maintenance is longer than that of vertical non-price restraints, it shows the same disregard of brands in formulating antitrust policy.[172]

As far back as 1911, the Supreme Court in *Dr. Miles* held that after title had passed from the manufacturer, any attempt to dictate the minimum price of an item was illegal.[173] The Court relied on the passage of title to reach this conclusion: the vertical price restriction was an unlawful restraint on alienation.[174] The Court rejected any defense based on the limited market position of the defendant or on the presence of trade secrets.[175] Although the Court did not speak specifically in terms of harm to competition, *Dr. Miles* became the basis of a per se rule against such restraints that lasted until *Leegin*.

The medicine in question was a so-called patent medicine, a tonic that calmed the nerves, probably through the alcohol that it contained. Such patent medicines were in fact not patented at all but secret formulas were developed by the manufacturer and sold under various brand names. The patent medicine industry began to rely on RPM strategies in the late nineteenth century at precisely the same time as the rise of branding and advertising that facilitated product differentiation began.[176]

It is not surprising that the Supreme Court did not discuss the branding aspects of *Dr. Miles* in formulating its rule. Brand management was still in its infancy. The Court saw the case more about property rights and the need to limit restrictions on the sale of products after title had passed.[177]

167 *Ibid.*, 118–19. 168 *Ibid.*, 107–13. 169 *Ibid.*, 113.

170 *Leegin Creative Leather Products, Inc.* v. *PSKS, Inc.*, 551 U.S. 877, 877 (2007).

171 *Ibid.*, 895–6. 172 *Ibid.*, 896–8.

173 *Dr. Miles Medical Co.* v. *John D. Park & Sons Co.*, 220 U.S. 373, 408 (1911).

174 *Ibid.*, 404. 175 *Ibid.*, 403–4.

176 B. Y. Orbach, "Antitrust Vertical Myopia: The Allure of High Prices", *Arizona Law Review*, 50 (2008), 262–3.

177 *Dr. Miles Medical Co.* v. *John D. Park & Sons*, 220 U.S., at 403–5.

This is a concern that modern intellectual property law addresses, if at all, through the first sale doctrine.[178] It is interesting to note, however, that the per se rule in *Dr. Miles* rejects the notion of any property rights remaining with the manufacturer after sale, despite the presence of a successful brand.

The severity of the per se rule from *Dr. Miles* against RPM waxed and waned for the next century. Almost immediately, the Court held that Section 1 of the Sherman Act did not apply to unilateral decisions to terminate a distributor for refusal to adhere to price levels.[179] The focus then shifted to what could be considered an illegal resale price agreement and what would be considered lawful unilateral decisions to terminate a contract with a dealer or distributor. Courts first expanded when an agreement could be inferred and then tightened the standard for finding an agreement to impose unlawful resale prices.[180]

As to substance of the per se rule from *Dr. Miles* against RPM, there was a similar expansion and contraction. The Court first explained that the *Dr. Miles* per se rule applied to both maximum and minimum RPM.[181] Then in 1997, the Court in *State Oil* v. *Khan* reversed course and held that the rule of reason would apply to maximum RPM.[182]

This set the stage for the *Leegin* case and the sea change eliminating the per se rule for even minimum RPM agreements. In *Leegin* the Court held that because RPM had the potential to increase inter-brand competition through the elimination of free-riding, case-by-case consideration under the rule of reason was justified.[183] Although the Court acknowledged the potential for RPM to be used as a facilitating device for either dealer or manufacturer cartels, it concluded that the rule of reason was flexible enough to handle these concerns.[184] To implement its holding in *Leegin*, the Court invited the lower courts to consider different presumptions and structured forms of the rule of reason as they gained experience in these cases to streamline review of the competitive consequences of RPM in different factual settings.[185]

178 Copyright Act, 17 U.S.C. § 106 (2010).

179 *United States* v. *Colgate & Co.*, 250 U.S. 300, 307 (1919).

180 *Monsanto Co.* v. *Spray-Rite Service Corp.*, 465 U.S. 752, 768 (1984); *Bergen Drug Co.* v. *Parke, Davis & Co.* 307 F.2d 725, 727–29 (3rd Cir. 1962).

181 *Albrecht* v. *Harold Co.*, 390 U.S. 145, 152 (1968).

182 *State Oil Co.* v. *Khan*, 522 U.S. 3, 22 (1997).

183 *Leegin* v. *PSKS*, at 882, 891–92 (2007). 184 *Ibid.*, 897.

185 *Ibid.*, 898–9. See generally C. A. Varney, "A Post-Leegin Approach to Resale Price Maintenance Using a Structured Rule of Reason", *Antitrust*, 24 (2009), 22.

Throughout the foregoing line of cases, the Supreme Court was obsessed with brands without ever seeking to define what brands were, how they functioned, why they mattered, or the effects of vertical restraints on the product differentiation critical to successful branding. The number of references to "brands," "inter-brand," and "intra-brand," or the total of all three, in the majority opinions of the Court's recent decisions addressing vertical restraints has risen dramatically without any fundamental attempt to grapple with the meaning of brands in the modern economy.

With this doctrinal evolution, brands have thrown off all antitrust constraints short of being used as a sham for traditional horizontal collusion among competitors. First, *Leegin* only applies where the manufacturer has parted with title.[186] Otherwise, the manufacturer is free to price at any level it wishes. Furthermore, the *Leegin* rule only applies when a manufacturer and a retailer make an agreement. A manufacturer is free to do anything it wishes under Section 1 of the Sherman Act regarding price if it acts alone.[187]

The debate over *Leegin* and RPM generally has also almost entirely ignored the role of brands. Of the many defenders and critics of *Leegin*, Professor Barak Orbach is one of the few commentators to note the centrality of brands to the RPM debate.[188] We wholeheartedly agree with him descriptively, even if we reach different normative conclusions for reasons discussed below. While the Supreme Court implies that brand image is the primary asset that should be protected from cradle to grave, and from creation though consumption, it never explicitly says so. This is a breathtaking proposition and a dramatic reversal from the historical assertion that the manufacturer lost all rights upon transfer of title. Now title is virtually meaningless, and the manufacturer's property-like interest in its brand is a strong justification for restrictions on price, marketing, and use long after the item has been transferred down the chain of distribution.

[186] *Leegin* v. *PSKS*, at 898.

[187] *United States* v. *Colgate*, 250 U.S. 300, at 307.

[188] See Orbach, "Antitrust Vertical Myopia", 266; see also B. Y. Orbach, "The Image Theory: RPM and the Allure of High Prices", *Antitrust Bulletin*, 55 (2010), 277; cf. P. E. Areeda and H. Hovenkamp, *Antitrust Law: An Analysis of Antitrust Principles and Their Application*, 2nd edn, 19 vols. (New York: Aspen Law and Business, 2004) vol. VIII, pp. 324–5 (arguing that presence of a strong brand is a factor favoring treating a particular resale price maintenance agreement as per se unlawful). But see generally G. R. Ackert, "An Argument for Exempting Prestige Goods from the Per Se Ban on Resale Price Maintenance", *Texas Law Review*, 73 (1995), 1185 (arguing in terms of prestige goods, but not directly engaging brands literature).

It is one thing to say that economics, rather than property law, should govern antitrust liability. It is another, far more troubling thing, however, in effect to propertize brands without explicitly saying so and strip downstream distributors and, potentially, consumers of their traditional property rights in the items they purchase and consume. If brands are going to become legal super-property, this stealth approach is an improper substitute for the robust public debate that such a dramatic change in the law should require.

Leegin was not a particularly compelling case to empower the brand in this fashion. The defendant in *Leegin* had only a middling brand for women's purses and belts,[189] with no significant free-rider issues to justify the resale price maintenance scheme in question. The defendant may not have had significant market power, whether measured traditionally or through a brand lens. But nor did it have many compelling arguments that the restraints in question were necessary or even useful in promoting its brand or creating further product differentiation within its retail category. Regardless of who should prevail in *Leegin* or future cases, antitrust will not have strong tools to deal with these types of issues under the rule of reason that the Supreme Court has announced without a more sophisticated understanding of brands and brands management.

5. Where brands take us

Our claim is simple. Brands are important tools in business competition; therefore, antitrust law (as well as trademark law) ought to catch up to this real-world practice. We have shown that brands are far more complex and robust than the legal conception of brands as merely trademarks. In addition, we have also shown how antitrust law has tried to manage brand practices, but only inadvertently, and without appreciating what it was doing. This willful blindness has enabled the power of brands to grow without asking whether such increased power was desirable. This chapter is a call to see the importance of brands and to begin to integrate understanding of brands into the law. We close with what we think must happen for that call to reach its full potential and set forth the benefits of such a shift.

So far, the significance of brands has eluded antitrust law. Brands are not a well-defined antitrust issue. This situation has allowed brands to

[189] *Leegin* v. *PSKS*, at 882.

grow in importance as part of business practice and strategy and misses the ways in which brands affect competition and society.

The law must recognize the transcendence of brands as a business strategy. A rich literature on brands exists and can aid in remedying the law's blind spot on brands. Brands are a fundamental business strategy designed to create artificial scarcity, economic rents, and consumer loyalty, and indeed to make brands a core aspect of consumer identity. Brands and the brand literature provide an important lens for analyzing and formulating legal policy.

This opportunity has rarely been seized. The law of antitrust has either pretended that brands don't matter or have discussed them indirectly by filtering this key business concept through the language of law and economics. For example, Professor Orbach is correct when he notes that "[t]he prevalence of RPM in markets for premium-brand goods has never drawn serious attention in the RPM literature."[190] But he is only correct with respect to the legal literature and the law and economics literature on this subject. As discussed throughout this chapter, the marketing and brand management literature is replete with discussions on this topic. This alternate body of literature is rarely drawn upon by either the proponents or the critics of the past or current legal rules on the myriad of business practices that antitrust and trademark law seek to regulate.

We are not calling for replacing the language of economics with the language of business literature. Economics is a vital and important language in the law, but it must be supplemented if we are to have a coherent legal regime with respect to brands. When law and economics first entered the legal academy, few had a background in economics; yet now some level of economic analysis travels with much of legal education.

The legal academy today faces a similar problem with brands. Most lawyers lack formal business or marketing training. Regardless of formal training, the business literature is challenging. It is large and often draws on other social science disciplines.[191] Some of the literature is anecdotal or motivational and aimed at a popular audience of either students or managers in the workforce. And as with almost any discipline, some of it lacks rigor.

Nonetheless, the field of marketing and brand management is a well-established and respected field with its own serious scholars,

[190] Orbach, "Antitrust Vertical Myopia", 266.

[191] See Heding *et al.*, *Brand Management Research*, pp. 246–7 (describing seven different scientific traditions found in brand theory).

journals, conferences, networks, vocabulary, and other means of transmission. An understanding of the field is necessary to understand fully the concepts of product differentiation, market segmentation, price discrimination, customer loyalty, and customer identity that are at the heart of modern brand management. Scholars, practitioners, policy makers, legislators, and judges need to be as familiar with the literature and language of marketing and brand management as they are with different strands of economic thought.[192]

Such a familiarity would likely result in a different language and vocabulary for both antitrust and trademark law – one that addresses the realities of how business operates. In antitrust, talk of cross-elasticity of demand and own elasticity would probably be replaced by analysis of "shoppers" or "switcher[s]" versus "loyals."[193] Survey data might be considered instead of or along with regression and simulation models. The focus would be on how companies compete to create loyal consumers who will return over and over again to the same brand or family of brands throughout their lifetime and trade up to the higher price, higher profit segments of the brand.[194] The competitive strategic techniques to be analyzed will vary from case to case, but would include brand extensions, increasing switching costs in different ways, RPM and other restrictions on distribution to maintain and enhance brand image, bundled discounts, loyalty rebates, increasing shelf space, and denying these same advantages to competitors in order to segment the market to the utmost degree possible. Few, if any, of these techniques emphasize price competition, which is the starting point for most economic analysis.

A deeper understanding of brands and brand discourse can yield a better picture of what the law is doing and a metric by which to see whether those results match the law's stated foundations. Insofar as the law champions a brand result, it should do so explicitly and be better equipped to say so. This, in turn, would permit clear, critical discussion regarding the normative desirability of such outcomes. We are in a world where the law fosters cradle-to-grave protection for companies' branded goods and

[192] See Waller, "The Language of Law", 337–8.

[193] See Griffin, *Taming the Search-and-Switch Consumer, passim*; Baye and Morgan, "Advertising in Online Markets", passim.

[194] See, e.g., Giorgio Armani, www.giorgioarmani.com/; Marc Jacobs, www.marcjacobs.com/; Pottery Barn, www.potterybarn.com (describing families of brands aimed at different age and income demographics).

services. The law must expand its horizons to appreciate what it is doing, articulate what it is doing, and answer whether it wants to be doing so in some other manner, if at all.

6. Conclusion

Brands may be discussed as part of competition and business strategy. Brands may be discussed as part of separate doctrines within the law. But uncoupling brands, competition, and the law is a mistake. The three operate together.

Companies use a combination of logos, packaging, advertising, distribution, and more to fashion a specific brand that functions as a company's identity, generates consumer loyalty, and affects the consumer's identity and self-image to reinforce that loyalty. The brand becomes a powerful tool, allowing businesses to affect demand, exert power within supply chains, control price, and more. Rather than simply functioning as a mark that identifies the source and quality of a good or service, a brand is a vital, dynamic part of a company's competitive repertoire.

Despite brands being a dominant way in which the business world conceives of a company's value and competition strategy, legal discourse has little to no understanding about these important, powerful business tools. This flaw has led to the law's permissive treatment of brands, with little appreciation for the implications of those behaviors as they affect the marketplace and competition in general. Specifically, two areas of the law – trademark and antitrust – that ought to operate as complementary parts of a coherent system to regulate competition, are giving corporate mark holders broad and increasing competitive brand power without either an explicit public policy debate or a conscious attempt to craft an appropriate legal regime to manage brands.

The current debate misses questions about the appropriate limits, if any, for the near absolute control of brand image, and the interaction of manufacturers, distributors, and consumers. Instead, strange doctrines with dubious theoretical foundations have arisen. For example, in trademark law odd results in confusion analysis and recent expansions of the law such as initial interest confusion and dilution, grow and upset the balance between competing producers and between producer and consumer. In antitrust law courts analyze questions of market definition, anticompetitive harm, barriers to entry, and vertical restraints, but fail to see how a brand, by design, directly affects these issues.

Competition law can and must begin to remedy the situation by simply drawing on the rich literature on brands and embracing a brand perspective as competition law confronts the realities of brands and competition. Such a perspective would allow all involved with competition policy to see more precisely what is at stake in a given issue.

Brands and competition travel together and will continue to do so well into the twenty-first century. As one commentator has said, the brand is the "reason, or 'logos' of the economy."[195] If legal systems and legal discourse wish to remain relevant and vibrant as they address competition, they must understand the brand. Failing to understand brands will lead to further confusion and dissonance as the law attempts to manage business realities with incomplete theoretical models. Understanding brands can only enhance the way in which brands and the law interact to provide a coherent, dynamic competitive system.

[195] Lury, *Brands: Logos of the Global Economy*, p. 6.

5

Brands and brand management

Insights from marketing for antitrust

GREGORY T. GUNDLACH AND JOAN M. PHILLIPS

1. Introduction

Brands have been all but ignored in antitrust. Informed by theory from neoclassical economics that finds that product differentiation, including that achieved through branding, yields ambiguous effects for economic efficiency, a widely held view is that "product differentiation merits special attention in antitrust only in limited circumstances."[1] Yet an emerging view is that product differentiation deserves more attention and greater concern when it involves brands and brand management.[2] Contending that neoclassical economics is limited in its capacity to fully comprehend the power of brands and citing the recent proliferation of prominent brands in the economy, scholars have called for re-examination of this marketing practice in antitrust.[3] These calls counsel that to fully understand the nature and implications of brands, antitrust must integrate insights from other fields including business theory and research.

This state of affairs provides the impetus for the current chapter. Our goal is to draw on insights from marketing thought and practice to investigate the implications of contemporary branding and brand management for antitrust. To accomplish this, we first summarize the understanding of product differentiation in neoclassical economics that has led to the

[1] P. E. Areeda, H. Hovenkamp and J. L. Solow, *Antitrust Law: An Analysis of Antitrust Principles and their Application* (New York: Wolters Kluwer, Law & Business, Aspen Publishing, 2007); see also E. H. Chamberlin, "Product Heterogeneity and Public Policy", *American Economic Review* 40 (1950), 85–92.

[2] See e.g., D. R. Desai, "From Trademarks to Brands", *Florida Law Review* 64 (2012), 981–99; D. R. Desai and S. W. Waller, "Brands, Competition, and the Law", *BYU Law Review* (2010), 1425–99; M. P. McKenna, "Testing Modern Trademark Law's Theory of Harm", *Iowa Law Review* 95 (2009), 63–117.

[3] See Desai and Waller, "Brands, Competition, and the Law", 1425–99.

conclusion that brands are of limited concern to antitrust. Our attention then turns to key features of modern branding and brand management as developed in the marketing literature. Our review of this literature identifies several insights for antitrust. These include:

(a) that consumer purchase choices combine complex bundles of tangible and intangible benefits and brands capture the meaningful differences reflected in the competing bundles of these benefits for consumers;
(b) that marketers employ sophisticated strategies of brand management to symbolize and communicate the differentiated value of products and services; and
(c) that successful brand management yields brands that possess significant value for the organizations that own them and considerable loyalty on the part of consumers who patronize them.

Drawing on the above insights we clarify views in antitrust concerning brands and then further develop them to better understand the implications of powerful brands for antitrust. Our effort reinforces the opinion of scholars who have called for greater attention to brands in antitrust. First, we describe how consumers make purchase choices based upon aspects of products that go well beyond their functional utility. This clarifies that brands are not an "artificial" form of product differentiation, but instead communicate meaningful differences to consumers that in turn influence their purchase decisions.[4] This understanding reinforces the idea that powerful brands can affect consumers' perceptions of competition. Second, we show that brands are an integral part of a firm's marketing efforts. This establishes that brands are not a way to "move beyond" marketing, but rather are fundamental to it. This insight bolsters the view that branding is an important and consequential competitive practice. Third, we explain how a powerful brand can decrease interbrand competition, but at the same time increase intrabrand competition. This makes clear that rather than "eliminating" competition, powerful brands affect competition in complex ways. This knowledge buttresses the view that powerful brands can affect competition in important ways. Together these insights bolster claims by scholars who contend that powerful brands warrant greater attention and more widespread concern in antitrust.

[4] *Ibid.*

2. Economics of product differentiation

In this section we briefly overview the economics of product differentiation. Product differentiation has been extensively studied in economics applying models of monopolistic competition. These models originate in the work of Edward Chamberlin, who distinguished monopolistic competition as a type of imperfect competition.[5] Models of monopolistic competition inform economic understanding of the efficiency of markets comprising goods and services that are considered imperfect substitutes for (i.e., differentiated from) one another. They have therefore been applied to aid in understanding mechanisms of product differentiation including brands and brand management. In this section we take an overview of the qualities of differentiated products that comprise monopolistic competition and the effects of monopolistic competition on firm profits and market efficiency. We then examine the application of these principles in antitrust to understand product differentiation, including that achieved through brands and brand management.

A. *Product differentiation*

In economics product differentiation refers to a situation in which potential buyers perceive differences in the products of rival sellers. As described in the economics literature these "differences may be real differences ... or they may be primarily the result of image differences."[6] Real differences are those found in the physical and design characteristics of a product such as size, styling, horsepower, and so on. Other differences are "subjectively" viewed by consumers and established through advertising and branding. In many markets the products of competing sellers are not homogeneous but differentiated to varying degrees, either in physical or design characteristics or else in the way consumers subjectively view them. Whether considered "real" or based on other differences, the main requirement is that consumers regard differences in competitors' products sufficiently important to be willing to pay a higher price for their preferred product.[7]

[5] E. H. Chamberlin, "The Theory of Monopolistic Competition", *Journal of Business & Economics Research* 4 (1933), 17–26.

[6] W. K. Viscusi, J. E. Harrington and J. M. Vernon, *Economics of Regulation and Antitrust*, 4th edn (Cambridge, MA: MIT Press, 2005), p. 87.

[7] *Ibid.*

Where product differentiation is present in a market, models of *monopolistic competition* demonstrate in mathematical terms that in the long run each competitor will earn zero profits. In the short run, product differentiation confers some market power to each competitor in the sense that each competitor can raise its price without a total loss of sales (because the firm's demand curve is slightly downward-sloping). However, over the long run profits acquired from this market power are squeezed out as competitors enter the market. The addition of competitors over time implies a smaller and smaller volume of sales for each competitor until such time as no excess profits remain to attract the entry of additional competitors. The result is that each firm will be able to recover its full costs but no more, resulting in zero economic profits.

Markets characterized by product differentiation and involving monopolistic competition can pose complex challenges to economic efficiency. These include static efficiencies in the form of allocative and productive efficiency. They also include dynamic efficiency in the form of innovation and growth. Each has been identified as an important component of economic efficiency. On the one hand, monopolistic competition results in the loss of economic efficiency, given that firms with market power are able to deviate from perfect competition through charging prices that exceed their marginal costs (reducing allocative efficiency), and operating with excess capacity, given their output is less than the output associated with minimum average cost (reducing productive efficiency). On the other hand, monopolistic competition can result in gains to economic efficiency through increases to product quality and product variety that better match the individual tastes of consumers (increasing allocative efficiency). Monopolistic competition involving differentiated products and loyal consumers may also allow firms to achieve economies of scale (increasing productive efficiency). Finally, monopolistic competition may also encourage research, development, and innovation when firms attempt to prolong the life of their brands through reinventing their appeal over time (increasing dynamic efficiency). Consequently, determining the net effects for overall economic efficiency resulting from product differentiation is difficult.

B. *Application in antitrust*

Given the ambiguous effects of monopolistic competition for economic efficiency, many antitrust scholars contend that product differentiation merits special attention only in limited circumstances.[8] This includes in the determination of market definition when considering mergers, and in instances of collusion.[9] However, other antitrust scholars view product differentiation as deserving more attention and greater concern where it involves powerful brands.

The opinion that brands as a form of product differentiation deserves increased attention in antitrust derives from the view that understanding the full impact of brands on competition is made difficult by antitrust analyses that rely on neoclassical models of competition.[10] Key limitations identified include the ability of these analyses to determine when brands confer meaningful market power and how brand management practices should be interpreted. As a consequence economic analysis is considered to have inhibited the development of sound principles for understanding brands in antitrust.

3. Marketing insights for understanding brand and brand management

Advocates for the re-examination of brands in antitrust counsel that to fully understand their effects for economic efficiency, antitrust can learn from insights developed in other disciplines, including business theory and research. In this section, drawing on key marketing literatures, we describe important insights that have implications for understanding brands in antitrust.

A. Consumers and brands

According to marketers, customers do not buy products; instead they buy the benefits of products.[11] The benefits, or value, that customers seek are reflected in the consequences of purchasing and using a product.[12] This idea is exemplified in the classic adage: "customers buy holes, not

[8] L. A. Sullivan and W. S. Grimes, *The Law of Antitrust: An Integrated Handbook*, 2nd edn (St Paul, MN: Thomson West, 2006).

[9] Areeda *et al.*, *Antitrust Law*; Chamberlin, "Product Heterogeneity", 85–92.

[10] See e.g., Desai and Waller, "Brands, Competition, and the Law", 1425–99.

[11] D. I. Hawkins and D. L. Mothersbaugh, *Consumer Behavior: Building Marketing Strategy*, 12th edn (New York: McGraw-Hill/Irwin, 2013), p. 358; P. Kotler and K. L. Keller, *Marketing Management*, 14th edn (Upper Saddle River, NJ: Prentice Hall, 2012), p. 326.

[12] P. E. Green, Y. Wind and A. K. Jain, "Benefit Bundle Analysis", *Journal of Advertising Research* (April 1972), 32–6; J. P. Peter and J. C. Olson, *Consumer Behavior and Marketing Strategy*, 9th edn (New York: McGraw-Hill/Irwin, 2010), p. 73.

drills." In this section we describe how consumer purchase choices combine complex bundles of tangible and intangible benefits and how brands capture the meaningful differences reflected in the competing bundles of these benefits for consumers.

Benefits sought by consumers can be tangible – the physical, functional, performance outcomes of using a product that consumers experience directly. Or they can be intangible – the internal, psychosocial, personal outcomes such as how the product makes you feel.[13] When making a purchase, customers think of their purchases as more than a collection of functional attributes, and rather as a complex bundle of tangible and intangible benefits that reflects "the sum of the physical, psychological, and sociological satisfactions the buyer derives from purchase, ownership, and consumption."[14]

Brands are designed to capture and reflect the benefit bundle sought by consumers. The American Marketing Association defines a brand as one or more visual elements, and explicitly that a brand is a "name, term, sign, symbol or design or a combination of them intended to identify the goods and services of one seller or group of sellers and to differentiate them from those of competition."[15] Historically, prominent brands emerged as mass-produced packaged merchandise that replaced locally produced merchandise sold from bulk containers.[16] Trademarks, the precursor to today's brands, were used to identify and communicate the differentiated value reflected in these offerings.

Today both consumers and marketers take a broader view of a brand that extends beyond a simple trademark or collection of visual elements (e.g., name, logo, symbol, etc.). Modern brands also represent aspirational brand identities that deliver both emotional and self-expressive benefits to consumers who use them;[17] that is, brands capture multiple levels of benefits sought by consumers. Consumer researchers believe that the mental representations that consumers have of a brand can be depicted as a hierarchical benefit-chain that begins with a brand's distinguishing attribute at the base, and then "ladders" up the chain as the tangible

13 Peter and Olson, *Consumer Behavior*, pp. 72–3.

14 J. P. Peter and J. H. Donnelly Jr., *A Preface to Marketing Management*, 13th edn (New York: McGraw-Hill/Irwin, 2013), p. 85.

15 American Marketing Association, *Dictionary*, available at www.ama.org/resources/Pages/Dictionary.aspx.

16 K. L. Keller, *Strategic Brand Management: Building, Measuring, and Managing Brand Equity*, 3rd edn (Mahwah, NJ: Pearson, 2008), p. 44.

17 D. A. Aaker, *Building Strong Brands* (New York: The Free Press, 1996), p. vii.

attribute (e.g., 1/4 in drill bit) provides the consumer with a functional benefit (e.g., hole), which provides one or more psychosocial benefits (e.g., accomplishment), which then ultimately satisfies some higher-order personal value (e.g., peace of mind).[18] It is this collective bundle of benefits – arrayed along a hierarchy – that consumers associate with a brand and consider in a choice context.

Branding is all about creating differences.[19] Indeed, branding has been used by sellers for centuries to differentiate one offering from another.[20] Marketing managers focus on developing points of difference that consumers will perceive as offering the most benefits. Points of difference are attributes or benefits that consumers strongly associate with a brand, evaluate positively, and believe they could not find in the same extent with a competing brand.[21] Consumers' brand choices frequently depend on the perceived uniqueness of brand associations. Points of parity, however, are attributes and benefits that are not unique to a particular brand, but are shared across a subset of brands.[22] Consumers identify competing brands through points of parity, but choose a brand based on points of difference. Marketers position their brands in the marketplace by choosing and establishing the brand's points of parity and points of difference.

To consumers, brands can provide several functions.[23] First, brands identify the maker of the product, allowing consumers to assign responsibility for the consumption experience back to the manufacturer, thereby reducing the consumer's risk. Brands also take on special meaning for consumers that is formed from prior experiences with the brand. Based on these experiences consumers learn which brands best satisfy their need and which brands do not. As a result, brands can provide a decision-making heuristic for consumers by simplifying the selection process and reducing search costs. The meaning that brands can hold for consumers can be profound, as consumers frequently form a deep exchange relationship with the brand. Consumers offer their trust and loyalty in exchange for the expected benefits that they will derive from

[18] See T. J. Reynolds and J. C. Olsen, *Understanding Consumer Decision Making: The Means-End Approach to Marketing and Advertising Strategy* (Mahwah, NJ: Lawrence Earlbaum Associates, Publishers, 2001), pp. 25–62; T. J. Reynolds and J. M. Phillips, "A Review and Comparative Analysis of Laddering Research Methods: Recommendations for Quality Metrics", *Review of Marketing Research*, 5 (2009), 130–74.

[19] Keller, *Strategic Brand Management*, p. 38.

[20] D. A. Aaker, *Managing Brand Equity* (New York: The Free Press, 1991), p. 7; Keller, *Strategic Brand Management*, p. 2.

[21] Keller, *Strategic Brand Management*, p. 107.

[22] *Ibid.*, p. 109. [23] *Ibid.*, pp. 6–9.

the brand. As noted earlier, these benefits are not solely functional, as brands can also serve as symbolic devices that allow consumers to project a certain self-image. When brands are publicly consumed, they allow consumers to communicate to themselves and others the type of person they are or desire to be. Finally, brands can also signal product quality and serve as an important tool for managing risk.[24]

B. Marketers and brand management

The objective of branding and brand management is to establish a differentiated presence in the market for a marketer's benefit bundles that attracts and retains loyal customers. In fact, a brand name is perhaps the single most important element on a product's package, as it is this insignia that serves as the brand's unique identifier.[25] In this section we describe how marketers employ sophisticated strategies of branding and brand management to symbolize and communicate the differentiated value of their products and services.

A distinguishing characteristic of modern marketing has been its focus on the creation of differentiated brands.[26] For many firms the primary focus of their marketing strategy is building, developing, and nurturing brands.[27] In fact, the term product strategy is often used synonymously with brand strategy. Firms characteristically use branding strategies to carry out their marketing strategy.[28] For example, firms often sell more than one product, and collectively those brands within a firm's "product mix" or "brand portfolio" are often sold or marketed jointly as part of a *co-branding strategy.* Firms deploy a *line extension strategy* when they use a brand name to facilitate entry into a new market segment (e.g., Diet Coke). A *brand extension strategy* is used when firms enter a new product category (e.g., extending Virgin Records to Virgin Airlines). *Family branding* is when a corporate name is used to enter a new market or product class (e.g., Honda Lawnmowers). A *multi-branding strategy* is used when firms assign a unique brand name to each product in its product line.

Although brands have long played a role in business and commerce, it was not until the twentieth century that branding and brand associations

24 *Ibid.*
25 Peter and Donnelly, *A Preface to Marketing Management*, p. 89.
26 Aaker, *Managing Brand Equity*, p. 7.
27 Peter and Donnelly, *A Preface to Marketing Management*, p. 88.
28 *Ibid.*, p. 90.

became central to marketplace competition.[29] More recently, branding and the marketing of brands has become more specialized and sophisticated, requiring the development of more advanced marketing techniques,[30] and market research is used to help identify and develop the bases for brand differentiation.[31]

Today's modern brand management system, first put into place by Procter & Gamble, assigns a manager to each brand and charges the brand manager with full responsibility for the financial success (or failure) of the brand. This current brand management system replaced an older model where managers were assigned to each functional area required to manage the brand (e.g., advertising, sales, research, regulation, etc.). The modern-day brand management system emerged as more sophisticated brand-nurturing organizational forms were needed to help coordinate brands across markets, products, roles, and context, as these challenges strained the conventional system.[32] More recently, marketers are managing entire brand systems that comprise brands and sub-brands that are intertwined.[33] The challenge facing today's marketers is to understand the role each brand plays in the firm's marketing strategy and to manage the system accordingly.

A brand is a strategic asset that is central to a firm's long-term performance and is managed as such.[34] The strategic brand management process involves the design and implementation of marketing programs and activities to build, measure, and manage the value of the firm's brands.[35]

Indeed, building and managing powerful brands is the cornerstone of many marketing programs. Modern-day marketing programs are geared toward building powerful brands that create customer interest and loyalty by providing tangible and intangible value that forms the basis of long-term customer–brand relationships.[36] For most organizations brands are the bases for their competitive advantage. However, strong brands do not just happen, but are a result of the successful implementation of sophisticated marketing programs.

Given the value of these brands and the growing complexity of the marketplace, sophisticated branding practices have become an

[29] Aaker, *Managing Brand Equity*, p. 7.
[30] Keller, *Strategic Brand Management*, p. 44.
[31] Aaker, *Managing Brand Equity*, p. 7.
[32] Aaker, *Building Strong Brands*, p. viii.
[33] *Ibid.*, p. 358. [34] *Ibid.*, p. vii.
[35] Keller, *Strategic Brand Management*, pp. 38–41.
[36] Aaker, *Building Strong Brands*, p. 357.

increasingly important part of a firm's marketing. It is not easy to build brands in today's environment. Among the many challenges marketers face are more savvy and informed consumers, brand proliferation, media fragmentation, increased competition, increased costs, and greater accountability.[37] In response to these challenges, marketers work to build, maintain, and manage the brand's value, or equity.

C. *The benefits of successful brand management*

To firms, brands represent enormously valuable pieces of legal property and their value, or equity, can be reflected in many ways. In this section we describe how successful brand management can yield brands that possess significant value for the organizations that own them and elicit considerable loyalty on the part of consumers who patronize them.

Brand equity is perhaps one of the most important marketing concepts to emerge in the 1980s and it has elevated the importance of the brand in marketing strategy.[38] Conceptually, brand equity can be thought of as a set of assets (and liabilities) linked to a brand's name and symbol that adds to (or subtracts from) the value provided by a product or service to a firm and/or that firm's customers.[39] More simply, brand equity refers to the value of a brand that emanates from its marketing, and much of marketing management involves enhancing brand equity.[40] In practice, marketers believe that brand equity comprises four major asset categories: brand name awareness, brand loyalty, perceived quality, and brand associations. In addition, brand management uses the design and implementation of marketing programs and activities to build, measure, manage, and endow a product with brand equity.[41]

Brand equity creates value for firms by generating marginal cash flows and by enhancing the efficiency and effectiveness of all aspects of marketing strategy – product (e.g., brand extensions), price (e.g., premium pricing), place (e.g., leverage in the distribution channel), and promotion (loyalty requires less promotional activity).[42]

The monetary value of brands continues to rise. The BrandZ™ Top 100 Most Valuable Global Brands 2014 added $310 billion to reach $2.9 trillion

[37] *Ibid.*, p. 27; Keller, *Strategic Brand Management*, pp. 30–1.
[38] Keller, *Strategic Brand Management*, p. 37.
[39] Aaker, *Building Strong Brands*, p. 8.
[40] Keller, *Strategic Brand Management*, p. 37.
[41] *Ibid.*, pp. 37, 636.
[42] Aaker, *Managing Brand Equity*, pp. 17–18; Aaker, *Building Strong Brands*, p. 8.

in brand value, a 12 percent increase following a 7 percent rise in 2013.[43] The combined brand value of the BrandZ™ Global Top 100 has almost doubled in eight years, since its inception in 2006. Most recently, Google ranked number one in the BrandZ™ Global Top 100. Google increased the most in dollar value, $45.2 billion, in the 2014 ranking. The brand had also increased significantly since 2006, $121.4 billion, second only to the gain of $131.9 billion by Apple during the same period. Microsoft also rose several spots, after a 29 percent brand value increase. The top four brands in BrandZ™ Global Top 100 are all in the technology category – Google, Apple, IBM, and Microsoft.[44]

The basic premise of brand equity is that the power of a brand lies in the minds of the consumers, and occurs when the consumer has a high level of awareness and familiarity with the brand and holds some strong, favorable, and unique brand associations in memory.[45] Therefore, a brand's value to a firm is largely created by the customer loyalty it commands. And brand loyalty is a key consideration when placing a value on a brand that is to be bought or sold, as loyal customers generate a predictable stream of sales and profits.[46] The impact of brand loyalty on marketing costs is often substantial: it is simply much less costly to retain customers than to attract new ones.[47] The loyalty of existing customers also represents a substantial entry barrier to competitors in part because the cost of enticing customers to change loyalties is often prohibitively expensive.[48]

Although brand loyalty is related to brand equity, it is distinct in that the brand loyalty of customers is most often measured as a behavior: namely, repeat purchases. The consistent demand generated by brand-loyal consumers gives the firm greater trade leverage as customers expect the brand to always be available.[49]

4. Implications for antitrust

Our examination of the branding and brand management literature from the marketing discipline yields important insights for antitrust. These insights both clarify and reinforce the viewpoints of scholars who contend

[43] Millward Brown, *2014 BrandZ Top 100*, 2014, available at www.millwardbrown.com/brandz/top_100_global_brands.aspx.

[44] *Ibid.* [45] Keller, *Strategic Brand Management*, p. 636.

[46] Aaker, *Building Strong Brands*, p. 21.

[47] *Ibid.* [48] *Ibid.*, p. 22.

[49] Aaker, *Managing Brand Equity*, p. 19.

that powerful brands warrant greater attention and more widespread concern in antitrust. In this section we elaborate upon these insights, the clarifications they offer, and the antitrust implications they provide.

A. *Brands involve "real" product differentiation*

Our examination clarifies antitrust understanding of the role of brands in product differentiation. The brand and brand management literatures indicate that brands are "real" forms of product differentiation. As seen in the overview above, these literatures show that brands are intended to capture the meaningful differences from competition reflected in the bundles of tangible and intangible benefits sought by consumers. These benefit bundles are wide-ranging in their composition and include not only the functional utility of a good or service, but also its quality and price, as well as additional perceptions, cognitions, associations, and other elements viewed to be important by consumers. The elements combine to create meaningful value to consumers that is captured in the brand. Moreover, while brands can help reveal unrecognized or unmet needs and wants, brands are generally not intended to make consumers pay for goods or services they do not want or in which they do not see value. Certainly confusion may surround the interpretation of brands and some offending firms may try to deceive consumers through their brands, but such outcomes are of limited benefit to marketers in the long run. The circumstances in which this is likely to occur have also been identified as circumscribed in their context. For these reasons brands should not be viewed as an "artificial" form of product differentiation intended to command a premium from consumers based on false or confused demand. Rather, brands should be understood as a real and calculated part of a consumers' interpretation of the differentiated value of a good or service.

Clarifying that brands are a real versus artificial form of product differentiation is important to antitrust. Understanding that brands capture the differentiated value offered by competitors and meaningfully perceived by consumers adds weight to the contention that brands can affect competition in important ways. To the extent that brands serve to create unique differences in competitors' goods and services, they affect the relevant domain of competitors and the relative influence of each competitor in the marketplace. Both are important considerations in the determination of a firm's market power.

B. Branding is integral to marketing strategy

Our examination also clarifies the role of brands in marketing strategy practice. The marketing literature shows that brands and brand management practices are an important and fundamental part of marketing strategy. As seen in the above overview, rather than being a separate strategy distinct from other elements of the marketing mix (i.e., the four P's – product, price, place, promotion), brands and brand management practices are integral to marketing strategy. Brands reflect the entirety of a consumer's experience with a good or service. This experience incorporates all elements of the firm's strategy. This includes each and every element of the marketing mix. Relative to a good or service, branding practices are intended to share with and facilitate consumers' overall perceptions of these strategies. From a strategy perspective, the desired outcome is that a brand reflects the coordinated efforts of a firm's marketing strategy; consumers find this effort sufficiently differentiated from that of the competition, and that as a result they are willing to pay for the value of these efforts.

Distinguishing that branding is an integral part of marketing strategy, rather than a separate practice distinguishable and apart from it, is important to antitrust. That branding is central to a firm's marketing strategy adds further weight to the contention that branding and brand management practices can affect competition in important ways. This argument is less persuasive if brands are viewed as a separate and distinct marketing practice from marketing strategy. The knowledge that brands are essential to marketing strategy, are an integral part of it, and that brands reflect a firm's overall marketing efforts relative to its competition, elevates the importance of brands and brand practices for understanding competition. The centrality of branding to a firm's overall strategy provides implications for understanding the ability of a firm to impact competition and therefore market power. In addition, the centrality of branding to a firm's strategy provides an added basis for understanding the exercise of this power through brand practices that may potentially be of concern to antitrust.

C. Brands pose complex effects for competition

Finally, our examination helps to clarify the impact of brands on competition. The marketing literature and related literatures in antitrust suggest that the effects of a powerful brand on competition are complex.

As described, the marketing literature offers support for propositions regarding the impact of influential brands on consumer loyalty. This literature demonstrates that brand management practices have yielded a growing number of influential brands that possess considerable value for the firms that own them. An important element of this value is the significant loyalty of consumers who patronize these brands. At the same time, related literatures in antitrust describe in greater detail how these effects impact competition. This literature shows that different forms of brand competition occur within the distribution systems through which many brands are marketed and sold. This includes horizontal competition in the form of interbrand rivalry among producers of different brands.[50] It also includes intrabrand rivalry between resellers of the same brand.[51] Finally, it includes vertical competition between manufacturers and resellers vying for their respective share of a brand's retail price.[52] The literature further shows that where these different forms of competition operate, a well-known brand that enjoys high customer loyalty can lower interbrand price competition. This occurs because customers of the brand are less prone to buying rival brands.[53] Narrowly considered, this leads to the conclusion that powerful brands "eliminate" price competition, or at least decrease it. However, focusing on only interbrand competition overlooks important effects for the other forms of competition. In particular, when a powerful brand reduces interbrand competition through consumer loyalty, further effects for intrabrand competition and vertical competition can result. In markets characterized by competition among resellers, a powerful brand that lessens interbrand competition will be accompanied by increases in intrabrand competition. This occurs because "a retailer will lose market share by charging more than other retailers for what consumers recognize as the same thing."[54] Reinforcing this effect is the vertical competition that can also result where powerful brands are involved. Resellers who carry a powerful brand have low elasticity of substitution. Thus they find it difficult to replace a powerful brand with a competing brand. Consequently, resellers engage in intrabrand competition or lose sales to rivals. Together, the literatures on marketing and antitrust

[50] See R. L. Steiner, "The Inverse Association Between the Margins of Manufacturers and Retailers", *Review of Industrial Organization*, 8 (1993), 717–40.

[51] *Ibid.* [52] *Ibid.*

[53] See W. S. Grimes, "Brand Marketing, Intrabrand Competition, and the Multibrand Retailer: The Antitrust Law of Vertical Restraints", *Antitrust Law Journal*, 64 (1995), 83–136.

[54] Steiner, "The Inverse Association", 727.

combine to demonstrate that the effects of powerful brands on competition are more complex than simply "eliminating" competition.

Understanding the complex effects brands pose for competition is important for antitrust. While reducing interbrand competition, powerful brands can increase intrabrand competition. Thus a view that powerful brands "eliminate" competition underspecifies the true impact of a powerful brand on competition. For antitrust, these complex effects also draw attention to extant focus on interbrand competition as the "primary concern" of the antitrust laws.[55] Scholars have questioned the basis of this focus and have raised concerns about the implications that it offers for antitrust thought and practice.[56] Scholars have also offered counsel regarding the importance of considering intrabrand competition in antitrust analysis.[57] The insights offered here add to these admonitions when considering powerful brands.

5. Conclusion

Brands have been largely overlooked in antitrust as an important form of product differentiation that can pose significant implications for competition. Scholars argue this is the result of narrow reliance on neoclassical economics for their antitrust understanding. Citing the proliferation of brands in the economy and contending that neoclassical economics is unable to fully comprehend the market power of brands, scholars have called for their re-examination in antitrust. These calls include the need to draw on insights from business strategy and research in order to fully understand brands. This chapter identifies and describes insights from marketing about branding and brand management practices to clarify their understanding in antitrust and to elaborate on the implications of powerful brands for antitrust. In doing so, it contributes to the growing literature on brands in antitrust.

[55] See e.g., *Continental T.V., Inc.* v. *GTE Sylvania Inc.*, 433 U.S. 36, 52 n.19 (1977).

[56] See Grimes, "Brand Marketing", 83–136.

[57] See *ibid.*

6

Brands and market power: a bird's-eye view

DANIEL A. CRANE

Introduction

Competition law has an ambivalent relationship with branding. On the one hand, competition law sometimes sees brand differentiation as positive for competition insofar as it makes collusion more difficult, and even goes out of its way to facilitate branding, for example by encouraging vertical restraints that facilitate brand promotion. On the other hand, competition law sometimes sees branding as a threat to market competitiveness, for example when it creates entry barriers or permits firms unilaterally to price above competitive levels.

In this chapter I introduce three challenges that characterize this ambivalent relationship. First, competition law must account for the fact that branding can sometimes diminish competition and enhance market power by creating space between rival products, but can also intensify competition by incentivizing producers and retailers to invest more heavily in product quality. Second, antitrust law – which generally assumes the sovereignty of consumer choice – has struggled with the possibility that excessive branding can create artificial distinctions in the minds of consumers and shift demand curves outward in ways that do not correlate with actual gains to consumers. Accepting this premise places in jeopardy the underlying consumer sovereignty assumption of antitrust law. Finally, competition law has to decide whether to deal with the phenomenon of post-contract lock-in to a particular brand. Is the power that comes from a consumer becoming technologically or contractually bound to a supplier the kind of market power with which competition law is rightly concerned?

Product differentiation and market power

Academic insights on the relationship between brands and market power go back to at least the 1930s and work on monopolistic competition and product differentiation by the British economist Edward Chamberlin.[1] Chamberlin was part of the coterie of mid-twentieth-century economists who responded to "ruinous competition" claims made by classical economists of the previous generation such as Alfred Marshall and Arthur Twining Hadley. The marginalists had argued that competition tended to force firms to price at marginal cost, which in turn prevented them from covering their sunk and fixed costs and thus invariably led to financial ruin in the long run.[2] Chamberlin responded that marginal cost pricing would only arise in circumstances of completely undifferentiated products and "that virtually all products are differentiated, at least slightly."[3] He observed that economists had conventionally viewed patents and copyrights as conferring market power, whereas trademarks had not.[4] Chamberlin argued that this was a mistake. Copyrights and patents might create "*pure* monopoly elements" insofar as the physical good could not be directly copied, but trademarks had the competitively pernicious tendency to "represent as *wholly* different two things which are, in fact, essentially alike."[5] Thus, for Chamberlin, the very function of trademarks was to create a degree of market power by artificially differentiating similar products.

It has thus been long understood that branding can diminish competition by creating space between rival products and even creating entry barriers that rival firms find difficult to overcome.[6] A firm that invests heavily in persuading customers to be loyal to its brand may make it difficult for new entrants to capture market share without making their own very large investments in new brands.

The observation that brand differentiation, through trademarks or otherwise, can create market power has not been lost to antitrust policy, but there has been a tendency in academic literature to minimize the importance of such market power. Commentators frequently distinguish between the limited pricing discretion that arises from branding and the

[1] E. H. Chamberlin, *The Theory of Monopolistic Competition: A Re-Orientation of the Theory of Value*, 5th edn (Cambridge, MA: Harvard University Press, 1946).

[2] See D. A. Crane and H. Hovenkamp, *The Making of Competition Policy: Legal and Economic Sources* (New York: Oxford University Press, 2013), pp. 125–7.

[3] Chamberlin, *The Theory of Monopolistic Competition*, p. 57.

[4] *Ibid.*, p. 60. [5] *Ibid.*

[6] See, e.g., R. Schmalensee, "Product Differentiation Advantages of Pioneering Brands", *American Economic Review*, 72 (1982), 349; D. R. Desai and S. W. Waller, "Brands, Competition, and the Law", *Brigham Young University Law Review*, (2010), 1425; M. A. Lemley and M. P. McKenna, "Is Pepsi Really a Substitute for Coke? Market Definition in Antitrust and IP", *Georgetown Law Journal*, 100 (2012), 2055.

more robust market power that arises from the absence of competition for the underlying products.[7] Others have argued that the pricing discretion that arises from branding is not attributable to market power at all, but rather to the fact that trademarks lower consumers' search costs.[8] Further, economists point out that trademark law has built-in features that diminish the likelihood that trademark protection creates market power. Trademarks lose their protection when they become generic – as happened in the case of Aspirin, Cellophane, Frisbee, and Thermos.[9] This diminishes the likelihood that firms retain market power through brands simply because customers conflate the product with the brand. Similarly, trademark law denies protection to marks that are functional. Richard Posner and William Landes argue that, economically, a good is non-functional when it has reasonable substitutes.[10] Since reasonable substitutability is the criterion to determine when goods compete with one another from an antitrust perspective, the functionality requirement may prevent firms from obtaining trademarks that limit the competitive choices of rivals.

In recent decades United States antitrust laws have tended to promote brand differentiation rather than oppose it. This is most visible in vertical restraints law, where over the last thirty years the Supreme Court has shifted toward legal rules that encourage manufacturers to restrict intrabrand competition through such practices as resale price maintenance and other non-price vertical restraints on downstream retailers. The Court has justified these restrictions as incentivizing retailers to invest in promoting the manufacturer's brand, which in turn strengthens the brand and intensifies competition between rival brands.[11] Thus, in this view, brand differentiation intensifies rather than reduces competition.

[7] See, e.g., E. Elhauge, "Defining Better Monopolization Standards", *Stanford Law Review*, 56 (2003), 258–61 (discussing distinctions between brand-created pricing discretion and monopoly power).

[8] W. M. Landes and R. A. Posner, "Trademark Law: An Economic Perspective", *Journal of Law and Economics*, 30 (1987), 265 ("Firms with strong trademarks ... will command higher prices for their brands not because of any market power but because the search costs associated with their brand are lower").

[9] W. M. Landes and R. A. Posner, *The Economic Structure of Intellectual Property Law* (Cambridge, MA: Harvard University Press, 2003), pp. 187–97.

[10] *Ibid.*, p. 198.

[11] See, e.g., *Leegin Creative Leather Products, Inc.* v. *PSKS, Inc.*, 551 U.S. 877, 890 (2007) ("A single manufacturer's use of vertical price restraints tends to eliminate intrabrand price competition; this in turn encourages retailers to invest in tangible or intangible services or promotional efforts that aid the manufacturer's position as against rival manufacturers").

A related aspect of antitrust policy concerning branding and product differentiation goes to the question of pricing and output coordination by rival firms. A central concern of antitrust policy – described by the United States Supreme Court as the "supreme evil of antitrust"[12] – is horizontal collusion. Product heterogeneity makes it harder for firms to coordinate tacitly or explicitly; thus product differentiation may reduce the likelihood of collusion.[13] To the extent that brand differentiation increases true product differentiation, in the sense that firms find it harder to standardize prices on their products because of differing features, brand differentiation may lessen the incidence of coordinated interaction and collusion. This suggests a further reason for antitrust law to favor brand differentiation. If firms are investing in differentiating their brands and increasing their market share and profits through product differentiation, they are less likely to be engaged in price fixing or tacit price coordination.

But then we come back to the original problem of unilateral market power created through sometimes artificial product differentiation – the insight that motivated Chamberlin to express greater concern over trademarks than patents and copyrights. Over the last few years antitrust enforcers have increasingly shifted the locus of their concerns from coordinated market power effects in homogenous goods markets to unilateral market power effects in differentiated goods markets. This is most visible in the Justice Department and Federal Trade Commission's 2010 revisions to the Horizontal Merger Guidelines.[14] The 2010 Guidelines represent a substantial shift away from earlier generations of merger guidelines that worried most that mergers would increase market concentration in a way that facilitated coordinated pricing and output decisions by the surviving firms.[15] The new Guidelines focus more on the potential that a merger will combine the two closest substitutes in a differentiated good market, enabling the merged firm to raise its prices unilaterally without any need to coordinate with rival firms.[16] Product differentiation is key to this sort

[12] *Verizon Communications Inc.* v. *Law Offices of Curtis V. Trinko, LLP*, 540 U.S. 398, 408 (2004).

[13] See L. Kaplow, "An Economic Approach to Price Fixing", *Antitrust Law Journal*, 77 (2011), 343, 359; W. S. Grimes, "Brand Marketing, Intrabrand Competition, and the Multibrand Retailer: The Antitrust Law of Vertical Restraints", *Antitrust Law Journal*, 64 (1995), 89–90.

[14] US Department of Justice and Federal Trade Commission, Horizontal Merger Guidelines (2010), available at www.justice.gov/atr/public/guidelines/hmg-2010.pdf.

[15] See D. A. Crane, "Rethinking Merger Efficiencies", *Michigan Law Review*, 110 (2011), 366.

[16] See generally C. Shapiro, "The 2010 Horizontal Merger Guidelines: From Hedgehog to Fox in Forty Years", *Antitrust Law Journal* 77 (2010), 49.

of unilateral market power; thus branding that creates product differentiation may give rise to heightened competitive concerns in horizontal merger cases.

Antitrust law thus has an unsettled and sometimes contradictory perspective on branding. On the one hand, investment in brand differentiation may stimulate interbrand rivalry and diminish the likelihood of collusion. On the other, it may create unilateral market power by diminishing the cross-elasticity of demand between rival products. Although there is not necessarily an inconsistency in worrying simultaneously about both problems, antitrust enforcers and judges are sometimes called upon to make choices between legal interventions that promote brand differentiation or treat it with suspicion. At present, branding has the sympathy of the courts and a somewhat less positive reception in the antitrust enforcement agencies.

Brand preference, consumer sovereignty, and paternalism

There is an intriguing interaction between judicial and academic wisdom buried in a footnote in, *GTE Sylvania*, one of the leading US Supreme Court precedents supporting vertical restraints because of their effect in stimulating brand promotion and interbrand competition. The majority opinion reacts to an argument by the economist William Comanor against vertical restraints as follows:

> Professor Comanor argues that the promotional activities encouraged by vertical restrictions result in product differentiation and, therefore, a decrease in interbrand competition. This argument is flawed by its necessary assumption that a large part of the promotional efforts resulting from vertical restrictions will not convey socially desirable information about product availability, price, quality, and services.[17]

Comanor's argument resonate with a broader social and economic critique of product branding in the capitalist system. The argument calls into question the assumption that any increase in consumer willingness to pay for goods resulting from branding enhances consumer welfare. Branding, in this view, may stimulate demand by creating a false impression in consumer minds that the products in question are more valuable due to their cosmetic differentiation. Branding may thus have the same

[17] *Continental T.V., Inc.* v. *GTE Sylvania Inc.*, 433 U.S. 36, 56, 56 n.25 (1977) (citing W. S. Comanor, "Vertical Territorial and Customer Restrictions: White Motor and Its Aftermath", *Harvard Law Review*, 81 (1968), 1422).

effect as deception and fraud – shifting out demand curves to diminish consumer welfare.

This negative perception of branding has exerted a modest effect on US antitrust enforcement, most notably in a Federal Trade Commission (FTC) enforcement action concerning the ReaLemon lemon concentrate brand. In 1974 the FTC brought a monopolization case against Borden, Inc., alleging monopolization of the concentrated lemon market.[18] Among the wrongful acts alleged by Borden was "[e]recting barriers to entry into the reconstituted lemon juice market through extensive trademark promotion and advertising which has artificially differentiated Borden's reconstituted lemon juice from comparable products of its competitors."[19] The administrative law judge found Borden had spent millions of dollars promoting its ReaLemon brand and had thus created entry barriers to competition by other lemon concentrate brands that were essentially identical to Borden's brand.[20] The FTC won the case on appeal, but ultimately settled the matter fairly lightly after a change in administration in Washington.

What is distinctive about the FTC's allegations in ReaLemon is that branding and trademark promotion were not merely alleged to evidence market power, as is true in many other cases. Rather, the fact of the investment in brand promotion was itself a key element of the claims of anticompetitive behavior. Overbranding ReaLemon – creating artificial distinctions from other physically identical products – was a species of unlawful exclusionary behavior.

ReaLemon rests on the implicit assertion that overbranding can dupe consumers into buying things they do not, or should not, really value. Whether or not justified in some way, the assumption that antitrust law should oppose overbranding as deleterious to consumer welfare creates a fundamental conflict with the baseline assumptions of competition policy. Antitrust law is built on an assumption of consumer sovereignty[21] – on the proposition that social welfare is maximized when consumer preferences direct the allocation of resources and describe their most valued uses. The demand curves conventionally used to describe the

18 Complaint, *In re Borden, Inc.*, 92 F.T.C. 669 (1978).

19 *Ibid.*, Para. 9(e).

20 ALJ Decision at § 85 ("Although no differences were mentioned between ReaLemon and the other products, both commercial and fresh users see ReaLemon as the brand that is proven and reliable and has captured their brand loyalty").

21 N. W. Averitt and R. H. Lande, "Consumer Sovereignty: A Unified Theory of Antitrust and Consumer Protection Law", *Antitrust Law Journal*, 65 (1997), 719.

anticompetitive effects of the exercise of monopoly power – deadweight losses and wealth transfers – are simply the aggregation of individual, idiosyncratic consumer preferences. If antitrust law calls into question these fundamental assumptions, it must offer a significantly different account of the relationship between consumer choice and market performance than it currently does.

Take, for example, the problem of so-called "Veblen goods," goods that signal the owner's social status through conspicuous consumption.[22] Veblen goods, which are typically heavily branded, may be characterized by an upward-sloping demand curve insofar as those who consume them obtain less value when they become cheap, widely available, and thus no longer able to convey elite class status. Buyers pay a premium price for exclusivity. One may very well find Veblen goods obnoxious, immoral, or evidence of the corrupting vanity of the wealthy, but it is impossible to condemn them as failing to create consumer welfare without adopting an objective theory of value. Once courts or antitrust agencies create such an objective theory of value – declaring what goods or services are objectively worth rather than simply calculating social welfare based on demand curves and consumer willingness to pay – the entire premise of antitrust law is called into question. For now antitrust regulators and judges in every case might be called on to decide what things are really worth and what attributes are more valuable than others, however consumers vote with their pocketbooks.

It is unsurprising that ReaLemon is close to unique as an antitrust precedent and that the majority's intuition in *GTE Sylvania* that brand promotion brings information to consumers that they do, and are entitled to, value remains the dominant perspective. Still, we surely have not seen the end of the road for arguments that excessive branding may harm consumer welfare. Advances in behavioral law and economics may lend new strength to claims that advertisers routinely exploit infirmities in consumer decision-making through branding essentially homogenous products.[23] Antitrust law is notoriously fickle in its fundamental assumptions, and further legal and social science developments in understanding consumer behavior and decision-making may return these issues to the fore.

[22] T. Veblen, *The Theory of the Leisure Class: An Economic Study of Institutions* (New York: The Macmillan Company, 1899).

[23] J. G. Hanson and D. A. Kysar, "Taking Behavioralism Seriously: The Problem of Market Manipulation", *New York University Law Review*, 74 (1999), 732–3.

Single-brand markets and the antitrust overexpansion

A final, but important, issue involving market power and branding concerns brand lock-in, or the power a seller in aftermarkets obtains over consumers once they have made an initial sunk investment in the seller's brand. The question is whether antitrust law should police the sort of power that arises in a bilateral monopoly situation due to customer lock-in. Under current law, there is an opening for antitrust policing of this sort of power within the brand, although it has been sharply criticized for overexpanding the domain of antitrust law.

At the outset, it is important to be clear about what is meant by competition within the brand. There are certain forms of intrabrand competition that antitrust law uncontroversially polices, as when two franchised retailers selling the same brand of product collude to fix retail prices. The anticompetitive effects of such collusion are felt within the brand insofar as the retail price of a particular brand of product increases, but the loss of competition is between rivals and retailers who have their own retail brands.

There is a different kind of intrabrand effect that arises when a manufacturer abuses its own customers, who have become locked into buying aftermarket services from that manufacturer. The Supreme Court's *Kodak*[24] decision illustrates this problem. Kodak manufactured photocopy and micrographic machines and sold them in a competitive market against other brands such as Xerox, Canon, and Minolta. Importantly, there was no allegation that Kodak had market power in the primary equipment market. The plaintiffs were Independent Service Organizations (ISOs), who alleged that Kodak monopolized the aftermarket for servicing Kodak copiers by refusing the ISOs access to its parts, over which it did allegedly have market power, in part due to patents. Kodak objected that, since it lacked market power in the primary market for equipment, it was economically and legally incapable of possessing market power in the aftermarkets. A five-Justice majority rejected this argument, finding it possible that Kodak was able to charge its customers supra-competitive prices for service because customers did not foresee lifecycle pricing and take it into their initial purchasing or leasing decision, and switching costs discouraged choosing a different brand of equipment once any monopolistic aftermarket practices by Kodak became known.

[24] *Eastman Kodak Co. v. Image Technical Services, Inc.*, 504 U.S. 451 (1992).

A conceptual problem with the ISOs' antitrust case is that it required defining a relevant market with specific reference to Kodak's brand. The plaintiffs could not allege a relevant market for servicing photocopiers in general, since then Kodak would have a relatively small share and would not possess market power. They had to allege that Kodak had a near-monopoly over servicing its own brand and thus to define the relevant markets service for Kodak-branded copy machines.

Critics of the decision have argued that allowing a plaintiff to define a relevant market with respect to a single brand misconceives the proper reach of antitrust law. In particular, Herbert Hovenkamp, a leading antitrust authority and editor of the influential Areeda antitrust law treatise, has sharply criticized the *Kodak* majority opinion as overextending antitrust law into post-contract lock-in.[25] Hovenkamp argues that it is problematic to make "antitrust the vehicle for fixing contracts that we might think unfair or, worse yet, for protecting people from their own carelessly made bargains."[26] Market power of this kind is ubiquitous in manufacturer–customer or manufacturer–franchisee relationships. It should ordinarily be avoided through carefully drafted contracts that protect the customer's or franchisee's interests in the aftermarket and, barring that, regulatory tools such as pro-consumer contract interpretation or franchisee protection statutes. Antitrust should, however, be understood as a species of public law intended to protect robust competition in markets between rival brands, not as a tool to protect the private interest in avoiding contractual exploitation.

Although *Kodak* remains on the books as good law, and plaintiffs sometimes bring antitrust cases claiming post-contract lock-in to a single brand, the lower courts have sharply circumscribed the reach of such theories. Courts have rejected single-brand lock-in theories for want of evidence of actual lock-in,[27] because the supposedly exploitative aftermarket practices were well disclosed in advance,[28] because customers could have

[25] H. Hovenkamp, *The Antitrust Enterprise: Principle and Execution* (Cambridge, MA: Harvard University Press, 2005).

[26] *Ibid.*, p. 101.

[27] See, e.g., *DSM Desotech Inc.* v. *3D Systems Corp.*, 749 F.3d 1332 (Fed. Cir. 2014); *PSKS, Inc.* v. *Leegin Creative Leather Products, Inc.*, 615 F.3d 412 (5th Cir. 2010); *Brokerage Concepts, Inc.* v. *U.S. Healthcare, Inc.*, 140 F.3d 494 (3rd Cir. 1998).

[28] See, e.g., *Smugglers Notch Homeowners' Association, Inc.* v. *Smugglers' Notch Management Co.*, 414 F. Appx. 373 (2nd Cir. 2011); *Michigan Division-Monument Builders of North America* v. *Michigan Cemetery Association*, 524 F.3d 726 (6th Cir. 2008); *PSI Repair Services, Inc.* v. *Honeywell, Inc.*, 104 F.3d 811 (6th Cir. 1997).

foreseen lifecycle pricing,[29] or because the only impediment to the customer switching aftermarket suppliers was a contractual undertaking to purchase exclusively from the manufacturer.[30] The single-brand lock-in theory is frequently invoked, but rarely successful.

The upshot is that plaintiffs typically must allege a relevant market that is wider than a single brand. It remains possible that a single brand is dominant in that market – for example, Borden having a very large share of the concentrated lemon juice market as a result of the strength of the ReaLemon brand, or Harley-Davidson having a dominant share of domestically produced motorcycles. However, the definition of the market ordinarily should not be limited to a particular brand; any evidence that the brand is dominant should ordinarily come through proof that the firm's strong brand gives it power over rivals selling or attempting to sell the same product.

Conclusion

The relationship between branding and market power remains complex and ambiguous. Different strands of antitrust policy can be understood as evidencing either hospitability or hostility to branding and brand differentiation. Perhaps the best that can be said is that contemporary antitrust law has no general theory with respect to branding, but rather considers the effects of branding on competition and market power in a context-specific, and sometimes contradictory, fashion.

29 *Harrison Aire, Inc.* v. *Aerostar International, Inc.*, 423 F.3d 374 (3rd Cir. 2005).

30 *Maris Distributing Co.* v. *Anheuser-Busch, Inc.*, 302 F.3d 1207 (11th Cir. 2002); *Queen City Pizza, Inc.* v. *Domino's Pizza, Inc.*, 124 F.3d 430 (3rd Cir. 1997); *Hack* v. *President and Fellows of Yale College*, 237 F.3d 81 (2nd Cir. 2000); *Forsyth* v. *Humana, Inc.*, 114 F.3d 1467 (9th Cir. 1997).

7

The two sides of brand marketing

Reconsidering competition law governing distribution restraints

WARREN S. GRIMES

Introduction

As a participant in an international intellectual property conference in the late 1970s, I had occasion to exchange thoughts about brand marketing with a Russian academic. As he described the distribution system in a socialist economy dominated by state-owned enterprises, there was little place for branded products. Yet, he pointed out, Russian consumers wanted the information that branding could provide. According to my colleague, savvy consumers in his country knew that a particular state enterprise in Kiev made comfortable and well-constructed shoes. Armed with this knowledge, consumers would inquire of their local shoe store when the next shipment of shoes from Kiev would arrive. Lines often formed when the word got out that the preferred shoes were available.

This story from the Soviet Union, it turns out, says a lot about why branding is an essential part of modern, efficient marketing. Without brands, consumers struggle to learn about reputation and quality. Producers who make a quality product, for their part, struggle to get that information out to the buying public. Once a product is branded, the producer has an incentive to use advertising to promote a brand's qualities. Indeed, word of mouth may allow the brand to sell itself. The producer can expand production to achieve economies of scale, and the consumer can more comfortably trust that the producer's incentive to maintain brand reputation will assure a quality product. That is brand marketing at its best – as it should work.

There is, however, a darker side. Exaggeration, obfuscation, and even outright deceit have long been associated with the sale of some branded products. The marketing of patent medicines in the late nineteenth and early twentieth centuries is an example. Most of these medications were not patented, although their ingredients, which often included alcohol, opiates, or both, were kept secret from buyers.[1] Advertising was intense, and laced with hyperbole and unsubstantiated claims about curative effects, but silent about ingredients. By 1906 investigative reports of ill effects and even death caused by consumption of these medications, along with Upton Sinclair's novel about meat packing abuses,[2] prompted Congress to enact the Pure Food and Drug Act.[3]

Today's brand marketing does not generally promote the sale of products that threaten death or serious injury. There remains, however, a strong non-informational side to modern brand promotion. Products are often promoted through image and appeals to status, not through hard information about the performance or tangible characteristics of the product itself. Disinterested ratings of products by organizations such as Consumer Reports, for example, frequently show lower-cost products with superior performance or characteristics to many higher-priced products. While appeals to status or image are common and by themselves not a basis for condemning brand advertising, the legal system governing brand selling should be designed, in addition to prohibiting counterfeiting, fraud, or misleading statements or omissions, to encourage the most beneficial features of branding: the conveyance of hard information and the creation of incentives for producers to maintain the quality of their branded products.

Competition law and the beneficial features of branding

In the United States, prior to the widespread proliferation of branding, producers had little control over distribution and retailing. Use of producer-imposed distribution restraints, however, expanded with the increase in branding. Resale price maintenance, for example, grew in the last decades of the nineteenth century as producers of branded products sought to control the retail prices at which their products were sold to the public. If the marketing of a brand is part of its overall image, it makes sense that producers would seek control over retail pricing. This rationale,

[1] For a description of the marketing of patent medicines in the United States during late nineteenth and early twentieth centuries, see R. J. R. Peritz, "'Nervine' and Knavery: The Life and Times of Dr. Miles Medical Company", in E. Fox and D. Crane (eds.), *Antitrust Stories* (New York: Foundation Press, 2007), pp. 61–73.

[2] U. Sinclair, *The Jungle* (New York: Doubleday Page & Company, 1906).

[3] Pure Food and Drug Act of 1906, Pub. L. No. 59–384, 34 Stat. 768, 768–70 (1906).

if carried to extremes, could lead to a very stultified retailing system in which efficient retailers would have little room to pass the benefits of their efficiency to consumers. A central purpose of branding is to create a distinct reputation for a product that increases consumer demand for that product, giving the producer a certain amount of control over pricing. The question, however, is whether that control should extend to downstream distribution methods and pricing by independent firms. If this is the result, there is a substantial departure from competition goals, which assume that competition will govern not only research, development, and production but distribution as well.

Although United States competition law took some time to catch up with the explosion of distribution restraints that accompanied branding, the Supreme Court's 1911 decision in *Dr. Miles Medical Co.* v. *John D. Park & Sons, Co.*[4] viewed contractually imposed resale price restraints on distributors and dealers as tantamount to horizontal price restraints, a conclusion easier to reach because the Court emphasized the venerable doctrine that accorded a property owner free rights to alienate on prices and terms that it chose. Although antitrust law governing resale price maintenance and other distribution restraints was hardly static over the next half century, after the Court's 1960 decision in *United States* v. *Parke, Davis and Co.*,[5] it was clear that vertically imposed minimum resale prices were per se unlawful. The high point of competition law restraints was *United States* v. *Arnold, Schwinn & Co.*,[6] which, with some exceptions, deemed both price and non-price restrictions on downstream dealers to be per se unlawful.

Current federal antitrust law has eliminated all per se rules governing distribution restraints (there is still a modified per se rule governing tie-ins). The parameters for the current paradigm were set by the Supreme Court in *Continental T. V., Inc.* v. *GTE Sylvania Inc.*,[7] where the Court emphasized that distribution restraints can have valuable promotion benefits for the seller of a branded product. Although the unraveling of the per se rule governing resale price maintenance took another three decades, the Supreme Court's 2008 decision in *Leegin Creative Leather Products, Inc.* v. *PSKS, Inc.*[8] completed this course. Still, the law in the United States remains unsettled, as courts grapple with vertical issues

4 *Dr. Miles Medical Co.* v. *John D. Park & Sons Co.*, 220 U.S. 373 (1911).

5 *United States* v. *Parke, Davis and Co.*, 362 U.S. 29 (1960).

6 *United States* v. *Arnold, Schwinn & Co.*, 388 U.S. 365 (1967).

7 *Continental T.V., Inc.* v. *GTE Sylvania Inc.*, 433 U.S. 36 (1977).

8 *Leegin Creative Leather Products, Inc.* v. *PSKS, Inc.*, 551 U.S. 877 (2008).

under the rule of reason standard that now governs price and non-price distribution restraints. Meanwhile, many of the fifty states have declined to eliminate the per se rule in their state competition law that governs resale price maintenance.

The *GTE Sylvania* paradigm, by recognizing that vertical restraints can have promotion benefits, was a step forward. The loss of intrabrand retail competition from a distribution restraint, for example, might be more than offset by brand promotion benefits that increase sales of a highly desired product. This might occur, for example, if dealer promotion efforts resulted in increased information and more rational buying decisions by consumers who receive that information. What is absent from the *Sylvania* paradigm, however, is a full recognition that while all distribution restraints can benefit brand promotion, they do so with vastly different negative effects on competition; they typically do so inefficiently when compared to other brand promotion tools; and they often do so while promoting the darker side of brand promotion that has nothing to do with conveying concrete information to the consumer. These considerations can be captured by assessing the following three factors:

(1) What is the extent of a distribution restraint's harm to competition?
(2) If there are any brand promotion gains from the distribution restraint, are they consistent with the beneficial effects of brand marketing?
(3) Are there more efficient and less competitively injurious tools for achieving the legitimate brand promotion goals?

The first question is pivotal. If a distribution restraint has only a minimal negative impact on intrabrand competition, the inquiry should end and the restraint should be declared lawful. If not, the nature of the fostered brand promotion ought to be an important part of the calculus. If the promotion involves conveyance of relevant information about the brand that assists consumers in making a wise purchasing decision, that favors more lenient treatment of the restraint. On the other hand, if the primary goal or effect of the brand promotion is non-informational (such as image or status enhancement), that is a far less compelling justification for the restraint. The efficiency of the brand promotion in achieving a legitimate promotion goal, a consideration absent from the *Sylvania* paradigm, is another critical issue. If there are more efficient and less competitively injurious tools for achieving the desired brand promotion, this increases the likelihood that the restraint is chosen not primarily for its information-based brand promotion but for the anticompetitive gains it brings to the brand holder.

As a general matter, the advertising of a branded product is the most obvious and efficient way for a producer to convey information to potential buyers. Even if the brand promoter wishes to convey image and status, non-informational packaging, product placement in high image stores, and advertising are efficient ways of achieving these ends. The use of vertical restraints can also promote these goals, but does so inefficiently. These observations are likely to hold for most distribution restraints. There are, however, differences that may justify different policy outcomes for various distribution restraints.

In the following section, I briefly analyze the likely benefits and injury flowing from three commonly used distribution restraints: (1) a dealer location clause that requires a dealer to operate out of a specified location; (2) exclusive retailing that limits the territory or class of buyers that a dealer can service; and (3) vertical minimum price fixing, commonly known as resale price maintenance.

The paradigm applied

Dealer location clause – A dealer location clause limits the dealer's operation to a specified location. This type of dealer restriction is, for example, common in the sale of motor vehicles. These restrictions are generally deemed lawful. While they limit intrabrand competition among dealers, they may do so insignificantly. Many consumers, when shopping for a particular automobile brand, will search widely among dealers for that brand. Internet access makes such comparative intrabrand shopping quite easy. It is true that location clauses may more effectively squelch intrabrand competition when the dealership is located in a relatively isolated community where buyers have less ready access to other dealers of the same brand. Still, given the substantial investment in buying a car, at least some of those buyers may be willing to travel a substantial distance to purchase a vehicle at a more attractive price.

The location clause example demonstrates the primacy of the first of the three operative questions: if a distribution restraint has only a relatively small impact on intrabrand competition, it should be deemed lawful without a need to address the second and third questions.

Exclusive retailing – A brand seller may define an exclusive class of potential buyers for a dealer. This may occur through geographic limits (the dealer may sell only to customers who reside within a defined geographic region) or through limits on customer classification (the dealer may sell only to customers who belong to a specified class, such as business customers). In its most extreme form, air-tight exclusivity (limiting each buyer to a single dealer) can eliminate all intrabrand competition for the buyer. There is, however, an ancillary question related to the degree of competitive harm: whether the brand is a relatively small player in the product market. A brand promoter can generally not achieve widespread distribution when exclusive dealerships are used. Hence, a promoter interested in maximizing distribution – and achieving a substantial market share – may disfavor exclusive dealership arrangements. If the promoter nonetheless chooses to designate exclusive dealers, because of the severity of the restraint on intrabrand competition, the court should proceed to measure both the nature of the promotion benefits and whether they can be achieved more efficiently by less anticompetitive means.

Exclusive dealerships can be a way to limit distribution to high-end outlets and thereby promote a premium brand image. Brand imaging is not directly linked to the conveyance of hard information that is a highly beneficial aspect of brand marketing. Thus brand imaging is not a compelling counterweight to the loss of intrabrand competition occasioned by the restraint. There are also a number of other efficient ways for a brand to achieve a high-end image, including advertising, packaging, and simply building a product with superior features or durability. These considerations weigh against allowing air-tight exclusive dealerships.

A court could nonetheless allow a certain degree of exclusivity when, despite being designated the only dealer in a geographic territory, customers remain free to shop outside the area. For many consumer products, the ability to buy through the Internet will make it difficult for a brand seller to achieve true exclusivity in dealerships. In addition, if the promoted brand is a small player in the interbrand market, stifling intrabrand competition will have minimal effect on retail competition among multi-brand dealers. On the other hand, if some form of exclusivity is linked to vertical minimum price fixing, the competitive harm (as discussed below) is likely to be more substantial

Vertical minimum price fixing (resale price maintenance) – The law in the United States and elsewhere has singled out resale price maintenance (RPM) for stricter treatment. Although *Leegin* has now set the rule of reason standard for assessing RPM under federal law, there is nothing in the Court's 5–4 decision that suggests that the setting of minimum resale prices does not warrant careful scrutiny. Indeed, measured against the three inquiries posed above, RPM is a prime candidate, if not for per se illegality, at least for a strong presumption of unlawfulness.

RPM ends intrabrand price competition among dealers that sell the brand. The impact of pricing restrictions could be widespread because RPM is often applied to open distribution systems and can affect many multi-brand dealers. As RPM becomes widespread in a particular product segment, efficient and innovative multibrand retailers could lose their competitive edge and consumers could pay more for products in that segment. Although disputed by some, there is substantial evidence that RPM does generate higher prices for consumers.[9] Defenders of RPM argue that even if higher retail prices follow, RPM pays for valuable distribution services.

The Supreme Court in *Leegin* identified three potential distributional benefits to RPM:

(1) creating an incentive for a retailer to promote the relevant brand (and lessening the impact of retailers who might free ride on the services of a non-promoting retailer);
(2) enhancing the image of the brand; and
(3) creating an incentive for a dealer to carry a full line of the seller's products.[10]

While any or all of these distributional benefits may occur because a dealer receiving a higher margin has an incentive to promote the brand, RPM is an inefficient way of achieving any of these distributional services. Some dealers will effectively promote the brand while others will sit back and reap the benefits of the higher margin without performing the desired promotion.

If a brand seller wants to promote its products through hard information, the most efficient way of doing so is to supply a good product and advertise it. Dealers will want to carry a product that consumers demand. In this way, the brand holder controls the flow of information and ensures that it is accurate and effective in achieving legitimate promotion goals. Granting a higher margin to the retailer may result in conveyance of more information at the point of sale, but the brand holder has little control over what the dealer does or does not do. The opportunities for

[9] W. S. Grimes, 'A Dynamic Analysis of Resale Price Maintenance: Inefficient Brand Promotion, Higher Margins, Distorted Choices, and Retarded Retail Innovation', *Antitrust Bulletin*, (2010) 55: 101.

[10] *Leegin* v. *PSKS*, 551 U.S. at 891–2.

non-conforming and non-informational promotion, including unlawful deceptive or misleading promotion, are heightened by this lack of control.

There are, of course, situations where the sale of the product will be enhanced by dealer efforts such as demonstration or prominent display. In these cases, a contractually based arrangement that gives promotion allowances to compliant dealers should more efficiently achieve the desired promotion and would do so without the loss of intrabrand competition.

RPM's inefficiency in ensuring legitimate retail promotion has often been overlooked in court decisions and theoretical analysis. If RPM is not an efficient promotion tool, there is a much greater likelihood that it is invoked by brand sellers who simply want to charge higher wholesale prices to their dealers. In order to maintain dealer loyalty in the face of higher wholesale pricing, the brand seller sets a high resale price that allows the dealer to share in some of the supracompetitive profit.

A final point is that widespread use of RPM in a product segment tends to nullify any promotional benefits for brand sellers. If most or all of the brands fix high resale prices, the dealer no longer has an incentive to promote one particular brand. Instead, the system operates as a subsidy for inefficient retailing. This might make sense if the goal is, as in some European and Asian nations, to subsidize a particular form of retailing, such as small bookstores. RPM as a subsidy device is still a relatively costly way of achieving this goal since it makes it less likely that natural market forces will allow efficient retailers to pass benefits on to consumers. A nation that wishes to sustain a culture of small book sellers might achieve its goal at lesser social cost by giving tax breaks or other subsidies targeted at small sellers, still allowing intrabrand price competition to flourish.

Conclusion

Brand selling is vital to an efficient and transparent distribution of the goods and services that consumers most want. Competition law governing distribution restraints should be set with an eye to allowing the positive aspects of branding to flourish, while limiting the use of distribution restraints that are not efficient purveyors of accurate and salient information and often are associated with non-informational and misleading promotion techniques. From this perspective, the most pernicious distribution restraint is RPM. It generates higher consumer prices, is not an efficient promoter of the informational benefits of brand selling, and, when widespread in a segment, can undermine efficient and innovative retailing.

8

Brands, product differentiation and EU competition law

IOANNIS LIANOS

Introduction

The term of the art 'brands' is often used in EU Competition law with the aim of providing factual information on the competitive, or not, relation between products or services provided by different economic actors. The European Commission often refers in its merger or antitrust decisions to the products (or services) of brand X that enter into competition on a relevant market with the products (or services) of brand Y. The term brand used in this context aims to provide a factual observation on the operation of the specific relevant market. No further inferences are made. Inquiring into the role of brands in this context is a simple exercise and offers little to the research question explored in this volume. However, the issue becomes more complex if one engages with the use of brands as an *operational concept* in EU competition law. Operational concepts connect theoretical concepts to simple factual observations. For instance, the operational concept of 'market power' connects a fact concerning the level of prices in a specific market at a certain point in time, which is partially an observable fact, with the theoretical construction of price theory, for instance the theoretical concept of monopoly or its antithesis, that of perfect competition, from which market power is a departure. These operational concepts help decision-makers to make inferences (they serve as analytical shortcuts) about the relation between the different facts they observe in order to assess causal relations and make predictions.

I would like to thank Nick Economides, Peter Davis and Spencer Weber Waller for their insightful comments on an earlier version of this chapter. Any errors or omissions are of the sole responsibility of the author. This chapter was written while on leave from UCL with support from the Leverhulme Trust. I also benefitted from the support of the Laboratory on Law and Development at the National Research University, Higher School of Economics.

It is now accepted that competition law makes extensive use of operational concepts transplanted from the discipline of economics, in particular neoclassical price theory.[1] Yet its receptivity to operational concepts developed in other disciplines, management studies in particular, has been relatively limited. And here lies the core of the problem with regard to the engagement of EU competition law with the *concept* of 'brands'. Although the discipline of economics and in particular neoclassical price theory perceives brands as a *fact* of economic life, until recently price theory has not made use of the term as an operational concept. Instead, economists prefer to focus on the semi-operational concepts of product differentiation,[2] advertising[3] or that of barriers to entry, which describe the consequences of the existence of brands, but do not engage directly with the concept of brand. However, marketing studies use 'brands' as an operational concept. Brands also extend to more than *product* differentiation, as they may be used by brand-owners in order to reinforce the 'emotional and cognitive appeal' of a certain brand to consumers, as is well explained in several of the contributions to this volume.[4]

One of the possible reasons of this relatively low analytical value of the concept of brand in neoclassical price theory comes from the relative ambiguity of the policy prescriptions of the theoretical models of 'imperfect competition' and 'monopolistic competition', which were the first to fully engage with product differentiation in the welfare economics tradition and to discuss the role of brands in the competitive process.

Although not ignored by Marshall, product differentiation really became the focus of economic inquiry starting in the 1930s. Two positions emerged in the literature. Relying on the welfare economics paradigm and having as a starting point for the analysis the concept of 'industries' producing a single/homogeneous commodity, Robinson's *Economics of Imperfect Competition* viewed product differentiation as a departure from

[1] See, I. Lianos, 'Lost in Translation: Towards a Theory of Economic Transplants', *Current Legal Problems*, 62(1) (2009), 346–404.

[2] Semi-operational as it describes an observable fact as well as serving the function of an operational concept.

[3] Which includes money spent on brands. It is also recognized that brands can be a source of across sub-market 'linkage'. See, J. Sutton, *Technology and Market Structure – Theory and History* (Cambridge, MA: MIT Press, 2001), chapters 11 and 12.

[4] See, for instance, Chapter 12 of this volume by Andrew Griffiths, noting that 'the identity that a brand confers on products gives a context to an individual act of consumption that may increase its emotional impact and turn it into the basis of a continuing relationship' and that 'branding can transform a product into a source of self-assurance or a means of self-expression or a symbol of status or of adherence to certain values'.

the ideal of perfect competition; hence the use of the term 'imperfect' to qualify the situation of product heterogeneity, the term 'imperfect' indicating the direction in which to go (that of 'perfect' competition).[5] In his *Theory of Monopolistic Competition*, Chamberlin took a different perspective, focusing on the concept of firm, rather than industry, and viewing product differentiation as a normal fact of economic life, with the concept of monopolistic competition describing the process of many sellers who produce heterogeneous products in response to divergent demands and preferences of consumers.[6] Chamberlin noted that:

> the consequences of product heterogeneity for welfare economics have been either ignored or seriously misunderstood. Monopoly elements are built into the economic system and the ideal necessarily involves them. Thus wherever there is a demand for diversity of product, pure competition turns out to be not the ideal but a departure from it.[7]

According to Chamberlin, 'if heterogeneity is part of the welfare ideal, there is no prima facie case for doing anything at all', the choice to be made being ultimately that of a 'less heterogeneous output as against a smaller, more heterogeneous one'.[8] This brings to the fore the idea that price is not the only, or the most important, parameter of competition and that quality and variety may also constitute important parameters that one should take into account.[9]

These contrasting views over product differentiation reflect the difficulties facing 'brands' and 'brand theory' in gaining acceptance as a useful operational concept in competition law.[10] This chapter aims, first, to

[5] J. Robinson, *The Economics of Imperfect Competition* (London: Macmillan, 1933).

[6] E. H. Chamberlin, *The Theory of Monopolistic Competition* (Cambridge, MA: Harvard University Press, 1933).

[7] E. H. Chamberlin, 'Product Heterogeneity and Public Policy', *The American Economic Review*, 40(2) (1950), 85–92, at 92.

[8] Chamberlin, 'Product Heterogeneity and Public Policy', 89–90. Two basic formalizations of product heterogeneity emerged in economics. The spatial model, which treats competition as a localized phenomenon, the assumption being that 'consumers purchase a limited number of brands (often one) from a small subset that are most preferred', and the representative consumer model, according to which 'a representative consumer purchases many brands, varying the proportions of each according to their prices and exogenously given utility weights': J. M. Perloff and S. C. Salop, 'Equilibrium with Product Differentiation', *Review of Economic Studies*, (1985), 107–20.

[9] Despite the different focus and policy prescriptions, Chamberlin's theory nevertheless forms part of the neoclassical price paradigm and shares with perfect competition 'the common neoclassical hard core': see S. J. Latsis, 'Situational Determinism in Economics', *The British Journal for the Philosophy of Science*, 23(3) (1972), 207–45.

[10] Although one should note the considerable progress that product differentiation-based oligopoly models brought to merger control and all other areas of competition law from

discuss the difficult normative choices that would entail the integration of 'brands' into the toolbox of competition authorities and the courts, in particular in view of the goals pursued by EU competition law, and second, to describe instances in which the concept of brands played an important role in the competition assessment conducted under EU competition law, and the limits it faced.

Normative choices

One of the most difficult issues to resolve when discussing about the added value offered by the concept of brand in competition law has to do with the role of consumers in the process of product differentiation that is inherent in the existence of brands. In competition law, the aim of protecting consumers implies that the outcome/consequences of a specific practice on consumers matters, before any decision on the lawfulness or unlawfulness of this practice has been reached. A different approach would take a deontological perspective and would emphasize competitive rivalry, irrespective of any actual or potential consequences of the specific practice/conduct on consumers or other protected interests, or some other 'political objective', such as the construction of an Internal Market in the EU context. So the question one should ask is how the constitution of brands and branding in general affects the interests that the specific competition law aims to protect.

For the benefits of comparison with other competition law regimes, taking the interests of consumers as a starting point,[11] one needs to take into account that there are various possible normative assumptions as to the relation between brands and consumer interest in this context.

If one takes the perspective of price theory, the protection of consumer surplus – the consumer part of the deadweight loss suffered as a result of the restriction of competition – will constitute the main focus of the analysis. As the development of a brand involves fixed costs that need to be recuperated over time, firms will not invest in it unless they are able to charge higher than competitive prices.[12] A price increase might lead

the early 1980s onwards. Yet these models do not engage systematically with the psychological aspect of consumer behaviour and the formation of consumer preferences, for instance the emotional and cognitive appeal of brands.

11 I. Lianos, 'Some Reflections on the Objectives of EU Competition Law', in I. Lianos, and D. Geradin (eds.), *Handbook in EU Competition Law: Substantive Aspects* (Cheltenham: Edward Elgar), pp. 1–85.

12 This is an assumption that may not always prove correct, as I will show later with the discussion about private labels, as in reality the introduction of a new brand may allow all

to a volume effect that would be suffered by a certain category of consumers: because of the price increase some consumers will no longer be able to buy the product, although past consumption patterns (revealed preferences) indicate that they would have preferred to do so, had the price not increased. Under this narrow definition of consumer surplus, the overcharge paid by the consumers, as a result of the price increase, should not be of concern for competition law enforcement, as it constitutes a wealth transfer from the buyers to the sellers. The suppliers may be in a position to compensate (hypothetically, not actually) the loss that consumers have suffered while still being able to compensate with this wealth transfer their own losses following the volume effect (producer surplus). Hence, if branding provides opportunities for more intensive product differentiation, this should not necessarily be a concern for competition law, even if that product differentiation leads to higher prices for certain categories of consumers, when, after factoring in the volume effect, it has also the effect of increasing the profits of the brand-owners to an extent that any loss of consumer surplus could be (hypothetically) covered. This is not the approach taken by EU Competition Law, in view of the emphasis it puts on the fact that, to be justified, restrictions to competition should at least be neutral from the point of view of those consumers directly or likely to be affected by the restrictive agreement.[13] One may also advance the view that product differentiation may reduce output, the classic dilemma being that of a 'less heterogeneous output as against a smaller, more heterogeneous one', in which case a total welfare standard approach would view branding with suspicion.

The matrix changes if we move beyond consumer surplus and include in the analysis the wealth transfer that consumers may have incurred because of the overcharges that resulted from the development of brands and increased product differentiation. These may not only relate to higher prices but could also cover any other parameter of competition, such as quality, variety and innovation. In this case, both the loss of consumer surplus and wealth transfers will be compared to the total efficiency

firms to raise prices, but an increase in competing brands of products may also tend to lower prices, as the firm would lose sales to the new brand (cannibalize its sales) and the rival's promotional activities may increase demand for the category or steal customers.

[13] Commission Guidelines on the application of Article 81(3) of the Treaty [2004] OJ C 101/97, para. 85. Although the Commission accepts that consumer harm assessed under Article 101(1) TFEU (e.g. higher prices) might be compensated by some benefits provided by the anticompetitive agreement assessed under Article 101(3) ('efficiency gains'), they require that these benefits *effectively* (and not only hypothetically) and *fully* compensate the consumer harm in one way or another.

gains pertaining to the supplier(s), thus enabling a cost–benefit analysis of the effect of the conduct on the welfare of a specific group of market actors, and direct and indirect consumers. In this case, one may argue that branding and the product differentiation that ensues may enable the brand-owner to increase the price of the branded good and thus to collect additional rents from the consumers that continue purchasing her products. The implicit counterfactual is that, in the absence of the brand and product differentiation, this price increase and the exploitation of this category of consumers would not have been possible. The assumption here is that brands and product differentiation lead to an increased ability and incentive for brand-owners to increase prices for consumers who do not switch to other brands or competing products (inframarginal consumers).

Some authors also argue that competition authorities should aim to preserve an optimal level of 'consumer choice', defined as 'the state of affairs where the consumer has the power to define his or her own wants and the ability to satisfy these wants at competitive prices'.[14]. They also refer to the term 'consumer sovereignty', which is defined as 'the set of societal arrangements that causes [an] economy to act primarily in response to the aggregate signals of consumer demand, rather than in response to government directives or the preferences of individual businesses'.[15] Consumer sovereignty may be preserved as the ability of consumers to influence the characteristics of the product bundle according to their own 'hypothetical' revealed preferences. Hypothetical revealed preference theory defines an agent's preferences in terms of what she would choose if she were able to choose, thus switching from actual to hypothetical choice.[16] The way this theory will work in practice is still a matter of speculation. It is clear that consumers are influenced in their decisions by choice architecture, that is 'the context of choice' as defined by the set of options under consideration. 'In particular, the addition and removal of options from the offered set can influence people's preferences among options that were available all along'.[17] The firms with their marketing

[14] R. H Lande, 'Consumer Choice as the Ultimate Goal of Antitrust', *University of Pittsburgh Law Review*, 62(3) (2001), 503–25, at 503.

[15] N. W. Averitt and R. H. Lande, 'Consumer Sovereignty: A Unified Theory of Antitrust and Consumer Protection Law', *Antitrust Law Journal*, 65 (1997) 713–56, at 715.

[16] For a critical analysis see, D. M. Hausman *Preference, Value, Choice, and Welfare* (Cambridge University Press, 2012), pp. 31–3.

[17] E. Shafir, I. Simonson and A. Tversky, 'Reason-Based Choice', *Cognition*, 49 (1993), 11–36, at 21.

activities may, for example, endogenously shape consumer preferences by establishing an artificial selection process – 'preferences are actually constructed – not merely revealed'.[18] A greater focus on consumer sovereignty may thus, in some cases, lead to more intensive competition law intervention to establish the parameters of independent (hypothetical) consumer choice and specific presumptions against commercial practices that deny the sovereignty of consumer choice. The consumer choice or consumer sovereignty standard may also accommodate the psychological aspect of the formation of these preferences, which is usually ignored in neoclassical price theory.

Transposing this debate over the issue of branding, it becomes essential to explore the origins of product differentiation. If product differentiation constitutes a natural outgrowth of consumer preferences, to which firms tend to respond by developing different brands, then one may argue that brands promote consumer choice.[19] If, however, product differentiation constitutes a way to manipulate consumer preferences, this may contradict the consumer sovereignty principle and brands may be perceived as limiting consumer choice, hence the need to understand how brands relate to the formation of consumer preferences, should the aim of competition law be the protection of the interest of consumers.

Similar concerns have also been expressed for another technique of product differentiation: advertising. As Kyle Bagwell argues in his study of *The Economic Analysis of Advertising*, advertising was 'almost entirely a 20th century project', in view of the focus of economic theory in the nineteenth century on the development of the perfect competition theory, which suggests no role for product differentiation.[20] Economic theory on

[18] *Ibid.*, 34.

[19] This seems to have been the view of Chamberlin ('Product Heterogeneity and Public Policy', 86), according to whom 'monopoly is necessarily a part of the welfare norm. In abstract terms it seems to follow very directly from the recognition that human beings are individuals, diverse in their tastes and desires, and moreover widely dispersed spatially. Insofar as demand has any force as a guide to production, one would expect entrepreneurs to appeal to them in diverse ways, and thus to render the output of the economy correspondingly heterogeneous, using this term in its broadest sense to embrace not only the qualitative aspects of the product itself, but also the conditions surrounding its sale, including spatial location. And since what people want – an elaborate system of consumers' preferences – is the starting point in welfare economics, their wants for a heterogeneous product would seem to be as fundamental as anything could be. Heterogeneity as between producers is synonymous with the presence of monopoly; therefore monopoly is necessarily a part of the welfare ideal.'

[20] K. Bagwell, *The Economic Analysis of Advertising*, Discussion paper No. 0506-01, Columbia University, Department of Economics, August 2005, pp. 1–2.

advertising emerged with Marshall in the later decades of the nineteenth century and early twentieth century and later developed in three distinct periods, depending on the dominant conception of the function advertising plays in relation to consumer preferences.[21]

During the first period, economists perceived advertising as a tool for altering consumer preferences and for creating product differentiation and brand loyalty, driving the demand curve of the advertised product to become more inelastic and thus leading to higher prices for consumers. The dominant perception at the time was that advertising led to a waste of resources, and had an 'entry-deterrence effect', as it aimed to manipulate the preferences of consumers in favour of the products of a particular firm ('the persuasive view').[22] Consumer preferences were thus endogenously determined. Joan Robinson represented this view when she argued that 'the customer will be influenced by advertisement, which plays upon his mind with studied skill, and makes him prefer the goods of one producer to those of another because they are brought to his notice in a more pleasing or more forceful manner'.[23] Empirical work has confirmed some of the intuitions of the 'persuasive view'. Comanor and Wilson performed a multi-variate regression analysis of the averaged profits of manufacturers in forty-one consumer-good industries for a period of three years and found 'empirical support for the conclusion that the heavy volume of advertising expenditures in some industries serves as an important barrier to new competition in the markets served by these industries'.[24] More recently, with regard to product differentiation Bronnenberg *et al.*

[21] *Ibid.*, p. 3. [22] *Ibid.*, p. 9.

[23] Robinson, *The Economics of Imperfect Competition*, p. 90. Among the different authors listed in the 'persuasive view', Bagwell (*The Economic Analysis of Advertising*) includes: D. Braithwaite, 'The Economic Effects of Advertisement', *Economic Journal*, 38 (1928), 16–37 (arguing that advertising may help to create 'reputational monopolies' while it has a modest quality-guarantee effect); N. V. Kaldor, 'The Economic Aspects of Advertising', *Review of Economic Studies*, 18 (1950), 1–27, at 18, (arguing that advertising provides a modest degree of information while wasting resources and that it also enhances concentration, as because of the economies of scale in advertising only the most profitable and larger firms are able to finance larger advertising expenditures and to develop direct connection with the consumers, by-passing other middlemen, such as retailers); J. S. Bain, *Barriers to New Competition: Their Character and Consequences in Manufacturing Industries* (Cambridge, MA: Harvard University Press, 1956) (noting that product differentiation constitutes the most important entry barrier and that advertising is the primary source of product differentiation); J. K. Galbraith, *The Affluent Society* (Boston, MA: Houghton-Mifflin Co., 1958) (criticizing the passive role of consumers in the process).

[24] W. S. Comanor and T. A. Wilson, *Advertising and Market Power* (Cambridge, MA: Harvard University Press, 1974), p. 239.

highlighted that brands, advertising or other past experiences and social milieu, such as childhood, lead to 'preference capital', which could be a valuable asset for incumbent firms and a source of long-term economic rents for them.[25] According to these authors, this explains why consumers have a high willingness to pay for particular brands, even when the alternatives are objectively similar.[26] This evidence indicates that brand loyalty may not always be a natural outgrowth of consumer preferences and that there is value for firms in using advertising, branding or other forms of product differentiation in order to establish some form of 'preference capital'. This strategy may generate high willingness to pay on the part of consumers and presumably steady economic rents for incumbents in the future, without that being justified by the objective characteristics of their product/service in comparison to the products/services of a new entrant. In other words, incumbent firms may have the incentives and the ability to alter the utility function of consumers in order to increase their profits. From this may result possible distortions of competition, which according to Nick Economides may fall into three categories:

> First competition in perception advertising may result in a larger number of brands at equilibrium than is optimal. Second, the tie in (of the brand and the product) produces an allocative distortion. Third, resources are wasted in the effort to link desired mental images with advertised goods.[27]

A different approach is advanced by the proponents of the 'informative view',[28] which considers that the principal function of advertising is to convey information to consumers, and from that perspective to help them choose the products/services that correspond the best to their preferences.[29] This view has been advanced by authors close to the Chicago School of

[25] Bart J. Bronnenberg, J.-Ph. Dubé and M. Grentzkow, 'The Evolution of Brand Preferences: Evidence from Consumer Migration', *American Economic Review*, 102(6) (2012), 2472–508.

[26] *Ibid.* See also, B. J. Bronnenberg, S. K. Dhar and J.-Ph. Dubé, 'Brand History, Geography, and the Persistence of Brand Shares', *Journal of Political Economy*, 117(1) (2009), 87–115. Yet these preferences are shaped over a considerable period of time.

[27] N. Economides, 'The Economics of Trademarks', *Trademark Reporter*, 78 (July–August 1988), 523–39.

[28] Although one should also note that even under the informative view, advertising can be a barrier to entry, as in any case it involves firms spending a lot of money to 'inform' customers rather than 'persuade' them. Yet this approach acknowledges the social value of these additional expenses, thus attempting to justify the possible barriers to entry that may emerge from advertising.

[29] Bagwell, *The Economic Analysis of Advertising*, p. 16.

economics.[30] Telser, a proponent of that view, argued that 'advertising is frequently a means of entry and a sign of competition', in view of its role as 'an important source of information' for consumers.[31] More importantly, although Telser recognizes that 'firms which have some monopoly power are more likely to advertise because they can obtain most of the increased sales stimulated by their advertising', he also finds a weak correlation between concentration or stable market shares and advertising, thus questioning the causal link earlier made by the proponents of the persuasive view.[32] Nelson also advances an informative view argument by distinguishing between search goods (whose quality can be determined prior to purchase, even if at high costs) and experience goods (whose quality can only be determined after consumption) and observing the benefits of advertising (and enhanced product differentiation) for experience goods (through the provision of indirect information on the product).[33] Advertising constitutes a way for the firms to signal to consumers that they are the most efficient (low-cost) firms, since they seek demand expansion (the 'signalling-efficiency effect' of advertising). Furthermore, '(a)dvertising increases the probability of a consumer's remembering the name of a brand', and therefore advertising assists the consumer by informing his choice ('the match-products-to-buyers effect'). Hence, advertising, as well as any mechanism of product differentiation (such as branding), stimulates price comparisons and therefore price competition. Finally, advertising, and brands in general, assist the consumer to draw positive associations between specific products and quality, reminding them of their previous experience with the product ('the repeat-business effect').[34]

The 'complementary view' constitutes the third tradition in the economics of advertising that is of relevance to our study.[35] Under this view, 'consumers possess stable preferences, and advertising directly enters these preferences in a manner that is complementary to the consumption of the advertised product', as consumers value 'social prestige' and

[30] G. J. Stigler, 'The Economics of Information', *Journal of Political Economy*, 69 (1961), 213–25.

[31] L. G. Telser, 'Advertising and Competition', *Journal of Political Economy*, 72 (1964), 537–62, at 558.

[32] *Ibid.*, 544.

[33] P. Nelson, 'Advertising as Information', *Journal of Political Economy*, 82 (1974), 729–54, 732–4.

[34] *Ibid.*

[35] Bagwell, *The Economic Analysis of Advertising*, p. 20, citing the work of G. J. Stigler and G. S. Becker, 'De Gustibus Non Est Disputandum', *American Economic Review*, 67 (1977),

'advertising by a firm may be an input that contributed toward the prestige that is enjoyed when the firm's products is consumed'.[36] Inspired by the Chicago School 'informative view', the 'complementary view' takes for granted the preferences of consumers for 'social prestige' and argues that consumer utility in this case derives from the consumption of various commodities, advertising or brand image being one of them. Advertising does not alter consumer preferences but 'instead enters as an argument in a stable utility function.'[37] Hence, it is possible that 'firms may compete in the same commodity (e.g. prestige) market even though they produce different market goods (e.g. jewellery and fashion) and advertise at different levels'.[38] Therefore, even uninformative advertising or branding may be beneficial to consumers, as consumers directly value the 'social prestige' image that this generates, which is part of the utility function.

Yet one may advance the familiar distinction between marginal and inframarginal consumers to partly counter this argument.[39] Marginal consumers value the additional 'social prestige' provided by the manufacturer's expenses on advertising or more generally the branding of the product, hence they may switch to the specific product/service from other products/services with which the specific supplier competes in the market for 'social prestige'. Inframarginal consumers do not value these additional expenses and the additional 'social prestige' these may generate, as they value the product as such more than the commodity of 'prestige'. Manufacturers may thus only consider marginal consumers and ignore inframarginal consumers, depending on whether the demand curve

76–90; L. M. Nichols, 'Advertising and Economic Welfare', *American Economic Review*, 75 (1985), 213–18.

[36] Bagwell, *The Economic Analysis of Advertising*, pp. 20–1.

[37] *Ibid.*, p. 143.

[38] *Ibid.*, p. 21. Households act in order to maximize their utility. This involves the reconciliation of their preference ordering (or utility function) with their given budget (income). The budget constraint, along with the agent's preferences, provide the necessary information required to determine the consumption bundle that would maximize the agent's utility up to a tangency point, which indicates that there is no possibility of increasing utility by moving along the budget constraint. Taking into account this budget constraint, a 'social prestige' preference may be satisfied by different products, associated with social prestige because of their brand, advertising and so on, the idea here being that 'preferences are ordered over characteristics, not over goods': Nichols, 'Advertising and Economic Welfare', 213.

[39] W. S. Comanor, 'Vertical Price-Fixing, Vertical Market Restrictions, and the New Antitrust Policy', *Harvard Law Review*, 98 (1985), 983–1002. One should not, however, ignore the possibility that firms make investments in advertising in order to credibly 'signal' product quality where this is hard to observe.

shifts with this additional investment in the prestige commodity and whether the consumer surplus generated is captured by the consumers who value 'social prestige'.[40] Consequently, for inframarginal consumers the additional 'social prestige' investment will not correspond to their preferences. However, the use of large amounts of data created on the Internet, including to some extent revelation of consumer preferences, can increase the category of marginal consumers, as opposed to that of inframarginal consumers.[41]

One could also refer to the issues raised by Veblen goods. Veblen, among others, has put emphasis on the phenomenon of 'conspicuous consumption',[42] which brings attention to the role interpersonal effects have on utility functions or the need to focus on the inner motivations of consumers.[43] Leibenstein proceeded to a classification of consumer demand for goods and services according to the motivation behind a consumer's demand. He distinguished between 'functional demand', which refers to the 'part of the demand for a commodity which is due to the qualities inherent in the commodity', and 'non-functional demand', which is 'the portion of the demand for a consumers' good which is due to factors other than the qualities inherent in the commodity'.[44] This relates to utility derived from the commodity, which 'is enhanced or decreased owing to the fact that others are purchasing and consuming the same commodity, or owing to the fact that the commodity bears a higher rather than a lower price tag'.[45] This non-functional demand may take different forms:

(i) the 'bandwagon effect', which refers to 'the extent to which the demand for a commodity is increased due to the fact that others are also consuming the same commodity';
(ii) the 'snob effect', which refers to the 'extent to which the demand for a consumers' good is decreased owing to the fact that others are also consuming the same commodity (or that others are increasing their consumption of that commodity)'; and finally

[40] Although one should also take into account instances of non-functional demand, such as 'bandwagon effects' and 'snob effects', which may relativize the importance of the distinction between marginal and inframarginal consumers in certain contexts. These effects are explored in the next paragraph.

[41] I am indebted to Nick Economides for making this last point.

[42] T. Veblen, *The Theory of the Leisure Class* (New York: Macmillan, 1899).

[43] H. Leibenstein, 'Bandwagon, Snob, and Veblen Effects in the Theory of Consumers Demand', *Quarterly Journal of Economics*, 64 (1950), 183–207.

[44] *Ibid.*, 189. [45] *Ibid.*, 189.

(iii) the 'Veblen effect', which refers to 'the phenomenon of conspicuous consumption, to the extent to which the demand for a consumers' good is increased because it bears a higher rather than a lower price', which is different from the 'snob effect' in the sense that it is a function of price, and not of the consumption of others.[46]

Typical Veblen goods are luxury products for which brand differentiation constitutes an important asset. Leibenstein found that if 'the Veblen effect is the predominant one, the demand curve is less elastic than otherwise, and some portions of it may even be positively inclined',[47] hence showing that higher prices may in some instances correspond to the preferences of consumers.

The decision to intervene in this context will therefore depend on the view one takes of product differentiation and its relation with the *real* preferences of the consumers. Those adept of the informative and/or the complementary view(s) will emphasize the value of product differentiation as an instrument to promote consumer welfare and consumer choice. The positive stance of the 'informative' and the 'complementary' views over advertising and brand differentiation was also echoed by other work focusing on the fact that product differentiation often responds to the heterogeneity of consumer demand[48] and on the need to reward 'pioneering brands' for risk-bearing innovation.[49] Those adept of the persuasive view will be more reticent to intervene in order to ensure that consumer welfare is preserved and that consumers are offered a choice that corresponds to their individual preferences. Behavioural economics or neuro-economics research has also highlighted how 'affective/hot-mode' decision-making, encompassing emotions and motivational drives may alter consumers' tastes and create brand loyalty, in comparison to a counterfactual where decision-making would have been entirely based on the deliberative effort of consumers to maximize their objective function, as this derives from their 'cold-state' preferences.[50] A regulator inspired by paternalistic objectives would strive in this case to ensure that brand differentiation responds to the 'cold-state' preferences of the consumers rather than being instigated by 'hot-mode' decision-making. However, it

[46] *Ibid.*, 189. [47] *Ibid.*, 207.

[48] K. J. Lancaster, 'Socially Optimal Product Differentiation', *The American Economic Review*, 65(4) (1975), 567–85.

[49] R. Schmalensee, 'Product Differentiation Advantages of Pioneering Brands', *The American Economic Review*, 72(3) (1982), 349–65.

[50] Bagwell, *The Economic Analysis of Advertising*, pp. 143–6.

remains difficult to distinguish, outside the laboratory, what constitutes a 'hot-state' or a 'cold-state' preference. Furthermore, a systematic reliance on some form of objective list of preferences that might reasonably be expected to promote an agent's well-being may be antithetical to the theoretical premises of mainstream competition law to rely on markets and revealed preferences through market behaviour, unless one takes a different paradigm relying on some form of soft paternalism, which is still uncharted territory in the area of competition law.[51]

Addressing the issue of consumer preferences does not constitute the only challenge that brand differentiation sets to competition law. The development of brands was initially instrumental to the emergence of manufacturer market power, as through the constitution of brand loyalty manufacturers were able to foster direct relations with consumers, without the intermediary of the middleman (e.g. wholesalers, retailers), thus reversing the balance of power between the two poles of the vertical distribution chain in favour of the manufacturers. Previously, products sold in retail stores were most often non-branded, access to a well-known retailer being the only way for a specific supplier to reach consumers. Advertising and other tools of product differentiation may thus be perceived as an effort to rebalance the relationship between manufacturers and retailers, shifting power to the manufacturers.[52] The growth in manufacturer advertising, by substituting for retail service, and the associated phenomenon of the multiplication of brands, has nevertheless over time facilitated the emergence of a more concentrated retail market.[53] Multi-brand retailers have emerged as a focal point of distribution in certain product categories.[54] Furthermore, retailers have developed private labels, which have increased their retail gross margins and have eaten market share from some national brand-owners, thus intensifying the 'vertical competition' between the two poles of the vertical chain.[55] Contrary to what

51 R. A. Thaler and C. Sunstein, 'Libertarian Paternalism', *The American Economic Review*, 93(2) (2003), 175–9. Most of the work on soft paternalism is in the area of regulation.

52 See, for instance, the work of R. Steiner, 'The Inverse Association Between Margins of Manufacturers and Retailers', *Review of Industrial Organization*, 8 (1993), 717–40.

53 R. L. Steiner, 'Marketing Productivity in Consumer Goods Industries – A Vertical Perspective', *Journal of Marketing*, 42 (1978), 60–70.

54 W. Comanor and P. Rey, 'Vertical Restraints and the Market Power of Large Distributors', *Review of Industrial Organization*, 17 (2000), 135–53.

55 Retailers with strong private labels have more leverage with manufacturers and this helps them to increase their gross margins. Private labels may also enhance consumer loyalty to retail brands and therefore reinforce the horizontal market power of the retailers. This will in turn strengthen retailers' vertical bargaining power against national brand

was usually the case with the use of brands in the past, private labels often indicate the presence of a lower-price substitute to national brands. They illustrate that brands and product differentiation may take two different directions: they either enable the firm to increase the price of the product and indicate higher quality for consumers likely to value this parameter of competition, or signal the presence of a low-cost alternative, for consumers who are more attentive to the price parameter of competition. The development of brands linked to low-cost retail products (e.g. Lidl, Aldi), low-cost airlines (e.g. Ryanair) or more generally the launching of 'fighter brands' indicates the multiple uses and effects of brands in a business context.

Last but not least, the emergence of 'social branding' promotes the idea that brands communicate vital consumer meaning and that consumers and brand-owners are interdependent to the extent that brands are connected, networked and socialized. The result is that people and communities identify with the brands they use and become co-creators to a certain extent of the brand meaning, along with the brand-owner. This perception of branding breaks with the 'broadcast' or 'one-way information transmission' model of the persuasive/informative/complementary views and perceives branding as a 'dialogic and iterative' interaction between active consumers and brand-owners.[56] Iconic brands resonate with the identity of large groups of consumers and lead to the formation of 'brand communities' that display brand loyalty, but which also expect that this loyalty will not be betrayed by the brand-owner, whose discretion as brand manager is restricted by the broader values and reference points of the specific brand community.[57]

manufacturers and will enable them to obtain better deals that will increase their profits; R L Steiner, 'The Nature and Benefits of National Brand/Private Label Competition', *Review of Industrial Organization*, 24 (2004), 105–27, at 106 (distinguishing between vertical competition – the competition between the different levels of the vertical structure, such as suppliers versus retailers over the sharing of the profits of the vertical chain – and horizontal competition – the competition between different vertical chains).

[56] See, for instance, D. R. Desai, 'From Trademarks to Brands', *Florida Law Review*, (2012), 981–1044, (noting the 'noncorporate dimension of branding', which 'involves consumers and communities as stakeholders in brands'); D. S. Ganjee, 'Property in Brands', in H. Howe and J. Griffiths (eds.), *Property Concepts in Intellectual Property Law* (Cambridge University Press, 2013), forthcoming. Available at SSRN: http://ssrn.com/abstract=2235721.

[57] A. M. Munir, Jr and T. C. O'Guinn, 'Brand Community', *Journal of Consumer Research*, 27 (2001), 412–31; D. Holt, *How Brands Become Icons* (Cambridge, MA: Harvard University Press, 2004).

The perception that brands are co-created by consumers and manufacturers or retailers renders more complex the discussion over the correspondence of product differentiation to consumer preferences and the complex interaction between consumer preferences and brand management by the brand-owner.

This complexity may explain the ambiguity of competition law, in particular EU competition law, to the phenomenon of branding and product differentiation. If one may find some illustrations of a hostile rhetoric of competition law to branding, it is also possible to uncover instances where the value of brands for consumer welfare and other objectives of EU competition law in general was duly recognized. It remains, however, that instances of the former are more numerous than instances of the latter, although one has to take into account the fact that product differentiation is prevalent in European markets and that *in fine* few competition cases investigated are selected on this basis.

Implementing the operational concept of brands in EU competition law

On several occasions the European Commission and the EU courts have made use of the concept of brand in order to derive specific inferences in the context of the competition assessment of business conduct. Confirming our earlier findings as to the ambiguous effects of branding and product differentiation more generally on competition, the inferences made were not always going in the same direction. In some cases, product differentiation was perceived as a positive development that had to be preserved, by enabling undertakings to protect the value of their brand (brands operating as a competition law defence). In most cases relating to product differentiation, however, it was viewed with suspicion and led to findings of anticompetitive effects, or raised concerns over restrictive competition practices that had to be tackled (brands operating as a sword). Most recently, the phenomenon of brands came to the epicentre of the competition law discourse with the focus on private labels, in particular in the food sector industry.

Brands, product differentiation and market power

In theory, by driving the demand curve of a branded product or service to become more inelastic, brands, and more generally product differentiation, may be considered as a source of market power in the economic sense of the word: the ability to raise prices profitably and reduce output.[58] Yet the development of low-cost brands in different economic sectors (e.g. air transport, clothing, food, retail services) may raise doubts as to the validity of this correlation. Michael Porter has observed that product differentiation and cost leadership 'are usually inconsistent, because differentiation is usually costly'.[59] He remarked that firms may pursue both low cost leadership and product differentiation as a strategy only in specific and temporary circumstances, when all competitors are stuck in the middle, where cost is strongly affected by market shares or when a firm introduces a major innovation. Other researchers have nevertheless emphasized the sustainability of the strategy of combining product differentiation and low-cost leadership, thus explaining the successful emergence of low-cost brands.[60] Hill has shown the benefits of differentiation as a way of achieving a low-cost position in certain market configurations, such as high-growth emerging industries that have significant learning and scale economies and the potential to differentiate the product, or mature industries experiencing significant technological change, which gives rise to new learning economies.[61] Major traditional 'quality-focused' brands are also launching low-cost 'no-frills' brands as a way to compete with mono 'low-cost' brands.[62] This increased product or service differentiation augments the elasticity of the demand curve and increases consumer choice.

The complex interrelation between low-cost and 'quality-focused' brands has not yet been thoroughly considered in EU competition law, which adheres to the assumption that brands and product differentiation lead to a more inelastic demand curve.[63] The objective of the firm may indeed be to use product differentiation (in variety or quality) to create a firm-specific demand curve that is more inelastic than the industry-wide

[58] This does not mean that branding will always drive the demand curve to become more inelastic. It may also increase demand.

[59] M. Porter, *Competitive Advantage* (New York: Free Press, 1985), p. 18.

[60] Charles W. L. Hill, 'Differentiation versus Low Cost or Differentiation and Low Cost: A Contingency Framework', *The Academy of Management Review*, 13(3) (1988), 401–12.

[61] *Ibid.*, 411.

[62] In the air transport sector, see, for instance, the plans of German carrier Lufthansa to launch in collaboration with Turkish Airlines a low-cost long-haul carrier: www.bloomberg.com/news/2014-07-09/lufthansa-to-expand-low-cost-push-as-spohr-mulls-long-haul-model.html.

[63] See, for instance, the classic CJEU judgment in Case C27/76 *United Brands* v. *Commission* (*Chiquita*) E.C.R., 1978, I-207 (where the brand was considered to be enhancing United Brands' dominant position).

demand curve. Competition authorities have relied occasionally on the inelastic demand curve of after-sales services or replacement equipment markets to define the brand as the relevant market, with the aim to protect from exploitation consumers who were 'locked in' to the specific brand. Although these cases concern after-markets, with the presence of information imperfections and asymmetries between sellers and purchasers, and the brands involved are not household names, they illustrate that in certain circumstances competition authorities and courts may define brands as a relevant market in order to protect consumers 'locked in' to a specific brand in certain contexts.

For instance, in *Hugin* a Swedish company, having at the time 13 per cent of the United Kingdom market for cash registers, was found by the Commission to have abused its dominant position for refusing to supply spare parts to its former exclusive distributor in the UK, which were needed to repair and maintain the large numbers of Hugin cash registers that it rented. Hugin had argued that the relevant market was 'cash registers' as a whole. The Court rejected this view and held instead that spare parts were separate products from the original equipment supplied, with the result that the relevant market was found to comprise only Hugin spare parts required by the independent undertakings repairing and servicing Hugin cash registers. By distinguishing the secondary market of spare parts from the primary market of the cash registers, the Court was able to ignore the possible competitive constraints that could be exercised on the conduct of the undertaking by its competitors on the primary market to which the independent retailers may have shifted their business.[64] No justification was provided for such finding and the Court did not elaborate further, as it found that the conduct did not affect trade between Member States.

The Commission set the principles of its aftermarkets analysis in its *Pelikan/Kyoecera*, *Info-Lab/Ricoh* and *EFIM* decisions, which related to complaints regarding the market for toners for printers and toners for photocopiers.[65] In its Notice on market definition the Commission

[64] For cases where similar issues were raised see, *Pelikan/Kyocera* in XXV Report on Competition Policy, point 87, and Commission Decision 91/595/EEC in Case No. IV/M.12 – *Varta/Bosch*, OJ L 320, 22.11.1991, p. 26, Commission Decision in Case No. IV/M.1094 – *Caterpillar/Perkins Engines*, OJ C 94, 28.3.1998, p. 23, and Commission Decision in Case No. IV/M.768 – *Lucas/Varity*, OJ C 266, 13.9.1996, p. 6.

[65] Case No. IV/34.330 – *Pelikan/Kyocera*, (1995) para. 6 (noting that the Commission will consider the following four elements: 'the extent that a customer (i) can make an informed choice including lifecycle-pricing, knowing of the warranty restrictions of the

explained this approach by noting the need, when defining a market, not only to assess the responses of customers based on their purchasing decisions when relative prices change, but also constraints on substitution imposed by conditions in the connected markets.[66] If the issue of compatibility between the spare parts and the primary product is important for consumers and the primary product has a long lifespan, there might be the risk that charging higher prices to 'locked-in' brand customers may be a profitable strategy, hence leading to the definition of a narrow secondary product market (e.g. spare parts, after-sales services). However, according to the Commission's Notice, 'a different market definition may result if significant substitution between secondary products is possible or if the characteristics of the primary products make quick and direct consumer responses to relative price increases of the secondary products feasible'. As it is further explained in the Commission's vertical restraints guidelines:

> [i]n practice, the issue to decide is whether a significant proportion of buyers make their choice taking into account the lifetime costs of the product. If so, this indicates there is one market for the original equipment and spare parts combined.[67]

Traditionally, economic analysis on after-markets has emphasized whether consumers 'full cost' at the outset in order to distinguish between the different cases.[68] A similar approach was adopted by the US Supreme Court in *Eastman Kodak*, which has been perceived as animated by post-Chicago principles that market imperfections (e.g. information imperfections) may lead 'unsophisticated' market participants to be exploited in after-markets for products to which they are locked in, even if the primary

various manufacturers, that he (ii) is likely to make such choice accordingly, and that, in case of an apparent policy of exploitation being pursued in one specific aftermarket, a (iii) sufficient number of customers would adapt their purchasing behavior at the level of the primary market (iv) within a reasonable time'; Case No. IV/E 2.36.431 – *Info-Lab/Ricoh* (1999), paras. 37 *et seq*.; Case COMP/C-3/39.391 *EFIM*, C(2009) 4125, para. 16. For cases where similar issues were raised, see Commission Decision 91/595/EEC in Case No IV/M.12 – *Varta/Bosch*, OJ L 320, 22.11.1991, p. 26; Commission Decision in Case No IV/M.1094 – *Caterpillar/Perkins Engines*, OJ C 94, 28.3.1998, p. 23; and Commission Decision in Case No IV/M.768 – *Lucas/Varity*, OJ C 266, 13.9.1996, p. 6.

[66] Commission Notice on the definition of the relevant market for the purposes of Community competition law, [1997] OJ C 37/5, para. 56.

[67] Commission Guidelines on Vertical Restraints, [2010] C 130/1, para. 1.

[68] See, P. Davis, L. Coppi and P. Kalmus, 'The Economics of Secondary Product Markets', OFT Discussion. Paper (2012).

market is competitive.[69] In its most recent case law, the CJEU confirmed the approach followed by the Commission in after-market cases.[70]

Because of their characteristics and lifespan, some products may be particularly conducive to such form of exploitation of market power. In this context, the EU Courts and the Commission have either found that the specific brand may constitute the relevant market, or have examined thoroughly the anticompetitive effects on the 'locked-in' customers, the brand therefore becoming an operational concept in the competition law assessment. For instance, one may understand the *Volvo* and *Renault* judgments of the Court of Justice of the European Union (CJEU) as relying on the assumption that the spare parts of each of these automobile manufacturers could be considered as a separate relevant market from that of the primary product, the automobile, the refusal by Volvo and Renault to deliver these spare parts to independent repairers constituting an abuse of a dominant position.[71] More importantly, in its Motor Vehicle Distribution Regulation and guidelines, the Commission defines a separate relevant market for the repair and parts of each brand, thus conceiving the after-sales market as a separate market to the primary one.[72] According to the Commission, '(b)ecause of the generally brand-specific nature of the markets for repair and maintenance services and for the distribution of spare parts, competition on those markets is inherently less intense compared to that on the market for the sale of new motor vehicle'.[73] Furthermore,

[69] *Eastman Kodak Co* v. *Image Technical Services, Inc*, 504 US 451 (1992). The judgment of the Supreme Court was criticized by some scholars (e.g. Herbert Hovenkamp, *The Antitrust Enterprise: Principle and Execution* (Cambridge, MA: Harvard University Press, 2005), p. 310, calling for the overruling of the *Kodak* precedent) and lauded by others (e.g. W. S. Grimes, 'Antitrust Tie-in Analysis After Kodak: Understanding the Role of Market Imperfections', *Antitrust law Journal*, 62 (1994), 263–325). Controversy notwithstanding, the *Eastman Kodak* precedent still seems to be good law, at least for some district courts: see, most recently, *Avaya, Inc.* v. *Telecom Labs, Inc.*, 1:06-cv-2490(JEI) (D.N.J., 2006) (27 March 2014). For a brief commentary, see Nicholas Economides, 'Avaya v. TLI Gives New Life to Aftermarket Monopolization Litigation A-La-Kodak', (8 August 2014), available at http://competitionacademia.com/2014/08/avaya-v-tli-gives-new-life-to-aftermarket-monopolization-litigation-a-la-kodak-2/.

[70] Case C-56/12 P, *European Federation of Ink and Ink Cartridge Manufacturers (EFIM)* v. *European Commission* [19 September 2013] ECLI:EU:C:2013:575, para. 37.

[71] Case C238/87, *AB Volvo* v. *Eric Veng* [1988] ECR 6211; Case 53/87, *CICRA and Maxicar* v. *Renault* [1988] ECR 6039 decided on the same day.

[72] Commission Regulation (EU) No. 461/2010 on the application of Article 101(3) of the Treaty on the Functioning of the European Union to categories of vertical agreements and concerted practices in the motor vehicle sector, [2010] OJ L 129/52.

[73] Commission Notice, Supplementary Guidelines on vertical restraints in agreements for the sale and repair of motor vehicles and for the distribution of spare parts for motor vehicles, [2010] OJ C 138/6, para. 15.

concerns over the exploitation of locked-in consumers may also be justified by the fact that 'repair and maintenance as a whole represent a very high proportion of total consumer expenditure on motor vehicles, which itself accounts for a significant slice of the average consumer's budget'.[74]

Although the above-mentioned cases may also be explained by the specific circumstances of market power in after-markets (thus not directly related to brand power), the vertical restraints guidelines summarize this tradition of hostility of EU competition law towards branding power by stipulating that:

> [v]ertical restraints agreed for non-branded goods and services are in general less harmful than restraints affecting the distribution of branded goods and services. Branding tends to increase product differentiation and reduce substitutability of the product, leading to a reduced elasticity of demand and an increased possibility to raise price.[75]

Brands are considered in several parts of the guidelines as indicating the existence of market power of the brand-owner and as barriers to entry.[76]

EU competition law has not, however, gone as far as developing a full-fledged theory of relational (or superior bargaining) market power, on the basis of the 'economic dependence' that some retailers may have on a well-known strong brand or group of brands, even if the supplier does not dispose of a high enough market share to be found in a dominant position or that provides him the ability to exercise market power, as it is the case in the competition law of some Member States (e.g. in German competition law: *sortimentsbedingte Abhängigkeit* or brand dependence).[77] For instance, in the famous *Rossignol* case, the German Federal Court (BGH) found that because of its commercial value and its market prestige, there were not sufficient switching possibilities for the customers of Rossignol ski equipment, here a leading specialized sport retailer, even if there was considerable competition between Rossignol skis and

[74] Commission Notice, Supplementary Guidelines on vertical restraints in agreements for the sale and repair of motor vehicles and for the distribution of spare parts for motor vehicles, [2010] OJ C 138/6, para. 15.

[75] Commission Guidelines on Vertical Restraints, [2010] C 130/1, para. 104.

[76] See, for instance, Commission Guidelines on Vertical Restraints, [2010] C 130/1, paras. 114, 117, 180.

[77] For a critical analysis of the superior bargaining power approach, see F. Jenny, 'The "Coming Out" of Abuse of Superior Bargaining Power in the Antitrust World' (2008), available at http://unctad.org/sections/ditc_ccpb/docs/ditc_ccpb0008_en.pdf. See also, I. Lianos, *La Transformation du droit de la concurrence par le recours à l'analyse économique* (Brussels: Bruylant, 2007).

other suppliers.[78] In particular, the Federal Court noted that, in addition to their price, the actual value of particular goods is determined by their quality and the producer's advertising activities, hence hinting at the role of product differentiation in providing some degree of (relative) market power. Although brands have been considered as reinforcing the finding of a dominant position, the European Commission and EU courts do not apply Article 102 TFEU on the simple basis of switching costs for consumers engendered by the appeal and reputation of a brand, in the absence of a dominant position on the relevant market.

Product differentiation nevertheless plays a more active role in EU merger control, in view of the recent emphasis put on unilateral (non-coordinated) effects theory and a significant impediment of effective competition below the levels of dominance.[79] In all these cases the merging firms may find it profitable to alter their behaviour unilaterally, following the acquisition, by elevating the price and suppressing output, and by acting independently of the remaining firms. Econometric techniques used in the context of differentiated products in order to assess these effects also take into account the multiple dimensions of consumer choice, as the parameters of the choice increase with the number of products considered. The literature provides different solutions regarding the existence of various dimensions of product competition (the dimensionality problem):[80] (i) multi-level demand models, (ii) spatial models and (iii) discrete choice models. Multi-level demand models, as well as spatial models, attempt to solve the dimensionality problem by dividing the products into smaller groups or sub-groups. The demand system applied has the Almost Ideal Demand System (AIDS) model formulation, under which it is assumed that consumers employ a multi-level decision-making process when purchasing a product. The actual application usually involves a three-stage system (although it is possible to

[78] German Federal Court, *Rossignol* (1976) WuW/E 1391, 1393 *et seq.*

[79] Council Regulation (EC) No. 139/2004 of 20 January 2004 on the control of concentrations between undertakings [2004] OJ L 24/1. For a recent account, see T. Mäger, 'Unilateral Effects in European Merger Analysis', in B. E. Hawk (ed.), *Annual Proceedings of the Fordham Corporate Law Institute 2010*, vol. 37 (New York: Juris Publishing, 2011), pp. 123–34; I. Kokkoris and H. Shelanski, *EU Merger Control: A Legal and Economic Analysis* (Oxford University Press, 2014), pp. 221–60.

[80] The brief analysis below draws on I. Lianos and C. Genakos, 'Econometric Evidence in EU Competition Law: An Empirical and Theoretical Analysis', in I. Lianos and D. Geradin (eds.), *Handbook in European Competition Law: Enforcement and Procedure* (Cheltenham: Edward Elgar, 2013), pp. 1–137, 15–23.

have as many levels as necessary):[81] the top level corresponds to overall demand for the product (for example, ready-to-eat cereal); the middle level involves demand for different market segments (for example, family, kids and adults cereal); and the bottom level involves a flexible brand demand system corresponding to the competition between the different brands within each segment. The discrete choice models take a more fundamental approach and project consumer preferences over the products' characteristics rather than the products themselves.

Nested logit models have also been used in order to examine the competitive interaction between brands in markets with differentiated products. In *Unilever/Sara Lee*, which concerned the sale of branded deodorants in a range of EU countries, the Commission estimated one- and two-level nested logit models for deodorants, with nests for male and non-male deodorants, and sub-nests depending on whether the deodorant was presented as skin-friendly. The Commission then combined the estimated elasticities of demand with standard supply-side assumptions (i.e., static Bertrand competition) to simulate the price effects of the merger. The nested logit model used relied overall on simplifying assumptions, a crucial feature of which is that within each nest, switching between individual brands is proportional to brand market share. Hence, in this case the Commission employed a two-level nest structure, which subdivided the male and non-male deodorants according to some further product characteristic, that is whether or not the male or non-male deodorants are branded as being 'skin-friendly', thus reducing reliance on market shares, as the assumption that consumers switch between products in proportion to market shares is limited to a narrower product set (e.g. non-male skin-friendly deodorants). Yet even with this modification, the nested logit model failed to take into account important aspects of differentiation across brands (such as the format of the deodorant, roll-on versus aerosol, fragrance, etc.).[82] The model could not thus identify the

[81] I. Small, 'Econometric Analyses of Unilateral Effects in Merger Cases', *Concurrences*, 2 (2009), 1–8.

[82] These are standard limitations of the standard nested logit model and may be overcome if one uses the random coefficients logit model (or BLP) developed by S. T. Berry, J. Levinsohn and A. Pakes, 'Automobile Prices in Market Equilibrium', *Econometrica*, 63(4) (1995), 841–90. According to this model random coefficients are incorporated 'for continuously measured product characteristics (and not just for the group dummy variables in the nested logit model)', thus creating more flexible substitution patterns, where products tend to be closer substitutes as they have more continuous characteristics that are similar. Yet these models are 'computationally more demanding': for a comparison, see L. Grigolon and F. Verboven, *Nested Logit or Random Coefficients Logit? A Comparison*

competitive interaction between brands within each category, as the simulation relied on estimates of substitution across all brands. It also did not include elements of dynamic competition, such as entry, product repositioning or retailer buyer power. The Commission recognized these limitations of the simulation method, yet it considered that the 'estimated effects are consistent with the rest of the available evidence and of a sufficient magnitude to be assigned a certain weight in the analysis'.[83] It is noted in the decision that, given the time frame of the investigation, it would have been prohibitively complex to introduce these additional factors into the model and the assessment was carried out by using the other qualitative and quantitative evidence on file.[84] Hence, there may be limits to a more systematic analysis of brands and their competitive interaction in this context.

One may conclude from the above that EU competition law seems to perceive branding as reducing elasticity of demand (and consumer switching), establishing barriers to entry and thus facilitating the exercise of market power to the detriment of consumers' welfare or choice. Yet this tradition coexists with a more positive perspective on the role of brands in promoting competition and the interest of consumers.

Product differentiation and brands as a defence tool

The *Metro I* judgment of the CJEU is particularly significant for emphasizing the important role of competition on quality and variety, rather than competition only based on the parameter of price. The Court held compatible to Article 101 TFEU the constitution of selective distribution networks, to which only dealers satisfying some objective, qualitative and proportional criteria will be accepted.[85] The CJEU declared that 'although price competition is so important that it can never be eliminated it does not constitute the only effective form of competition or that to which absolute priority must in all circumstances be accorded'.[86] Following this judgment, as a matter of principle, product differentiation leading to

of Alternative Discrete Choice Models of Product Differentiation, Center for Economic Studies Discussions Paper Series (DPS) 11.24 (September 2011), available at www.econ.kuleuven.be/ces/discussionpapers/default.htm.

[83] Case No. COMP M.5658, *Unilever/Sara Lee* (2010), para. 182, available at http://ec.europa.eu/competition/mergers/cases/decisions/m5658_20101117_20600_2193231_EN.pdf.

[84] *Ibid.*, para. 10.

[85] Case 26/76, *Metro SB-Großmärkte GmbH & Co.* KG v. *Commission* [1977] ECR 1875.

[86] *Ibid.*, para. 21

higher prices would not be deemed anticompetitive in EU competition law if it has the effect to increase the level of competition on parameters other than price, such as quality, product variety and innovation.[87] This hospitable tradition to product differentiation and consequently branding may lead to the finding that some restrictions of price competition may not infringe Article 101 TFEU if they aim to promote the brand image of the product (thus increasing product variety) and its overall quality.

The CJEU has accepted that restricting the number or types of retailers in a selective distribution framework may be a necessary evil in order to create a brand image, should the nature of the product justify such investment.[88] Similarly, the Court recognized the specific characteristics of franchise agreements in *Pronuptia*,[89] where it held that a franchisor should have the freedom to select his franchisees and to impose on them the obligation to obtain the contract products only from a designated source when it is not possible to formulate objective quality specifications, or more generally obligations as to the nature of any advertising and promotion of the products. These restraints broadly rely on the need to protect the brand reputation of the franchise network. Indeed, a common feature of franchise contracts is the transfer of intellectual property rights (trademark) and know-how from the franchisor to the franchisee. This may create a risk of *ex post* opportunism. Indeed, 'if one franchisee allows the quality of his establishment to deteriorate, he benefits by the full amount of the savings from reduced quality maintenance' but 'he loses only part of the costs, for part is borne by other franchisees'.[90] It follows

[87] See, more generally, Commission Guidelines on the application of Article 101(3), [2004] OJ C 101/97, paras. 16, 24, 69–72 and 86 (noting that '[i]f a restrictive agreement is likely to lead to higher prices, consumers must be fully compensated through increased quality or other benefits'). Qualitative selective distribution systems do not infringe Article 101(1) TFEU and quantitative restrictions may be justified under Article 101(3) TFEU: Case T-19/92 *Leclerc* v. *Commission ('YSL')* [1996] ECR II-1851; Case T-88/92 *Leclerc* v. *Commission ('Givenchy')* [1996] ECR II-1961.

[88] This is the most controversial aspect of the EU case law on selective distribution, as it accepts the constitution of selective distribution systems only for certain types of products, in essence luxury, complex, experience and credence goods. Commission Guidelines on Vertical Restraints, [2010] C 130/1, para. 185. For a critical discussion of the guidelines and the case law of the EU Courts, see T. Buettner, A. Coscelli, T. Vergé and R. A. Winter, 'An Economic Analysis of the Use of Selective Distribution by Luxury Goods Suppliers', *European Competition Journal*, 5(1) (2009), 201–60.

[89] Case 161/84, *Pronuptia de Paris GmbH* v. *Pronuptia de Paris Irmgard Schillgallis* [1986] ECR 414.

[90] P. H. Rubin, 'The Theory of the Firm and the Structure of the Franchise Contract', *Journal of Law and Economics* 21 (1978), 223–33, at 227.

that the franchisor will have to select his franchisees carefully, institute a quality control mechanism, introduce early termination clauses in the franchising agreement and impose further restrictions necessary for the protection of the identity and reputation of the network and the value of the assets, such as the trademark, which are also used by the other members of the franchise network.

More generally, EU competition law recognizes that:

> [a] vertical restraint may help to create a brand image by imposing a certain measure of uniformity and quality standardisation on the distributors, thereby increasing the attractiveness of the product to the final consumer and increasing its sales.[91]

However, this does not go as far as accepting that the protection of brand image and the promotion of the brand constitutes a justification for any type of anticompetitive conduct. Already in *Consten & Grundig*, the CJEU had ignored the possible positive effects to inter-brand competition of the strategy of the German brand of electrical equipment Grundig to offer an exclusive distribution agreement to French distributor Consten, coupled with a trademark licence agreement for France, because of its potential to affect intra-EU trade and parallel imports with the establishment of an absolute territorial protection.[92] The Court did not consider the possibility that such territorial protection could be the only way for a not-well-known brand to gain access to the market of another Member State.[93] The possibility for new, not so well-known brands to impose restrictions of passive sales by other distributors into an exclusive territory, or to an exclusive customer group, has nevertheless been accepted by both the CJEU[94] and the European Commission,[95] when it is necessary for the distributor to recoup the substantial investment that needs to be made where there was previously no demand for that type of product in general or for that type of product from that producer in particular.

However, the recent case law of the CJEU and the decisional practice of some national competition authorities on the prohibition of online sales in the context of a selective distribution network reminds us that,

[91] Commission, Guidelines on Vertical Restraints, [2010] C 130/1, para. 107(i).

[92] Cases 56 & 58/64, *Etablissements Consten S.A. and Grundigverkaufs-GmbH.* v. *E.E.C. Commission* [1966] ECR 419. Contrast the Opinion of Advocate General Roemer.

[93] V. Korah and D. O'Sullivan, *Distribution and the EC Competition Rules* (Oxford: Hart Publishing, 2002).

[94] Case 161/84, *Pronuptia de Paris GmbH* v. *Pronuptia de Paris Irmgard Schillgallis* [1986] ECR 414, para. 24 (interpreted *a contrario*).

[95] Commission Guidelines on Vertical Restraints, [2010] C 130/1, para. 61.

in the presence of hardcore restrictions, it is not possible to rely successfully on the need to protect brand image as a competition law defence.[96] More generally, the CJEU held in *Pierre Fabre* that '(t)he aim of maintaining a prestigious image is not a legitimate aim for restricting competition and cannot therefore justify a finding that a contractual clause pursuing such an aim does not fall within Article 101(1) TFEU'.[97] One may think of these broad restrictions as based on some form of industrial policy aims to develop an e-commerce or m-commerce that is not entirely in the hands of brand manufacturers and to provide possibilities for innovative, low-cost distributors to emerge, or more simply as a way to enhance the opportunities of parallel trade. The vertical restraints guidelines nevertheless attempt to reach a balance between these different objectives by recognizing the possibility of a supplier requiring that its distributors have one or more bricks and mortar shops or showrooms as a condition for becoming a member of its distribution system.[98]

Private labels and the emergence of a new rhetoric on brands

The development of private labels, as well as that of 'low-cost' brands, challenges the premise that branding and product differentiation render the demand more inelastic and hence lead to higher prices for consumers. Private label is a term referring to all products sold under a retailer's brand, which could be the retailer's own name (store brands) or a brand created by a manufacturer exclusively for the retailer, who defines the characteristics of the product (generic brands). Private label products are generally exclusively distributed by the retailer along with national brand products, which are marketed by manufacturers throughout the national market, not just in the specific retailers' outlets. Private labels usually appeal to consumers because of their lower price. Hence, product differentiation by private labels may counteract the effect of differentiation strategies employed by national brands suppliers who aim to increase their prices and improve their profitability. This brings a horizontal dimension into the relationship between

[96] For a recent discussion, see G. Monti, 'Restraints on Selective Distribution Agreements', *World Competition Law and Economic Review*, 36(4) (2013), 489–511; A. Font Galarza, E. L. Dziadykiewicz and A. Guerrero Perez, 'Selective Distribution and e-commerce: An Overview of EU and National Case Law', *Concurrences*, 2 (2012), 2–8.

[97] C439/09, *Pierre Fabre Dermo-Cosmétique SAS* v. *Président de l'Autorité de la concurrence and Ministre de l'Économie, de l'Industrie et de l'Emploi* [2011] ECR I9419, para. 46.

[98] Commission Guidelines on Vertical Restraints, [2010] C 130/1, para. 54.

suppliers and retailers, as private labels may compete for market share with national brands.[99] Private label brands' market share has been constantly growing, in particular in the food sector,[100] and represents a significant volume of retail sales in Europe. From simple generics in the 1970s, the quality of private label brands considerably improved in the late 1980s and early 1990s.

Private labels are generally perceived by consumers as being of lower price and quality than national brands. In addition, national labels benefit from a 'reputation premium', as a result of more extensive advertising campaigns than private labels enjoy, and also from brand loyalty-building. This leads to lower prices for private labels than equivalent – in terms of quality – national brand products. Despite this retail price differential, retailer's gross margins for private labels are more important in comparison to national brand products.[101] It follows that the commercialization of private labels is more profitable for retailers, in comparison to national brands.

This constitutes the main reason for the introduction of private labels by retailers and often leads to the exclusion of second-tier national brands from the market.[102] Two reasons explain the higher retail gross margins for retailers. Steiner notes that retailers with strong private labels have more leverage with manufacturers and this helps them to increase their

[99] Although the issue of private labels being in the same market as national brands depends on a number of circumstances, recent case law has not excluded the possibility that private labels may be in the same relevant market as national brands at the retail level but not at the wholesale level because of differences in the functioning of the markets for national and private labels: Case IV/M.623, 16 January 1996; Case COMP/M.2097, *SCA/Metsä Tissue*, 31 January 2001, para. 20–8, available at http://ec.europa.eu/comm/competition/mergers/cases/decisions/m2097_en.pdf.

[100] M. B. Ward *et al.*, 'Effects of the Private-Label Invasion in Foods Industries', *American Journal of Agricultural Economics*, 844 (2002), 961–73. This is also highlighted in the recent UK Competition Commission report into the grocery sector: UK Competition Commission, Final Report, Groceries Market Investigation 30.4.2008, available at www.gov.uk/cma-cases/groceries-market-investigation-cc (hereinafter, Groceries Market Report). Some retailers have also developed a strong private-label identity as they sell only own-label goods (e.g. Aldi, Marks & Spencer) and the development of private labels constitutes an important aspect of their commercial strategy against other retailers. It seems that the development of private labels is an important aspect of horizontal competition between retailers: Groceries Market Report, at p. 71, footnote 2. See also Appendix 9.10 ('consumer research indicates that around 20 per cent of shoppers choose their grocery retailer on the basis of own-label ranges').

[101] In addition to these higher gross margins, private labels also create loyalty to the supermarket chain.

[102] Ward *et al.*, 'Effects of the Private-Label Invasion in Foods Industries', 963.

retail gross margins, compared to what they would have been in the absence of strong private labels.[103] Private labels may also enhance consumer loyalty to retail brands and therefore reinforce the horizontal market power of the retailers. This will in turn strengthen the retailers' vertical bargaining power against national brand manufacturers and will enable them to obtain better deals that will increase their profits.[104] These distributional effects are ambiguous from the point of view of consumers. Steiner observes the generally positive effect of competition between private labels and national brands, what he calls the 'mixed regimen':

> [i]n this structure a group of [national brands] receive vigorous competition from the [private labels] of the major chain retailers – contest that tends to maximize social welfare in consumer goods industries. That is, it brings about a high level of total surplus while also stimulating innovation by manufacturers. It produces these benefits because of a combination of horizontal and vertical relationships that are unique to this structure.[105]

The commercialization of private labels obviously increases consumer choice by offering a lower price substitute to consumers. The system may also introduce an effective countervailing power for retailers against the market power of national brand-owners. Nevertheless, private labels may also produce important anticompetitive effects, in particular if they end up dominating the market. First, they may increase retail prices for consumers. Private labels will increase search costs for consumers and will therefore offer the opportunity for a higher mark-up at the supply or retail level.

Empirical studies have also showed that competition from private labels might not lead to lower prices for national brand products.[106] Consumers with a high degree of loyalty to the manufacturer's brand will not benefit from the introduction of private label products:

> [t]he trade-off for the national brand producer facing a private label is between exploiting the loyal consumers with a high price and competing

[103] Steiner, 'The Nature and Benefits of National Brand/Private Label Competition', 113–4. Retail gross margins are defined as 'the difference between the brand's retail price and its factory, or manufacturer's price – which difference is its dollar retail gross margin ($RGM) – divided by its retail price and expressed as a percent': R. L. Steiner, Intrabrand Competition – Stepchild of Antitrust, *The Antitrust Bulletin*, 36 (1991), 155–200, at 162.

[104] Steiner, 'The Nature and Benefits of National Brand/Private Label Competition', 112–13.

[105] *Ibid.*, 105.

[106] T. Staahl Gabrielsen and L. Sørgard, 'Private Labels, Price Rivalry, and Public Policy', *European Economic Review*, 51 (2007), 403–24, at 404.

> for the switching consumers with a lower price. When the fraction of loyals is high, the national brand will concentrate on the loyal segment and a private label will be introduced at a lower price. On the other hand, when the fraction of loyals is relatively low, the national brand finds it optimal to offer an exclusivity contract to the retailer at a low price and no private label is introduced … If the national brand producer serves both loyal and switching consumers initially, the price of the national brand will be relatively low. In such a situation private label competition would lead to an increase in the price of the national brand. The reason is that the national brand producer decides not to serve the switching consumers to which the private label is offered and instead sets a high price to serve only loyal consumers … Loyal consumers are worse off due to a higher price on the national brand, while switching consumers are better off when offered a low-price private label. It turns out that in some cases consumers on aggregate benefit from private label introduction, in other cases they are worse off.[107]

It follows that the effect of private labels on consumers is ambiguous and largely depends on the characteristics of consumer demand for the specific product. Depending on the circumstances, restricting the commercial freedom of retailers may have a positive or a negative welfare effect for consumers.

Second, because of the gatekeeper role of the retailers, consumer choice and product variety may be affected if private labels exclude all but the leading national brands. As the European Commission remarked in its merger decision *Procter & Gamble/Gillette*:

> [i]f a retailer refused to carry a brand of the parties, the brand would risk disappearing from the customers' awareness. As a consequence, it would be detrimental to a leading brand of the parties to be excluded from a major retailer for a longer period, as it would entail significant losses in customer awareness, whilst the costs would be relatively minor for the retailer (whose sales with this brand represent only a small fraction of its turnover). It should also be noted that the parties' overall sales represent on average not more than 2% of the retailers' sales, while for the parties certain retailers represent 10% and more of the sales in a given country.

However, the Commission also noted that this is unlikely to happen in practice as leading national brands ('must-stock brands') may play a role of quality certification for the retailer in inter-store competition. Private labels change the power relation between suppliers and retailers to the benefit of the later. The retailers establish their control over the suppliers,

[107] *Ibid.*, 406.

which see no reason to develop their own brands and finally are marginalized as independent players in the market (they could still supply goods for the retailers' private labels).

It is not clear what will be the effects of private labels for innovation. Copycat packaging is an important concern for suppliers of national brands and may lead to fewer investments in R&D and less innovation. Private labels may also be a source of buyer power, which in certain circumstances, if this is associated with selling power, may produce anti-competitive effects.

Commission Regulation 330/2010 on vertical agreements applies only in situations where the undertakings are competing distributors, for example independent retailers competing with supplier-owned outlets, but does not cover situations where the supplier and the retailer are competing manufacturers. This excludes from the scope of the block exemption situations instances where the retailer sells private labels that compete with the national brand of a supplier, except in circumstances where the distributor provides specifications to a manufacturer to produce particular goods under the distributor's brand name and both parties conclude a subcontracting agreement. The existence of own brands including private labels and the brand image of the undertaking concerned among final consumers are elements to be considered in assessing if the customers of one of the undertaking possess buyer power.[108] Buyer power is viewed positively, as it 'may prevent the parties from exercising market power and thereby solve a competition problem that would otherwise have existed', which 'is particularly so when strong customers have the capacity and incentive to bring new sources of supply on to the market in the case of a small but permanent increase in relative prices'. Private labels are also mentioned a second time with regard to category management agreements that may lead to distortions of competition, as 'in most cases the distributor may not have an interest in limiting its choice of products, when the distributor also sells competing products under its own brand (private labels), the distributor may also have incentives to exclude certain suppliers, in particular intermediate range products'.[109]

The issue of private labels has, and will continue to be, a central issue of the recent national and EU initiatives with regard to the retail supply chain and the emerging bargaining power gap between retailers and suppliers, in

[108] Commission Guidelines on Vertical Restraints, [2010] C 130/1, para. 116.
[109] Commission Guidelines on Vertical Restraints, [2010] C 130/1, para. 210.

particular in the food sector.[110] The European Commission has commissioned research on the effect of private labels on competitiveness, innovation and choice,[111] following up the work undertaken by some national competition authorities on this issue.[112] A 'Task Force Food' was put in place at the DG Competition at the European Commission in 2012, hinting of the possibility of competition law investigations and eventually a sector enquiry in this sector. However, the complexity of the problems raised by unequal bargaining power between retailers and suppliers cannot be solved only by competition law and a more integrated framework is needed,[113] combining the enforcement of competition law, when there is conduct that enters its scope – including provisions on abuse of economic dependence in some Member States – but also unfair trading practices laws,[114] provisions of contract law and more generally civil law (tort law, European sales law), which

110 Commission Communication, 'A better functioning food supply chain in Europe', COM(2009) 591; Commission Staff Working Document, Competition in the food supply chain, (28 October 2009), available at http://ec.europa.eu/economy_finance/publications/publication16065_en.pdf; Commission Decision of 30 July 2010 establishing the High Level Forum for a Better Functioning Food Supply Chain (2010/C 210/03); Commission Decision of 19 December 2012 amending the Decision of 30 July 2010 as regards its applicability and the composition of the High Level Forum for a Better Functioning Food Supply Chain, [2012] OJ C396/17; ECN Report on competition law enforcement and market monitoring activities by European competition authorities in the food sector, May 2012.

111 See, for instance, the DG Enterprise and Industry commissioned report on The Impact of Private Labels on the Competitiveness on the European Food Supply Chain (Luxembourg: Publications Office of the European Union, 2011), available at http://ec.europa.eu/competition/publications/KD0214955ENN.pdf. The DG Competition has also recently launched a study on choice and innovation in the food sector focusing on the shift of bargaining power from suppliers to retailers, following the introduction of private labels: see European Commission – Press Release, IP/12/1356 (December 2012). The study was published in October 2014: European Commission, The Economic Impact of Modern Retail on Choice and Innovation in the EU Food Sector (Final Report), available at http://ec.europa.eu/competition/publications/KD0214955ENN.pdf.

112 See, for instance, in the UK the Competition Commission investigation on the supply of groceries in the UK market investigation, 30 April 2008, which was followed up by the implementation of the UK Groceries Code Adjudicator Act 2013.

113 On the interrelation between the different approaches, in particular competition law, unfair commercial practices legislation and soft law, see I. Lianos, 'New Kids on the Block – Retail Driven Practices and the New Regulation of Vertical Restraints in EU Competition Law', (2010) June Competition Policy International, available at www.competitionpolicyinternational.com/new-kids-on-the-block-retailer-driven-vertical-practices-and-the-new-regulation-of-vertical-restraints-in-eu-competition-law/.

114 Green Paper on unfair trading practices in the business-to-business food and non-food supply chain in Europe COM(2013) 37; Communication of the Commission, Tackling unfair trading practices in the business-to-business food supply chain, COM(2014) 472 final.

aim to deal with abusive use of unequal bargaining power, and finally soft law and self-regulatory initiatives by the industry that have emerged in several Member States.[115]

Its seems, therefore, that private labels and their competitive relation with national brands may lead to some cross-fertilization between these different areas of law and the development of a more holistic paradigm of retail regulation that will engage more closely with the concept of brand, than what is currently on offer. While there are significant differences between the objectives of each of these different areas of law and their instruments, their current emphasis on retailer power, in particular its relational dimension of 'bargaining power', offer real opportunities to the concept of 'brand' to gain operational concept status in various areas of the law, including competition law.

Conclusions

While not adopting a clear and unambiguous perspective on the concept of brand, EU competition law has engaged in multiple instances with branding and product differentiation. It is, however, too early to conclude if brands will gain operational concept status in EU competition law and if the multiple understandings of branding, developed by management or business studies, will finally make their entry into EU competition law's sources of wisdom. The concerns raised by retailer power and the development of private labels indicate that the existing economic theory on product differentiation may not provide the complete picture on the effects of brands on the competitive process and ultimately on consumers. Competition law will also need to tackle the issues raised by the development of 'social branding' and the dialogic interaction between brand-owners and consumers in the constitution of their brand identity, which breaks with a unidirectional view of the power relations between brand-owners and consumers. The importance of normative choices and assumptions on the interaction between brands and the formation of consumer preferences will also be a key parameter in the integration of the concept of brands in EU competition law and other related areas of law (e.g. unfair trade practices law).

[115] On a discussion of the possible combinations between these different tools across Member States, see Final Report, Study on the Legal Framework Covering Business-to-Business Unfair Trading Practices in the Retail Supply Chain, Final Report (26 February 2014), available at http://ec.europa.eu/internal_market/retail/docs/140711-study-utp-legal-framework_en.pdf.

9

Private labels, brands and competition law enforcement

ARIEL EZRACHI AND KETAN AHUJA

Introduction

Private labels have become a common phenomenon in retail outlets. These labels, procured and sold by the retailers, increasingly dominate shelf space and benefit from brand power in their own right. In the majority of outlets, private labels compete alongside traditional brands to satisfy consumers' need for economy or premium products.

This chapter explores the nature of competition between private labels and brands. Commentators generally see the proliferation of private labels as contributing to a more competitive environment, to the benefit of consumers. However, at times private labels may lead to mixed effects and could reduce consumer welfare in the long run. This chapter considers the unique characteristics of label/brand competition, which combine horizontal, vertical and market power elements. These mixed characteristics pose a challenge to traditional competition analysis. An interesting question subsequently emerges – can traditional competition analysis capture the complex competitive landscape and accurately weigh the short- and long-term effects of private labels on competition?

The first section of the chapter describes the proliferation of private labels and the central role played by supermarkets and other retailers in brand competition. The second section explores the unique characteristics and the possible welfare effects of label/brand competition. The third section explains the limitations of traditional competition analysis and reflects on possible enforcement options.

The proliferation of private labels

A private label is a brand owned by a retailer, and which upstream manufacturers produce according to the retailer's specifications. Private labels are brands in their own right, and often have significant consumer following and associations. This chapter will therefore refer to private labels as 'private brands' to distinguish them from 'traditional brands'.

Over the past five decades retailers have steadily grown in size, from local, specialised shops, to large supermarkets. The largest supermarket chains now achieve similar or greater sales to the largest manufacturers of consumer goods. For example, in 2005 the French retailer Carrefour achieved sales of $94 billion, while the largest manufacturer of consumer goods (Nestlé) achieved sales of $75 billion.[1] CocaCola, the eighth largest manufacturer of consumer goods, only achieved sales of $23 billion.[2]

Retailers have made use of this market power: they have significantly developed their private brand offerings.[3] According to a recent survey, across Europe private brands have a market share of 36.7 per cent of sales by value, and 47.1 per cent of sales by volume, and a number of retailers almost exclusively sell private brands, including Marks & Spencer and Aldi.[4] This represents significant growth since 2008, when private brands commanded roughly 23 per cent of the market share.[5] Private brands command a higher market share in the UK than in any other European country, with 51.1 per cent of sales by value, and 57.6 per cent of sales by volume.[6] Nonetheless, private brands markets are not equivalently mature in all EU member states: for example, in Greece private brands only accounted for 14.6 per cent of sales by value.[7]

This trend is global, with private brands' market share growing significantly in all regions worldwide.[8] Private brands will continue to gain market power for the foreseeable future: they are growing at a faster rate than traditional brands in almost all Western economies, except for the USA and France.[9]

[1] N. Kumar and J. Steenkamp, *Private Label Strategy: How to Meet the Store Brand Challenge* (Boston, MA: Harvard Business Review Press, 2007), p. 3.

[2] *Ibid.*

[3] R. Herbert, 'Private Labels – What Drives Them Forward', in A. Ezrachi and U. Bernitz (eds.), *Private Labels, Brands and Competition Policy: The Changing Landscape of Retail Competition* (Oxford University Press, 2009).

[4] IRi Special Report, 'Private Label: Balancing Quality and Value' (November 2013), p. 3, available at www.iriworldwide.eu/Portals/0/articlepdfs/PrivateLabel_2013_ExecutiveSummary.pdf#zoom=75, accessed 1 June 2014.

[5] European Commission, 'The Impact of Private Labels on the Competitiveness of the European Food Supply Chain' (January 2011), p. 11, available at http://ec.europa.eu/enterprise/sectors/food/files/study_privlab04042011_en.pdf, accessed 1 June 2014.

[6] *Ibid.*, p. 4. [7] IRi Special Report.

[8] Kumar and Steenkamp, *Private Label Strategy*, p. 6.

[9] IRi Special Report, p. 10.

Previous orthodox wisdom suggested that private brands are a recessionary phenomenon: they do well when the economy is weak, but lose any gains when the economy strengthens.[10] Private brands do perform well in weaker economies:[11] for example, Spain had the highest rate of private brand growth in Europe in 2013, buoyed by its struggling economy.[12] However, many consumers never return to traditional brands when the economy strengthens: a portion of private brand growth in recessions is permanent.[13]

Importantly, retailers have the financial and logistical capabilities to offer an ever-expanding range of private brands, which can cater to all levels of price, quality and sophistication. Decades ago, private brands were viewed as 'a cheap and nasty substitute for the real thing',[14] but they have expanded beyond that role, and now compete aggressively against traditional brands on quality and other non-price parameters.[15] Indeed, in mature private label markets private brands offer more than the 'economy' alternative and cater for a range of qualities using different branding to signal the difference in cost and quality.[16] For example, in 2005, Tesco Premier Cru was named the best non-vintage champagne in the UK, and it beat traditional brands Tattinger and Lanson in blind taste tests.[17] What is more, a product's complexity is no longer a bar to retailers who wish to develop a private brand for that product: Aldi even offers its own brand of PCs (Medion).

This increase in quality is driving growing consumer acceptance of private brands. In the USA 54 per cent of consumers say they intend to buy more private brands in the future.[18] Similarly, only 29 per cent of US consumers believe that traditional brands are worth the price premium, and only 16 per cent believe that private brands are generally of lower quality than traditional brands.[19] Private brands carry no social stigma,

[10] J. Quelch and D. Harding, 'Brands versus Private Labels: Fighting to Win', *Harvard Business Review*, 1 (1996), 99–109.

[11] L. Lamey, B. Deleersnyder, M. Dekimpe and J. Steenkamp, 'How Business Cycles Contribute to Private Label Success: Evidence from the US and Europe', *Journal of Marketing*, 71 (2007), 1–15.

[12] IRi Special Report, p. 3.

[13] L Lamey *et al.*, 'How Business Cycles Contribute to Private Label Success', p. 11.

[14] 'Make it your own', 4 March 1995, *The Economist*, p. 8.

[15] Kumar and Steenkamp, *Private Label Strategy*, p. 8.

[16] For example, Sainsbury's has a high-value private brand (Taste the Difference), a mid-value brand (By Sainsbury's), and a low-value private brand (Basics), as well as a number of other specialist brands (including SO Organic and Be Good to Yourself).

[17] Kumar and Steenkamp, *Private Label Strategy*, p. 8.

[18] *Ibid.*, p. 11. [19] *Ibid.*, p. 15.

with only 6 per cent of consumers reporting that they would feel uncomfortable serving private brands in their home.[20]

Management literature accounts for this proliferation of private brands by dividing them into four sub-categories.[21] While the reality on the outlet floor may be more complex, this division helps appreciation of the breadth and sophistication of retailers' private brand offerings. The first category includes 'generic' brands of poor quality, which are generally the cheapest products on offer. The second category includes 'copycat' brands, which attempt to imitate brand leaders' packaging and quality as closely as possible, but sell for a lower price. A third category includes 'premium' brands, which offer high-quality products, and differentiate themselves from traditional brands. Retailers use them to engender store loyalty, and price them comparably with brand leaders. The last category includes 'value innovators'. These products offer high quality without frills and with significant price-saving innovation.

The characteristics of 'private' and 'brand' competition

The growing market share of private brands has transformed the landscape of retail competition in developed countries. Major retailers are no longer confined to their traditional roles of purchasers and distributors of branded goods. By selling their own label products within their outlet, they compete with their upstream brand suppliers on sales and shelf space.[22]

This unique vertical/horizontal relationship is key to understanding private and traditional brand competition. While private and traditional brands compete against each other, the retailer that owns the private brand also controls the arena in which they compete (the outlet). As illustrated below, the retailer can therefore determine pricing, shelving, promotion and access.[23]

The gatekeeper role

Traditional brand manufacturers depend on retailers, which control their access to customers. At times, the retailer may derive unfair advantages and

[20] *Ibid.* [21] *Ibid.*, p. 28.

[22] A. Ezrachi, 'Unchallenged Market Power? The Tale of Supermarkets, Private Labels and Competition Law', *World Competition*, 33(2) (2010), 257–74.

[23] For a review of these points, see: Ezrachi 'Unchallenged Market Power?'

high levels of market power from its 'gatekeeper' position. For the traditional brand producer, switching between distribution channels is difficult, costly and generally impossible in the short term.[24] As a result, it can only replace main distributors 'at the cost of very heavy financial losses, if at all',[25] and may suffer detrimental outcomes even if a small distribution channel is eliminated.[26]

This dependency is amplified where customers' loyalty to the retailer overrides their brand loyalty. As private brands gain prominence, customers exhibit greater loyalty to particular retailers at the expense of loyalty towards traditional brands. Between 1975 and 2000 the percentage of Americans aged between 60 and 69 who said they stuck to well-known brands declined from 86 per cent to 59 per cent.[27] Another US study found that between 1992 and 2007 brand loyalty declined in ten of fifteen product categories.[28] Indeed, consumers are increasingly loyal to specific retailers.[29] As customers trade brand loyalty for store loyalty, brands become even more dependent on retailers to distribute their products.

Importantly, a retailer's gatekeeper role gives it a very high degree of market power, which its market share may not reflect. A small number of retailers have enormous bargaining power over suppliers, and can deny market access to new or existing products.[30] This power of retailers to foreclose the market particularly threatens secondary brands, which consumers do not view as 'must have' products.

Just as significantly, retailers can also use their buyer power to combat competition from other retailers, and foreclose the retail market for consumers. Illustrative of this are comments made by a Vice President of Procurement of a large European retailer, who stated that if a traditional brand manufacturer supplied the hard discounter, the retailer would substantially reduce the shelf space allocated to the brand in question.[31]

[24] H. Laaksonen and J. Reynolds, 'Own Brands in Food Retailing across Europe', *Journal of Brand Management*, 2 (1994), 37–46, 97, 102.

[25] *Ibid.*, 101.

[26] W. S. Grimes, 'Buyer Power and Retail Gatekeeper Power: Protecting Competition and the Atomistic Seller', *Antitrust Law Journal*, 72 (2004–5), 563–88.

[27] Kumar and Steenkamp, *Private Label Strategy*, p. 14.

[28] *Ibid.* [29] *Ibid.*

[30] J. Berasategi, 'Supermarket Power: Serving Consumers or Harming Competition' (February 2014), p. 10, available at www.supermarketpower.eu/documents/38179/39950/Supermarket+Power.pdf/9c0ed73f-37db-4d23-bd2d-1f583bf501e9, accessed 10 June 2014.

[31] *Ibid.*, p. 19.

Switching costs

Outlets face low switching costs when procuring supplies for private brands: they can source from more than one supplier, and face minimal consumer backlash as consumers are rarely aware of the ultimate manufacturer's identity.[32] Private brand manufacturers are substitutable, and have virtually no product differentiation, because they build products to retailers' specifications. They also generally have low individual market shares, and retailers are well informed about product quality and cost.[33] The European Commission noted in *Rewe/Meinl* that low switching costs give retailers a high degree of market power when negotiating with private label manufacturers.[34] It is worth noting that markets for private label production are highly competitive, and manufacturers often have difficulty sustaining their prices significantly above marginal cost.[35] Instruments such as real-time-online-bidding enable the retailer to increase pressure on producers, driving their price down, to the benefit of consumers. Note, however, that the improvement in range and quality of private brands may limit the number of producers capable of delivering the product specifications. In these cases, retailers develop close relationships with particular private label manufacturers, and switching costs may increase as producers are less easily substitutable.[36]

Quality erosion

The intensive competition among private label manufacturers forces them to accept intensive downward pressure on prices. This produces welfare benefits for consumers, but it may also erode quality in a way that hurts consumer welfare. Aggressive downward pressure on prices may force manufacturers to bid for contracts at a loss, forcing them to reduce quality to regain profitability. They may also pre-emptively erode quality to sustain profit margins. Significantly, manufacturers' ability to erode quality

[32] H. Smith and J. Thanassoulis, 'Bargaining between Retailers and their Suppliers', in A. Ezrachi and U. Bernitz (eds.), *Private Labels, Brands and Competition Policy, the Changing Landscape of Retail Competition* (Oxford University Press, 2009), p. 47.

[33] Kumar and Steenkamp, *Private Label Strategy*, p. 111.

[34] *Rewe/Meinl* (Case IV/M.1221) Commission Decision 1999/674/EC [1999] OJ L274/1 at [76].

[35] Kumar and Steenkamp, *Private Label Strategy*, p. 111.

[36] A. Braak, M. Dekimpe and I. Geyskens, 'Retailer Private-Label Margins: The Role of Supplier and Quality-Tier Differentiation', *Journal of Marketing*, 77(4) (2013), 86–103.

is often limited and depends on the nature of the product, the retailer's quality control mechanism and the customer's ability to detect a reduction in product quality. Quality erosion can cancel out welfare gains that result from lower prices: 'although the customer pays less, it receives less than it bargained for.'[37] As private brands manufacturers do not own the brands that adorn their products, they externalise part of the risk associated with quality degradation. It is the retailer that owns the brand that may suffer the consequences of quality erosion on its brand loyalty.[38] It is important to note that quality degradation is not a leading strategy for a private brand manufacturer. It may, however, become a necessary strategy if it forms the only means to stay active on the market. In such a case, the benefit from quality erosion outweighs the risk of detection.

By contrast to private brands manufacturers, traditional brand manufacturers are less likely to engage in quality erosion. Product quality is often an essential feature of traditional brands' reputations, so brands will suffer if customers detect a reduction in product quality.

Buyer power and competing brands

Private brands increase a retailer's buyer power when negotiating the purchase of traditional brands. A retailer's buyer power depends not only on its size and economies of scale, but also on whether the manufacturer can confidently expect the retailer to purchase the product. Absent private brands, a supplier that produces a 'must stock' brand can expect to conclude deals with all major retailers. It therefore knows roughly what its final output will be, and will be unwilling to sell to a large retailer at below a profitable price.[39]

However, private brands may provide retailers with good alternatives to leading traditional brands. Leading brand manufacturers are therefore not certain that large retailers will purchase their products. As a result, manufacturers see large retailers as incremental business. Large retailers can therefore negotiate better deals because manufacturers will not rely on them to bear as large a share of the manufacturer's fixed costs. Note that as a result, prices for small retailers may increase. The UK Competition Commission's empirical evidence supports this analysis.[40]

37 A. Ezrachi and K. De Jong, 'Buyer Power, Private Labels and the Welfare Consequences of Quality Erosion', *European Competition Law Review*, 33(5) (2012), 98.

38 *Ibid.*, 259.

39 Smith and Thanassoulis, 'Bargaining between Retailers and their Suppliers', pp. 49–50.

40 *Ibid.*, pp. 47–8.

At times, a retailer may benefit more from the buyer power it gains from a private brand than from selling the private brand itself. A retailer's threat not to purchase a leading traditional brand is more credible if it already carries an alternative private brand than if it threatens to procure an alternative private brand, because creating a private brand involves significant up-front costs.[41] This explains why supermarkets maintain unsuccessful private brands. For example, two Unilever brands dominate the Dutch market for cooking margarine. Leading supermarket chains Albert Heijn and C1000 introduced unsuccessful private brands, which command very low market shares. What is more, inventory costs for margarine are very high, because it has to be chilled. Nonetheless, they continue allocating expensive chiller space to their unsuccessful private brands to give them negotiating power against Unilever.[42]

Store and brand loyalty

A supermarket's private label offering is unique to that chain, and is therefore one of the main variables in a customer's choice of outlet. In contrast, traditional brands are available at every major retailer, and so do not provide customers with a reason to choose one retailer above another. Retailers therefore develop private label offerings that engender store loyalty, often at the expense of secondary and slower-selling traditional brands. Market research demonstrates the success of this strategy. Studies of American and French consumers show a strong correlation between their store loyalty and the number of privately branded goods they purchase.[43] This increase in store loyalty comes at the expense of loyalty to traditional brands.

In this context, it is noteworthy that the cost of switching outlet often is higher than the cost of switching product. In other words – once consumers are accustomed to a certain retailer – they will not easily switch to another just because a certain traditional brand is not on offer. Unless it is a 'must stock' brand, the customer is likely to accept a private brand substitute.

41 Kumar and Steenkamp, *Private Label Strategy*, p. 116.

42 *Ibid.*, p. 117.

43 *Ibid.*, p. 119.

Pricing private and traditional brands

The offering of private brands increases competitive pressure and often results in lower prices for all brands, to the benefit of consumers. As for the relative pricing of private and traditional brands, it is interesting to note that the retailer controls the price difference between its private brand and the traditional competitor. It can therefore manipulate the perceived value of goods to benefit its private brand. For example, the leading Parisian supermarket Casino overprices traditional brands compared to other retailers, but prices its private brands competitively. 'The French Competition Authority has concluded that this practice restricts consumers' freedom of choice and competition.'[44]

Retailers can also manipulate the price difference between private and traditional brands to improve their margins, or foreclose traditional brands from retail markets. Retailers often earn higher margins on private brands than on traditional brands. However, note the reported practice of Spanish supermarkets, which overprice traditional brands to extract maximum value from brand-loyal customers, while rendering traditional brands uncompetitive for other customers. If they matched traditional brand margins with private brand margins, the average price of traditional brands would fall by 20 per cent.[45] Nonetheless, retailers' control over pricing of leading brands is not unlimited. Market forces, including competition between retailers and advertising of traditional brands, determine the pricing of leading traditional brands to a large extent.

By contrast, retailers have greater control over pricing of private brands. Private brands differ in size, nature and quality between supermarket chains, which makes it difficult for consumers to engage in price comparison. This reduced transparency tends to soften price competition between the private brands of different retail chains.[46] However, prominent private brands are likely to be priced competitively and form a visible part of retail competition,[47] as are private brands that retailers use to engage in price competition against other retailers.

[44] Berasategi, 'Supermarket Power', p. 203.

[45] The Brattle Group, 'Competitive Assessment of the Spanish Food Supply Chain' (6 April 2012), available at. http://brattle.com/system/publications/pdfs/000/004/816/original/Competitive_Assessment_of_the_Spanish_Food_Supply_Chain_Garcia_Delgado_Apr_6_2012.pdf?1378772132, accessed 10 June 2014; see also Berasategi, 'Supermarket Power', p. 11.

[46] UK Competition Commission Grocery Market Inquiry, 'The Supply of Groceries in the UK Market Investigation', Final Report (2008) Appendix 9.10, [20].

[47] *Ibid.*, 25.

Finally, retailers can create pricing structures that encourage customers to buy higher-margin products. Generic brands attempt to offer consumers very cheap options, and often are not profitable enough to justify their shelf space. Retailers often use them to attract customers, in the hope that customers ultimately purchase both generic brands and other higher-margin products.[48]

Shelf space

Retailers are able to arrange their shelves in a way that promotes their private brands. They can, for example, place products at eye level to draw customers' attention. More significantly, they can arrange products in ways that allow consumers to make certain comparisons. This is particularly relevant for copycat brands, which retailers generally place next to the leading brand to allow consumers to make favourable price and quality comparisons with the copycat brand. Retailers can also arrange shelving to prevent their low-margin generic brands from competing with higher-margin premium or traditional brands. The US retailer Target positions its premium private brands next to other premium products, while its generic private brands sit next to lower-priced products, to prevent the consumer from directly comparing its two private brands.[49] What is more, retailers can use shelf arrangements to put pressure on traditional brands, and thereby increase their bargaining power.[50]

Marketing

Retailers control product displays and in-store marketing. As consumers make many decisions in-store, particularly for low involvement goods, this control gives the retailer a decisive advantage over brand suppliers.[51] As a result, traditional brands must engage in extensive out-of-store marketing to ensure consumers notice their products, whereas this is not necessary for retailers who wish to draw consumers' attention to private brands. In addition, retailers can afford to adopt general 'umbrella' private brand lines that cover a wide range of products: they do not need to invest in

[48] Kumar and Steenkamp, *Private Label Strategy*, p. 33.

[49] *Ibid.*, p. 87. [50] *Ibid.*, p. 19.

[51] A. Ezrachi and J. Reynolds, 'Advertising, Promotional Campaigns, and Private Labels', in A. Ezrachi and U. Bernitz (eds.), *Private Labels, Brands and Competition Policy: The Changing Landscape of Retail Competition* (Oxford University Press, 2009), p. 259.

highly focussed brands or expensive marketing strategies for each product category.[52]

Retailers also have significantly lower marketing costs when introducing new private brands. A retailer can ensure that its new private brand reaches consumers, while a manufacturer must put significant effort into marketing its products to ensure that retailers distribute them.[53] In addition, new products will benefit from the retailer's 'umbrella' range, making specific advertising unnecessary.

Copycat brands, and to a lesser extent value innovators, are also designed to free-ride off traditional manufacturers' promotional activities, further reducing marketing costs for the private brand. Private brands that copy a leading brand's packaging may increase their market share by up to 55 per cent above a private brand that uses dissimilar packaging to a leading rival's product.[54] Copycat packaging may lead consumers to believe that the product is produced by the traditional brand manufacturer, is of a similar quality, shares the same characteristics or is in fact the traditional brand itself.

Intellectual property law limits a retailer's ability to copy another brand's packaging. However, the threshold for intervention under intellectual property law does not eliminate weaker forms of copying, which may still influence consumers. A traditional brand may also not wish to damage its relationships with its major distributors by rigorously enforcing its copyrights. Moreover, not all private brands attempt to free-ride off traditional brands' reputations. Some retailers develop highly distinctive premium private brands to compete on quality with leading brands, and engender customer loyalty to the retailer.[55]

Finally, the existence and market power of private brands means that traditional brands must invest more heavily in marketing to protect themselves.[56] This further strengthens the inbuilt cost advantage that private brands have over traditional brands.

Access to information and innovation

As the distributor, the retailer has access to confidential information from the suppliers ahead of new product launches. This may enable the retailer

52 *Ibid.* 53 *Ibid.*

54 UK Competition Commission Grocery Market Inquiry, 'Working Paper on the Competitive Effects of Own Label Goods' (Final Report published 30.04.08), 31–6.

55 Kumar and Steenkamp, *Private Label Strategy*, p. 41.

56 *Ibid.*, pp. 92–101.

to produce private brands that incorporate innovations faster than traditional manufacturers can. This can weaken manufacturers' incentive to invest in innovation, for it undermines the innovator's profitability.[57] The European Commission noted in its *Kesko/Tuko* decision that retailers' access to confidential product and strategic information gives them considerable leverage over traditional brand producers.[58] Yet, arguably, retailers will *self-police* the extent to which they follow up innovation, since in the long term their profitability will benefit from the presence of the leading brand.

Conversely, however, traditional brand manufacturers' incentive to innovate may increase as they lose market share to private brands, because innovation offers them a chance to restore high levels of profitability. Studies conclude that new products released by traditional brands will boost the brand's market share. Innovation is more likely to hurt secondary traditional brands than private brands, and it is only innovation in the leading traditional brands that is likely to steal significant market share from all tiers of privately branded products. Generally, innovations with new intrinsic benefits, which maintain a large price gap, are more likely to affect premium private brands, while innovations with a lower price gap and fewer intrinsic benefits are more likely to affect generic private brands.[59] Nonetheless, innovation does significantly help traditional brands maintain market power: private brands have on average a 56 per cent higher market share in product categories with low innovation than in product categories with high innovation.[60]

A retailer also has access to detailed market information, which is not available to traditional manufacturers. This may enable retailers to identify gaps in the market more readily than branded manufacturers. This has been the case in the UK in the chilled food, fresh pasta and ethnic food categories. In those instances, retailers identified a gap in the market, which they filled with new product categories.

[57] As reported by the Competition Commission, some suppliers have reacted to this risk by delaying the release of sensitive information to retailers and limiting its scope. See UK Competition Commission Grocery Market Inquiry, 'The Supply of Groceries in the UK Market Investigation', 40.

[58] *Kesko/Tuko* (Case IV/M 784) Commission Decision 97/409/EC [1997] OJ L 174 02/07/1997 P. 0047 – 0050 [152].

[59] K. Gielens, 'New Products: The Antidote to Private Label Growth?', *Journal of Marketing Research*, 49(3) (2012), 408–23.

[60] Kumar and Steenkamp, *Private Label Strategy*, p. 168.

Risk management

When engaging in follow-on innovation, retailers generally face lower risks of failure when introducing their new product as they control marketing and shelf space. This gives retailers an in-built cost advantage.[61] By contrast, when retailers develop more complicated premium brands and value innovators, they take on failure risks that are similar to those manufacturers face when introducing new products. For example, 'Saks Fifth Avenue launched three new private label brands in 2004, but none did as well as expected, [which] forced higher markdowns and lower margins.'[62] To ensure premium brands are successful, retailers must invest in significant market research, and must engage in expensive marketing to create brand imagery. They have a more limited ability to recoup these costs than traditional brands because the private brand will only sell at that retailer's stores.[63] Failure can have serious consequences for a retailer as private brands are often closely associated with the retailer's image or umbrella range.[64]

Retailers also use their buyer power to transfer trading risks to suppliers of traditional brands. Common practices include negotiating for guaranteed margins, agreeing that the retailer can return unsold items to the manufacturer, and trading on credit from manufacturers.[65] As a result, retailers can be seen more like providers of distribution services rather than customers who purchase the manufacturers' products outright.

Assessment of private labels under traditional competition analysis

On one hand, private brands produce significant verifiable short- and mid-term welfare benefits. On the other hand, their long-term exclusionary effects are more speculative and harder to quantify. In what follows we consider the possible pro- and anti-competitive effects of private brands and the way traditional competition law assesses these effects.

Verifiable positive effects

Private brands usually offer consumers a range of products at *lower prices* than those of competing brands. Evidence from studies in the USA and France indicates that traditional brands generally sell for 37 per cent

[61] *Ibid.*, p. 98. [62] *Ibid.*, p. 56. [63] *Ibid.*

[64] *Ibid.*, p. 87. [65] Berasategi, 'Supermarket Power', pp. 42–3.

more than private brands of equivalent quality.[66] According to the UK Competition Commission, 40 per cent of consumers who purchase private brands do so because of their lower prices. Moreover, 30 per cent of consumers believe private brands are better value than the branded equivalent.[67] This increases the competitive pressure on brand leaders and generally reduces the price of branded goods across the board.

Retailers can achieve these cost-savings on private brands because they have significant in-built marketing advantages, which generally make expensive advertising unnecessary.[68] Copycat brands in particular are able to free-ride on traditional brands' marketing investments. Private brands also generally undertake lower risks of failure than traditional brands, so they can adopt generally lower prices as they do not have to compensate the brand-holder for the costs of previous failures. Retailers have significant bargaining power as a result of their 'gatekeeper' role, low switching costs and private brand offerings, which allow them to negotiate better prices with manufacturers, which they will then pass on to consumers as long as retail markets remain competitive. Finally, as retailers grow, they benefit from significant economies of scale that allow them to source goods at lower prices, and reduce processing costs.[69]

Private brands may also *stimulate innovation* from traditional brand manufacturers, as innovation offers a traditional brand manufacturer a chance to regain lost market share, higher margins and ultimately profitability. Nonetheless, private brands do not universally increase traditional brands' incentive to innovate. The innovations of traditional brands are more likely to harm rival traditional brands than private brands, and only the leading brand in any given product category is able to significantly harm private brands with new innovations. While innovations are successful against premium private brands, they offer fewer benefits against generic private brands.[70]

What is more, private brands can stimulate innovation by retailers. Retailers have extensive market information that is unavailable to traditional manufacturers, which allows them to more easily identify demand patterns and gaps in the market that private brands may satisfy. This has

[66] *Ibid.*, p. 98.
[67] UK Competition Commission Grocery Market Inquiry, 'Working Paper on the Competitive Effects of Own Label Goods', p. 8.
[68] Ezrachi and Reynolds. 'Advertising, Promotional Campaigns and Private Labels', p. 270.
[69] Kumar and Steenkamp, *Private Label Strategy*, p. 70.
[70] Gielens, 'New Products', p. 420.

been the case, for example, in the UK for chilled food, fresh pasta and ethnic food. In addition, recall that manufacturers of private brands operate in an extremely competitive market, and must therefore focus on efficiency, flexibility and innovation in manufacturing to remain profitable.[71]

A private brand can also help *counterbalance the leading brand's market power* in product categories that are dominated by a traditional brand. Other traditional brands might find it impossible, too expensive or too risky to enter a product category dominated by a leading brand. The retailer may be in a better position to take on the dominant brand because of its in-store marketing advantage, price advantages, control over shelving and label reputation. In this respect, private brands may provide more viable competition for the leading brands than do secondary and tertiary brands.[72]

Potential negative effects

Conversely, private brands produce a number of possible adverse effects that competition analysis may take into account. As indicated above, these are longer term effects and as such are less certain. They stem predominantly from the unique competition landscape discussed in the second section of this chapter.

Possible adverse effects include the *risk of foreclosure*. Retailers' gatekeeper role, low switching costs and private brands give them significant buyer power, which they can use to foreclose the market to traditional brands. What is more, stores have the incentive to foreclose the market to secondary traditional brands, and replace them with private brands. A retailer's private brands help it engender loyalty among customers, and can produce higher profit margins than traditional brands. Accordingly, the retailer may have the incentive to push out branded goods as long as this does not undermine the volume of sales in the outlet.

Retailers can also foreclose traditional brands by offering them less favourable price and non-price trading conditions than they offer to their

71 Kumar and Steenkamp, *Private Label Strategy*, p. 154.

72 See the submission by Morrisons describing Morrisons' advantages over secondary and tertiary brands when facing the leading brand: 'Secondary brands tend not to have the marketing support of the brand leaders and find it difficult to compete against own-label products. Own-label products acquire the well-known reputation of the retailer, which promotes sales over less well-known secondary and tertiary brand reputations.' UK Competition Commission Grocery Market Inquiry, 'The Supply of Groceries in the UK Market Investigation', 23.

own private brands. Retailers can price their private brands in ways that are less advantageous to traditional brands. By manipulating the quality, quantity and positioning of shelf space that a retailer gives to a traditional brand, it can ensure the traditional brand does not sell as well as its private brand.

In exchange for lower competition among traditional brands, some secondary brand producers may shift from traditional brand to private brand production, thereby increasing competition among private label suppliers. Secondary brands may therefore regain market access on a large scale and with lower risks, which may yield efficiencies. However, markets for private brand suppliers are already highly competitive, and it is unclear that additional competition upstream yields welfare benefits. What is more, added pressure in private brands supply markets may force suppliers to consolidate or result in quality degradation. Other secondary brands that are foreclosed from large supermarkets may access retailers through alternative, smaller distribution channels or may simply exit the market. Significantly, loss of a major retail channel can devastate a traditional brand: a loss of 22 per cent of turnover involves a serious risk of bankruptcy for the brand producer.[73] Overall in the long term, private brands could lead to high levels of concentration to the detriment of consumers.

Private brands may also *chill innovation*. Private brands that act as innovation-followers may weaken traditional brands' incentive to innovate. Retailers have access to confidential product information before new product launches, and can therefore produce copycat private brands faster than traditional brands can incorporate innovations.[74] Copycat brands that quickly incorporate innovations undermine the innovator's profitability and incentive to innovate. Yet, arguably, retailers will self-police the extent to which they follow up innovation, since in the long term the leading brand's presence will boost their profitability.

Moreover, private brands may suffer from *quality erosion*, as a result of the retailer's high market power when negotiating with private label manufacturers. This may occur when downward pressure on price forces the manufacturer to accept negligible profits, or even losses, and customers have difficulty detecting changes in product quality. Quality erosion

[73] *Ibid.*, [101]; Grimes, 'Buyer Power and Retail Gatekeeper Power', 563.

[74] See *Kesko/Tuko* (Case IV/M 784) Commission Decision 97/409/EC [1997] OJ L 174 02/07/1997 P. 0047 – 0050, [152].

directly harms the final consumer, and may cancel out the benefits of lower prices.[75]

Competition law analysis

Traditional competition law analysis does not easily take account of the nature of competition between private and traditional brands, as described above. As this chapter focuses on retailers' unilateral conduct, this section will assess the ability of current competition law rules on unilateral conduct to regulate competition between private and traditional brands. Nonetheless, we note that the nature of private label and brand competition may also have implications for competition law rules on anticompetitive agreements and mergers.

Article 102 TFEU controls *dominance and the abuse of dominance.* Dominance is defined as an undertaking's position of economic strength, which enables it to prevent effective competition being maintained on the relevant market by affording it the power to behave, to an appreciable extent, independently of its competitors, customers and consumers.[76] Findings of dominance require high market shares: the European Commission considers undertakings will generally not be dominant if they have market shares below 40 per cent.[77] In the context of this chapter it is important to note that in most jurisdictions a single retailer is unlikely to meet this threshold, because it is likely to operate in generally competitive markets, with a number of strong market players, none of which are overwhelming. Accordingly, under traditional analysis retailers' conduct will rarely trigger Article 102 TFEU.

However, one may argue that conventional economic benchmarks should be adjusted when applied to large retailers, because of their gatekeeper role, low switching costs and private brand offerings. These features give retailers a greater degree of market power on upstream markets than companies with equivalent market shares would have in different industries. In other words, market shares and market concentration do not provide a good proxy for market power. A retailer may have a relatively low market share, and face strong competitors on downstream

75 Ezrachi and De Jong, 'Buyer Power, Private Labels and the Welfare Consequences of Quality Erosion', 262.

76 Case 27/76 *United Brands* v. *Commission* [1978] ECR 207, [1978] 1 CMLR 429.

77 Guidance on the Commission's enforcement priorities in applying Article 82 of the EC Treaty to abusive exclusionary conduct by dominant undertakings [2009] OJ C 45/7, [14] [hereinafter European Commission Guidance].

markets, and yet it may still have the power to foreclose upstream producers from reaching consumers. The retailer may therefore be able to behave independently of upstream traditional brand manufacturers that compete with its private brands, even if it cannot behave independently of competitors on downstream retail markets. Note on this point that a retailer's market share on upstream procurement markets may be more relevant to assessing its dominance than its share of downstream retail markets, as the European Commission recognised in *Rewe/Meinl*.[78]

To address these concerns, one may argue in favour of lowering the threshold of dominance. For example, Finland now deems that any grocery retailer with a market share of more than 30 per cent is dominant.[79] Such an approach, however, provides a sub-optimal solution. It is under-inclusive, for it does not address non-grocery retailers, or retailers with less than 30 per cent market share, that may still be able to foreclose competition. Its ultimate failing, however, is that it attempts to use rigid market share thresholds to establish dominance in an industry where an undertaking's market power comes from its gatekeeper role and strong bargaining position, which are only loosely related to its market share.

Even if a retailer has a position of dominance, one needs to consider whether it has *abused* that position. Here one may find it difficult to balance between verifiable short-term benefits and speculative long-term effects. This would make it difficult to establish that retailers abused their dominance. The Commission's Guidance on Article 102 TFEU indicates that the Commission will intervene to prevent foreclosure on intermediate or final-consumer markets.[80] When establishing foreclosure, the Commission states that it will take into account general market evidence (such as the dominant undertaking's position in the market), as well as evidence on specific types of exclusionary practices (for example, loyalty-inducing rebates).[81] Although general market evidence may point to foreclosure, it is unlikely that any existing exclusionary practices will support arguments that retailers foreclosed traditional brands. Retailers may foreclose products by refusing to buy them on fair terms, or by manipulating shelving, in-store marketing or pricing. It is not clear that existing exclusionary practices cover these types of conduct, and one may find it hard to establish consumer harm when such practices result in the

[78] *Rewe/Meinl* (Case IV/M.1221) Commission Decision 1999/674/EC [1999] OJ L274/1, [76].

[79] M. Oinonen, 'The New 30% Rule: A Viable Solution to Detrimental Buyer Power in the Finnish Grocery Retail Sector?' (2014) 10(1) *European Competition Journal*, 97–121, at 98.

[80] European Commission Guidance, p. 19.

[81] *Ibid.*, [21].

offering of cheaper alternatives. The long-term effects may be too speculative to be taken into account in the analysis of abuse.

Buyer power

Part of the reason competition law underestimates retailers' market power is that it generally assumes *buyer power* benefits consumer welfare. In the context of Article 102 TFEU the European Commission recognises that countervailing buyer power can constrain undertakings that might otherwise be dominant. In its Guidance on Article 102, the Commission notes that 'Even an undertaking with a high market share may not be able to act to an appreciable extent independently of customers with sufficient bargaining strength … [who] may deter or defeat an attempt by the undertaking to profitably increase prices'.[82] The Commission is also evidently aware of countervailing buyer power arguments in merger cases: it found that the *Friesland Coberco/Nutricia* merger would not significantly impede effective competition in part because retailers had significant countervailing buyer power as a result of their large market shares and private label ranges.[83] Overall, European competition law has developed a clear approach to assessing countervailing buyer power arguments, which takes into account market share, ability and incentive to switch suppliers, and the likelihood that savings would reach most consumers.

In contrast, competition law does not have as clear an approach to assessing arguments that buyer power harms competition. The Commission's Article 102 Guidelines do not specifically address the anti-competitive effects of buyer power, and only a few of its merger cases discuss the negative effects of buyer power in detail.[84] Most notably in *Kesko/Tuko*, the Commission blocked Kesko's proposed acquisition of Tuko, in part because the merged entity would have significant buyer power as a result of its large market share, customer loyalty schemes and private label ranges.[85] The Commission's primary concern was that the merged entity could use its buyer power to disrupt retail competition, rather than to foreclose competition at the supplier level.[86] Notably, the merged entity

[82] *Ibid.*, [18].

[83] *Friesland Coberco/Nutricia* (Case COMP/M.2399) [2002] OJ C18/14.

[84] A. Ezrachi and M. Ioannidou 'Buyer Power in European Union Merger Control', *European Competition Journal*, 10(1) (2014), 69–95, at 75.

[85] *Kesko/Tuko* (Case IV/M.784) Commission Decision 97/277/EC [1997] OJ L110/53 [133].

[86] *Ibid.*, [150].

would have been dominant even under a traditional analysis (with a 55 per cent share of the Finnish grocery market).[87]

In practice, however, buyer power will rarely constitute grounds for blocking a transaction, but will more likely force merging parties to offer commitments.[88] Applying similar reasoning, under the Commission's current approach, misuse of buyer power is unlikely to constitute a stand-alone abuse under Article 102 TFEU, and the Commission may be more inclined to address buyer power arguments with behavioural remedies.

Theories of harm regarding the negative welfare effects of buyer power currently provide imperfect analytical tools for competition enforcement agencies.[89] This may explain the European Commission's reluctance to seriously address arguments that buyer power harms competition.[90] In any case, competition law fails to take sufficient account of the potential for buyer power to foreclose competition.

Concluding remarks – enforcement choices

It is important to note that our analysis does not argue in favour of intervention. We illustrate the range of effects that private brand competition generates and the limited capacity of traditional competition analysis to take them fully into account.

We note the mismatch between the unique characteristics of the vertical competition between private and traditional brands and the benchmarks for intervention as outlined in Article 102 TFEU. Indeed, the relationship between private and traditional brands produces a unique set of competitive conditions that result from the retailer's position as a horizontal competitor to and vertical distributor of traditional brands. This position allows the retailer to control competition between products, and gives the retailer a higher degree of market power than its market share would reflect in another industry. Traditional competition law is ill designed to deal with this sort of vertical competition, and as a result will rarely trigger intervention.

The challenges described above, and the limitations of traditional competition analysis, lead to a number of key enforcement choices.

[87] *Ibid.*, [106].

[88] Ezrachi and Ioannidou, 'Buyer Power in European Union Merger Control', 83.

[89] *Ibid.*, 70–4. [90] *Ibid.*, 83.

One option is to focus on the short-term benefits and conclude that the use of private brands by retailers does not give rise to a competition problem. On the contrary, private brands vigorously compete with traditional brands, producing significant short-term benefits in the form of lower prices, wider choice and better quality. Accordingly, as long as traditional competition law benchmarks are not satisfied, intervention is not required as there is no competition problem.

Another approach is to accept that competition law may need to evolve to capture vertical competition. It should find market power with limited market shares, and intervene despite the short-term benefits of private brands. Competition law errs by treating distribution channels as analytically neutral, and should recognise that firms compete when they can 'take sales, margins and market shares from each other'.[91] Intensive vertical competition may harm welfare without any significant changes in retail market structure. As retailers unilaterally introduce and strengthen their private brands, they generate a cumulative effect upstream, which may have detrimental results in the long term on consumer welfare. Such an approach calls for a change in our analytical benchmarks and theories of harms. It may lead to a novel approach to dominance, abuse and remedies.

An alternative approach may reject the call to widen the competition law toolbox and change its analytical benchmarks. Such changes risk creating legal and business uncertainly and would be based on controversial theories of harm. Accordingly, while it is accepted that some anticompetitive effects may exist, the prism of competition law cannot easily process the complexity of vertical brand competition and should therefore not play a leading role in this matter. The solution is to be found outside the competition law landscape, in the form of soft or binding tools or sector regulation. These tools would more adequately deal with the risk of foreclosure and long-term upstream and mid-stream effects while taking into account social, economic and industrial considerations.

[91] R. Steiner, 'Market Power in Consumer Goods Industries', in A. Ezrachi and U. Bernitz (eds.), *Private Labels, Brands and Competition Policy: The Changing Landscape of Retail Competition* (Oxford University Press, 2009), p. 76.

PART III

Brands and IP law

10

Trademark dilution and the management of brands

Implications of the Trademark Dilution Revision Act for marketing and marketing research

JOHN D. MITTELSTAEDT

Introduction

A trademark is made up of any word, name, symbol, or device, or combination thereof, adopted and used by a manufacturer or merchant to identify its products and to differentiate them from those manufactured or sold by others.[1] Trademarks are an important form of intellectual property protection for companies, as they serve as the legal foundation for brands. While the definition of a "brand" is similar to a trademark ("name, term, design, symbol, or any feature that identifies one seller's good or service as distinct from those of other sellers"),[2] the concept of brand is more encompassing than its legal foundation. Although brands distinguish goods "so as to source," they also serve as promises to consumers. Marketers talk about brands as market-based sources of firm equity,[3] and as strategic assets.[4] Marketers also talk of brands as having personalities,[5] as sources of emotional attachment,[6] and as entities

[1] 15 U.S.C. § 1127 (2014).

[2] P. D. Bennett, *Dictionary of Marketing Terms*, 2nd edn (Chicago: American Marketing Association, 1995), p. 27.

[3] See K. L. Keller, *Strategic Brand Management*, 3rd edn (Upper Saddle River, NJ: Prentice Hall, 2008).

[4] See D. A. Aaker, *Building Strong Brands* (New York: Free Press, 1995); D. A. Aaker and E. Joachimsthaler, *Brand Leadership: The Next Level of the Brand Revolution* (New York: Free Press, 2009); P. Kotler and K. L. Keller, *Marketing Management*, 13th edn (Upper Saddle River, NJ: Pearson Prentice Hall, 2009).

[5] See J. L. Aaker, "Dimensions of Brand Personality", *Journal of Marketing Research*, 34 (1997), 342–52.

[6] See M. Thomson, D. J. MacInnis and C. W. Park, "The Ties that Bind: Measuring the Strength of Consumers' Emotional Attachments to Brands", *Journal of Consumer Psychology*, 15(1) (2005), 77–91.

around which consumers form communities.[7] So while brands find their legal foundation in trademarks, they possess values to organizations that have never been protected under trademark law, because a brand's equity extends far beyond a firms' ability to reduce consumer confusion.

Legal protection of trademarks in the United States grew out of the common law concept of "passing off" as a form of unfair competition, through the copying of products.[8] Historically, trademark protection was intended to prevent confusion among consumers by ensuring that they were able to distinguish among different competitors, and so that they could identify particular products with particular craftsmen and manufacturers. Trademarks benefit consumers, and by extension producers, by eliminating confusion in two ways. First, trademarks serve as indicators of quality to consumers, since the ability to tie a product to a source enhances the likelihood that a firm will stand behind its product. Second, trademarks allow firms to differentiate their products from competitor products, creating variety and assortment, to the benefit of heterogeneous segments of consumers. Trademark protection, like copyright and patent protection, serves as an incentive for firms to produce products of the highest quality, to the benefit of consumers. In the USA the primary mechanism for trademark protection today is section 43(a) of the Lanham Act of 1946, as it has been interpreted by the United States Supreme Court.[9] Like other regimes of intellectual property protection, trademark protection serves to encourage fair competition in the marketplace. Unlike patents or copyrights, however, trademark law provides only indirect protection of a firm's intellectual property. Trademark law has always protected first the interests of the consuming public, and then firms only through the interests of their consumers. And in this way the law's interest in protecting trademarks has always differed from the managerial interests of a brand.

This changed in 2006, when Congress passed the Trademark Dilution Revision Act (TDRA),[10] which revised, clarified, and reinstated the trademark dilution protection of the Federal Trademark Dilution Act of 1995 (FTDA), which had been vacated by the United States Supreme Court in 2003. As a result, the institution of dilution protection more closely aligns

[7] See A. M. Muniz, Jr. and T. C. O'Guinn, "Brand Community", *Journal of Consumer Research*, 15 (2005), 77–91.

[8] J. T. McCarthy, *McCarthy on Trademarks and Unfair Competition*, 3rd edn (New York: Clark Boardman Callaghan, 1996), p. [5.02, P. 5-4].

[9] 15 U.S.C. § 1125(a) (2014).

[10] 15 U.S.C. § 1125(c) (2014).

the concepts of trademarks and brands, and changes how firms should think about the management of their brands.

The purpose of this chapter is to consider the implications of this important change in trademark protection on brands and brand management. While there has been much discussion about the legal implications of dilution protection,[11] few have considered the marketing implications of this change in jurisprudence. This chapter will review trademark protection regimes and the change in law. Then it will consider two questions of importance to marketers and marketing scholars. First, how does trademark dilution protection change the way we manage brands and brand equity? Second, what implications does dilution protection have for how we measure brands in the marketplace and in the courtroom?

A marketer's historical perspective of brand protection

Trademarks protect the signs, sounds, or images by which consumers recognize producers in the marketplace. The intent of trademark law is to protect the customer, not the producer. The legal philosophy of trademark law has its historic origins in the principle of confusion: the intent of the protection of marks is to provide the consumer with an assurance of knowledge "so as to the source" of the products and services they purchase. As Itamar Simonson, Sebastian S. Kresge Professor of Marketing at Stanford, puts it, trademark infringement is the equivalent of cashing a check on someone else's bank account, where the teller (consumer) cannot distinguish between the identity of the casher of the check and the

[11] See R. C. Bird, "The Impact of the Moseley Decision on Trademark Dilution Law", *Journal of Public Policy & Marketing*, 26 (2007), 102–17; R. C. Bird, "Making Sense of Trademark Dilution (again): The Trademark Dilution Revision Act of 2006", *Journal of the Academy of Marketing Science*, 36 (2008), 434–35; E. Goldman, 'Trademark Dilution Revision Act of 2006', *Technology & Marketing Law Blog*, 10 October 2006, available at http://blog.ericgoldman.org/archives/2006/10/trademark_dilut_3.htm; K. Goodberlet, "The Trademark Dilution Revision Act of 2006: Prospective Changes to Dilution Definition, Claim Analyses, and Standard of Harm", *Journal of High Technology Law*, 6 (2006), 249–79; J. Jacoby, "The Psychological Foundations of Trademark Law: Secondary Meaning, Acquired Distinctiveness, Genericism, Fame, Confusion and Dilution", *Trademark Reporter*, 91 (2001), 1013–71; J. Jacoby, "Dilution in Light of Victoria's Secret: The Psychology, Varieties, and Measurement of Trademark Dilution", New York University Center for Law and Business Working Paper Series CLB-03-020, (2003), pp. 9–11; K. M. Saunders, "Dilution Revisited: A First Look at the Trademark Dilution Revision Act", *Pennsylvania Bar Association Quarterly*, 20 (2007), 69–76; Kaye Scholer, 'The Trademark Dilution Act of 2006: A Major Overhaul of Federal Trademark Dilution Law', *Intellectual Property Update*, October 2006, available at www.kayescholer.com.

holder of the account.[12] "From the buyer's perspective, confusion between trademarks implies that consumers do not get the brand they intended to buy."[13] From the trademark holder's perspective, a sale is lost, to the detriment of the original (senior) brand. The consequences of confusion for marketers have a long history in the marketing literature.[14] Ironically, firms bring grievances on behalf of their customers, but rarely share the spoils of victory directly with their customers.

Throughout the twentieth century, however, there was a second perspective on trademark infringement that was discussed among legal scholars and philosophers – the principle of dilution. The idea of dilution was first introduced by Frank Schechter.[15] At the time, the view of the United States Supreme Court was that the purpose of a trademark was "to identify the origin or ownership of the article to which it is affixed."[16] This was the basis of the confusion perspective, and would become the basis of the Lanham Act in 1946, which codified intellectual property law in the United States.

Schechter argued that the confusion standard served only to indicate ownership or origin, but that the complexities of commerce of the day had moved well beyond these notions.

> It has been repeatedly pointed out by the very courts that insist on defining trademarks in terms of ownership or origin that, owing to the ramifications of modern trade and the national and international distribution of goods from the manufacturer through the jobber or importer and the retailer to the consumer, the source or origin of the goods bearing a well known trademark is seldom known to the consumer.[17]

What becomes important to the consumer is not that the product came from a particular place known to the user, but that "the goods in connection with which it is used emanate from the same – possibly anonymous – source or have reached the consumer through the same channels as certain other goods that have already given the consumer satisfaction, and

[12] I. Simonson, "Trademark Infringement from the Buyer Perspective: Conceptual Analysis and Measurement Implications", *Journal of Public Policy & Marketing*, 13 (1994), 181.

[13] *Ibid.*, 181.

[14] G. Miaoulis and N. D'Amato, "Consumer Confusion and Trademark Infringement", *Journal of Marketing* 42 (1978), 48–55; D. Cohen, "Trademark Strategy", *Journal of Marketing*, 50 (1986), 61–74.

[15] F. I. Schechter, "The Rational Basis of Trademark Protection", *Harvard Law Review*, 40 (1927), 813–33.

[16] *Hanover Star Milling Co.* v. *Metcalf*, 240 U.S. 403, 412 (1916).

[17] Schechter, "The Rational Basis of Trademark Protection", 814.

that bore the same trademark."[18] From Schechter's perspective, the power of a trademark was as a signifier of *quality*, rather than as a signifier of *source*.

> The true functions of the trademark are, then, to identify a product as satisfactory and thereby to stimulate further purchases by the consuming public ... but today the trademark is not merely the symbol of good will but often the most effective agent for the creation of good will, imprinting upon the public mind an anonymous and impersonal guaranty of satisfaction, creating a desire for further satisfactions. The mark actually *sells* the goods. And, self-evidently, the more distinctive the mark, the more effective is its selling power.[19]

It is not the assurance of source that matters to the consumer, as much as the assurance of quality that emanates from the source that is important. In short, by the early part of the twentieth century a trademark was valued by the consumer because it had become what we in marketing call a "brand."

What the theory of dilution adds to our understanding of trademark infringement is the acknowledgement that the value of a brand comes from the efforts of the producer, as much as it does from the consent of the consumer. This is a compelling argument, and has found its way into state statutes governing intellectual property. Massachusetts passed the first dilution statute in 1947, and by the beginning of the twenty-first century thirty-seven states had provisions for trademark dilution, although they differed in form and coverage.[20] What was lacking was a uniform statute governing trademark dilution.

The Federal Trademark Dilution Act and *Moseley*

The FTDA of 1995 was intended to unify dilution protection across the United States. It defined dilution as "the lessening of the capacity of a famous mark to identify and distinguish goods or services, regardless of the presence or absence of (1) competition between the owner of the famous mark and other parties, or (2) likelihood of confusion, mistake or deception."[21] The intent was to extend to famous marks protection against

[18] *Ibid.*, 816. [19] *Ibid.*, 818–19, emphasis in original.

[20] C. Chicoine, D. Atlas, S. Getzoff, S. Kayser, R. E. Lyon, D. M. Perry, S. D. Philips, A. A. Rubenstein and H. J. Shire, "U.S. State Dilution Laws", INTA Dilution and Well-Known Marks Committee, U.S. State Dilution Law Subcomittee Report, International Trademark Association Report #2394308, 2004, available at www.inta.org.

[21] *Moseley* v. *V Secret Catalogue, Inc.*, 537 U.S. 418, 421 n.1 (2003) (citing 15 U.S.C. § 1127).

dilution, over and above protections already afforded under provisions regarding confusion of the Lanham Act. Standards for famousness were not included in the statute, as it was anticipated that these would emerge through court interpretation.

The first major challenge under the FTDA was *Moseley* v. *V Secret Catalogue, Inc.*[22] In *Moseley*, the issue in the case centered on a dispute between the lingerie retailer Victoria's Secret and a retailer of adult products called Victor's Secret. While all agreed that no one would reasonably mistake a Victor's Secret store for a Victoria's Secret store (i.e., no confusion), Victoria's Secret Catalogue, Inc. argued that their trademarks could be associated with Victor's Secret stores in the minds of consumers, tarnishing Victoria Secret's reputation, and in doing so, diluting its brand.[23]

In *Moseley*, the United States Supreme Court ruled that no actual dilution had been shown, and that no standards for either likelihood of dilution or dilution by tarnishment were offered.[24] In its unanimous ruling the Court narrowed the provisions of the FTDA in two important ways. First, it required evidence of actual dilution. Second, it limited the form of dilution to blurring, excluding tarnishment. What this meant was that a famous brand could only claim dilution protection if it could show actual blurring of its trademark. This set the standard so high as to eliminate dilution as a practical form of intellectual property protection.

The Trademark Dilution Revision Act

In 2006 Congress passed the TDRA to clarify the intent of the FTDA in light of the ruling in *Moseley*. The TDRA includes several important provisions that shape dilution protection.

First, dilution protection is afforded to (and only to) "famous" marks. Famous is defined in the statute as one that is "widely recognized by the general consuming public of the United States as a designation of source of the goods or services of the mark's owner."[25] Excluded from dilution protection are niche, regional, or similar brands that may have significant meaning to a specific audience, but that are otherwise anonymous to the general public.

Second, the TDRA provides protection against both dilution by blurring and by tarnishment. Dilution by blurring is the result of an association arising from the similarity between the famous brand and the

[22] *Moseley*, 537 U.S. at 418–36.
[23] *Ibid.*, 423–4. [24] *Ibid.*, 434.
[25] 15 U.S.C. § 1125(c)(2)(A) (2014).

diluting mark "that impairs the distinctiveness of the famous mark."[26] Dilution by tarnishment, on the other hand, is an association arising from the similarity of marks "that harms the reputation of the famous mark."[27] The former diminishes the ability of a firm to control the destiny of its brands, while the latter recognizes that the equity of its brand can be compromised by the actions of others.

Third, the TDRA overturned the "actual" standard set in *Moseley*, allowing for restrictions of junior marks in cases where the likelihood of dilution of the senior mark can be shown. This means injunctive action can be pursued if the possibility of dilution exists, rather than waiting for actual dilution to occur. The likelihood standard is borrowed from infringement by confusion, where the Court recognized that in cases of consumer perception, damage to a trademark cannot easily be undone. The law sets out six factors to assess the likelihood of blurring, but no factors to assess the likelihood of tarnishment.[28]

Implications for business practice

The TDRA of 2006 reverses the decision in *Moseley*, and clarifies the intent of Congress in the FTDA of 1996. The practical effect of this is to bring into closer alignment the legal notion of a trademark and the managerial notion of a brand. Trademarks are recognized as signifiers of quality to consumers, not just of source. Trademarks are to be protected as assets of an organization, and are not just signifiers that reduce confusion. In short, brands can be protected for the good of the firm, not just the good of the consumer.

Managers and attorneys have very different views of brands and trademarks.[29] Managers see brands as a source of firm equity to be managed, while attorneys see trademarks as property to be protected from infringement by others. These are very different views of property, its value, and its use. And while definitions of trademarks and brands appear similar, the protected dimensions of a trademark have always been more narrowly defined than the managerial dimensions of a brand. One important consequence of Federal dilution standards, as they are now codified in the TDRA, is that trademarks

[26] 15 U.S.C. § 1127(c)(2)(B) (2014).

[27] 15 U.S.C. § 1127(c)(2)(C) (2014).

[28] 15 U.S.C. § 1127.

[29] R. A. Peterson, K. H. Smith and P. C. Zerrillo, "Trademark Dilution and the Practice of Marketing", *Journal of the Academy of Marketing Science*, 27 (1999), 255–68.

and brands are more closely aligned, and attorneys and managers need to be more cognizant of each other's views of brands as property and as equity. Two important marketing implications arise from this: the management of fame, and the need to monitor brand health for legal purposes.

Two classes of brands

The TDRA effectively creates two classes of legal protection for brands – "famous" and "not famous" – with different managerial latitude and different standards of legal protection. While all brands enjoy protection against infringement by confusion, brands that rise to the standard of famous enjoy protection against dilution as well.[30] This means that if you hold a famous mark, you can align your legal thinking of trademark protection with your branding strategies, where non-famous brands that want to achieve the same effect must launder their protection through the facade of customer confusion. With the inclusion of dilution as a legal recourse, trademark protection becomes brand protection for famous brands, but not for the non-famous brands.

For famous brands, dilution becomes the best first line of brand defense. One need not show that the image of one's brand is confused, or likely to be confused, with the image of someone else's. Instead, it suffices to show that the actions of another affect, or are likely to affect, the distinctive brand image cultivated by one's marketing efforts. One need not show that the consumer is harmed, only that the brand is harmed.

For brands that do not rise to the standard of "famous," the picture is more complex. Managers of brands that are less than famous must decide if the costs of fame are worth the protection it affords. If your brand is distinctive but not famous, should you take the (expensive) steps necessary to establish fame? If your brand is well known within a niche market or subpopulation, are the legal benefits of dilution protection worth the investment of the resources to become a broadly recognized brand? Managers must calculate the value and likelihood of dilution protection against the cost of establishing famousness. In addition, they must consider the legal risks associated with challenging more famous brands for market share or market leadership, expecting that the more famous mark will argue that any erosion of market share represents dilution of its own brand. Nothing in the standards for dilution requires confusion, or even its suggestion. While no one would confuse Victor's Secret with Victoria's Secret, one can see how the former is suggestive of the latter, and therefore holds the potential to

[30] Goodberlet, "The Trademark Dilution Revision Act of 2006".

dilute. If, on the other hand, Automaker A runs a series of aggressive advertisements against Automaker B, and Automaker B's research indicates a shift in some measure of effect – for example, awareness, liking, or consideration – can B argue that A's efforts have blurred the image of its brand, and therefore diluted its value? A good attorney would consider making such an argument.

If fame is to serve as a tool for brand management and legal protection, then one must answer the following questions: how is it measured, and by whom? Peterson, Smith, and Zerrillo offer two standards for famousness, typicality, and dominance.[31] Typicality means the extent to which a brand is considered "typical" of its product category. Typicality can be operationalized as the extent to which a trademark elicits recall of its product category.[32] "When you think of McDonald's, what product category comes to mind?"[33] Dominance, on the other hand, is a measure of the strength of a brand as representative of a category. "When you think of airlines, what brand comes to mind?"[34] The greater the typicality of a brand, the greater its famousness. The greater the dominance of a brand, the greater its famousness. Typicality and dominance are both top-of-mind questions, the form that Simonson found generated the highest rates of confusion in trademark infringement studies.[35] While all this represents a start, no commonly accepted, valid measure of fame exists in the marketing domain.

Tracking brand health

The expansion of the legal notion of trademarks through the use of the standard of dilution means that brand managers must now take into account legal aspects of brand tracking and brand health that were previously their exclusive domain. Most of the academic research on the effects of dilution is experimental in nature.[36] While valuable for understanding how and to what extent blurring and tarnishment occur, they rely on the ability

[31] See Peterson *et al.*, "Trademark Dilution and the Practice of Marketing", *Journal of the Academy of Marketing Science*, 27 (1999), 255–68.

[32] A. F. Simonson, "How and When Do Trademarks Dilute: A Behavioral Framework to Judge 'Likelihood' of Dilution", *Trademark Reporter*, 83 (1995), 149–74.

[33] Peterson *et al.*, "Trademark Dilution and the Practice of Marketing", 261.

[34] *Ibid.*, 262.

[35] Simonson, "Trademark Infringement", *Journal of Public Policy and Marketing*, 13(1994), 181–99.

[36] See M. Morrin and J. Jacoby, "Trademark Dilution: Empirical Measures for an Elusive Concept", *Journal of Public Policy & Marketing*, 19 (2000), 265–76; M. Morrin, J. Lee and G. M. Allenby, "Determinants of Trademark Dilution", *Journal of Consumer Research*, 33 (2006), 248–57; C. Pullig, C. J. Simmons and R. G. Netemeyer, "Brand Dilution: When Do New Brands Hurt Existing Brands?", *Journal of Marketing*, 70 (2006), 52–66.

to measure the associative networks of brand images both before and after the experimental treatment. The effects of dilution are captured in the difference between before and after conditions.

In reality, at the point a brand manager believes that their brand has been diluted, either by blurring or tarnishment, it is too late to measure the "before" condition. This means that a brand manager must be able to demonstrate, at any point in time, whether or not their brand is famous – the precondition for dilution protection – through metrics of brand recognition, distinctiveness, and health. The ability of a firm to show that its brand is famous, and has been for some time, and to have benchmarks as support, strengthens its hand if and when an issue of dilution arises. For firms with famous brands, it is likely worth the investment to track brand health over time, in accordance with the needs of both the legal department and the marketing department. The needs of legal representation may well differ from the needs of the brand manager, but all are probably discoverable documents in legal proceedings.

Tests of dilution are more complex than tests of famousness. Both are summarized in Table 10.1. Scholars argue that dilution is best understood in the context of associative network theory.[37] Associative network theory is built on the premise that memory is made up of nodes, which hold concepts and links that constitute relationships or associations.[38] Cognitive representations of brands are held in nodes, and around them are associative networks that constitute perceived brand image, personality, and the like. When a node is activated, the network of associations is activated. Blurring occurs when the strength of associations is weakened. Morrin and Jacoby measured blurring by accuracy and speed of response to associative questions, and found both weaken in the presence of diluting brands,[39] while Morrin, Lee, and Allenby found that dilution through logos reduced brand exclusive recall.[40] Pullig, Simmons, and Netemeyer found that blurring was least likely to occur when copycat strategies were employed,[41] and Howard, Kerin, and Gengler found significant involvement effects.[42]

[37] See Morrin and Jacoby, "Trademark Dilution", 267; Morrin *et al.*, "Determinants of Trademark Dilution", 249; Pullig *et al.*, "Brand Dilution", 53.

[38] See Jacoby, "Dilution in Light of Victoria's Secret", *The Psychology, Varieties and Measurement of Trademark Dilution*, 9–11 (NYU Ctr. for Law & Bus. Working Paper No. CLB-03-020, 2008).

[39] See Morrin and Jacoby, "Trademark Dilution", 'Trademark Dilution: Empirical Measures for an Elusive Concept', *Journal of Public Policy and Marketing*, 19 (2000) 265–76.

[40] See Morrin *et al.*, "Determinants of Trademark Dilution", *Journal of Consumer Research*, 33 (2006), 248–57.

[41] See Pullig *et al.*, "Brand Dilution", *Journal of Marketing* (2006), 52–66, 70.

[42] See D. J. Howard, R. A. Kerin and C. Gengler, "The Effects of Brand Name Similarity on Brand Source Confusion: Implications for Trademark Infringement", *Journal of Public Policy & Marketing*, 19 (2000), 250–64.

Table 10.1 *Summary of measures of fame and dilution*

Construct Tested	Study	Approach	Finding
Famousness	Peterson, Smith, and Zerrillo (1999)	Offers two approaches to measuring famousness: Typicality – the extent to which the brand is able to elicit recall of its own category, and Dominance – the strength of the brand to category relationship; Telephone Survey.	Offers metrics for typicality and dominance
Dilution by Blurring	Morrin and Jacoby (2000)	Speed and accuracy of response; Experiment.	Recognition accuracy decreases when diluted; reaction time varies when diluted, depending on the category similarity and familiarity; familiarity is used as proxy for famousness.
Dilution by Blurring (weakening of the associations between a brand and its distinctive aspects)	Pullig, Simmons, and Netemeyer (2006)	Brand name accessibility (aspect → brand name) and aspect accessibility (brand name → aspect); Test of associative network theory; Experiment.	Blurring is least likely to occur in copycat strategies, when a junior brand emerges in a similar category to the senior brand and with other similar aspects.

Table 10.1 (*cont.*)

Construct Tested	Study	Approach	Finding
Dilution by Blurring	Morrin, Lee, and Allenby (2006)	Logos diluted, then asked to freely recall the original product category associated with brands; Experiment.	Logo dilution reduces exclusive brand recall.
Confusion	Howard, Kerin, and Gengler (2000)	Tested similarity of sound and meaning in high and low involvement conditions; Experiment.	Find that similarity of sound leads to highest brand source confusion in low involvement conditions; similarity of meaning leads to highest confusion in high involvement conditions.

To date no research has been done on methods of assessing dilution by tarnishment. Perhaps this reflects the complications of experimental testing of these concepts without doing actual damage to a brand image. More likely, it reflects a sense that tarnishment is apparent only after it happens. Solid benchmarks of attitude toward a brand would go a long way toward assessing tarnishment *ex post facto*.

Combined, these two managerial implications for trademark dilution suggest that good brand management practices should include threshold and benchmark measures for fame, association, and attitude toward the brand, and should be tracked over time. While each serves a managerial purpose in the context of brand health, they would also serve the legal purpose of establishing the context of, and the commitment to, brand dilution and its prevention.

Concluding thoughts on the role of marketing in assessing implications of the TDRA

The TDRA serves as acknowledgement of the evolving perception that the value of a trademark comes from the efforts of the producer, not just the consent of the consumer. The impact of this shift is yet to be known. After more than a decade of legislative and court involvement, it appears that trademark dilution is now, and is likely to be, a key component of brand management, having substantial effects on how firms manage and protect high profile brands.

The true impact of the TDRA on the practice of law and brand management will depend on the benchmarks and metrics used by industries and courts to understand the boundaries of dilution on the behavior of consumers and organizations. Marketing scholars should play a role in establishing the standards by which courts and companies evaluate the extent and form of trademark dilution. Questions for future research are offered here.

First, what standards should measure the threshold for fame? The standards for typicality and dominance are different.[43] If consumers were asked for brands of airlines, and Delta was frequently mentioned, then a case can be made for its dominance. If asked to describe the product category of Delta, and the answers are split between airlines, faucets, and dental insurance, then is the standard of typicality met? Conversely, when

[43] Peterson *et al.*, "Trademark Dilution", 262.

asked what brand of MP3 player one thinks of most (dominance), Apple may come to mind. But when asked to indicate the product category for which Apple is typical, computers, music, or cell phones may be most frequently mentioned. Here, Apple meets the criteria for dominance, but does it meet the criteria for typicality. Must a brand be both typical and dominant to be famous? Which serves as a necessary condition for fame?

Second, what constitutes likelihood of dilution? While standards and methods for assessing likelihood of confusion exist,[44] we need to understand the threshold points for dilution. While Morrin and Jacoby offer valuable metrics,[45] we need benchmark measures for associative networks.

Third, are there universal standards for threshold effects on fame, or dilution by blurring or tarnishment, that transcend product or service categories? If so, then marketing scholarship should play a role in establishing regulatory standards.

Finally, how will dilution protection change the way we think about brands? While the concept of a trademark has been constrained by law, the notion of the brand has not. Will the effective merger of trademarks and brands constrain how we think about brands?

[44] Simonson, "Trademark Infringement", 181.

[45] Morrin and Jacoby, "Trademark Dilution", 254.

11

Trade mark law meets branding?

ILANAH FHIMA

Introduction

Although trade marks and brands are broadly concerned with the same subject matter, it is often felt that there is a disjunction between what trade mark law protects and what trade mark owners need, not just to protect their trade marks as legal phenomena, but also their brands as holistic, socially constructed entities. This chapter tracks the development of two lines of the Court of Justice of the European Union (CJEU)'s case law. These suggest that trade mark law is moving towards protecting aspects of image and branding in a way that recognises how consumers respond to trade marks and the brands that they are a part of, while at the same time acknowledging what trade mark owners need in order to preserve the relationship between their brands and consumers. In the first line of case law, the CJEU is moving relatively rapidly towards protecting trade marks not just as indications of trade origin, but also as carriers of a protectable image built up through promotion and advertising. However, there is a mismatch between the principle, which the Court recognises, and what the court is willing to offer in terms of concrete protection in individual examples of harm to a brand's image. In the second line of case law, which is very much at its starting point, the CJEU is beginning to show a willingness to treat aspects of brand image as a holistic whole in judging distinctiveness, use and infringement, allowing brand owners more successfully to capture the benefit of the entirety of their brand, rather than just the individual elements that are registered as trade marks.

Brand image

While trade mark lawyers think of product names, logos and other characteristics as indicators of trade origin, marketers think of them as contributing to brand equity, defined by Aaker as 'a set of assets (and liabilities) linked to a brand's name and symbol, that add to (or subtract from) the value provided by a product or service to a firm and/or that firm's customers'.[1] Brand equity contributes to a brand's 'identity' – a set of associations connected to the brand that, if favourable, will influence purchasing decisions[2] and differentiate a brand owner's product from other physically similar products, allowing the brand owner to charge a price premium.[3] Trade mark law has primarily concerned itself with the source-signifying functions of the constituents of brands. However, there is a growing trend for European trade mark law to recognise these image-signifying functions as well, at least on a conceptual level.[4]

The CJEU's early case law

The value of a brand's image was recognised, at least in principle, from the earliest CJEU cases defining the role and scope of trade marks. In *Centrafarm* v. *Winthrop*[5] and subsequent cases,[6] the CJEU defined the 'specific subject-matter' of a trade mark as:

> the exclusive right to use that trade mark, for the purpose of putting products protected by the trade mark into circulation for the first time, and is therefore intended to protect [the trade mark owner] against competitors

[1] D. Akker, *Building Strong Brands* (London: Pocket Books/Simon Schuster, 2010), pp. 7–8.

[2] Although current literature tends to view the formation and maintenance of a brand's identity as a two-way process. Rather than brand owners dictating brand image, consumers help to form the image through their relationship with the brand – see D. Desai, 'From Trademarks to Brands', *Florida Law Review*, 64 (2012), 981, 1000. Arguably, though, the CJEU's recognition of brand image has been limited to the top-down approach, dictated by the brand owner – see further D. Gangjee, 'Property in Brands: the Commodification of Conversation,' Chapter 2 in H. Howe and J. Griffiths (eds.), *Property Concepts in Intellectual Property Law* (Cambridge University Press, 2013).

[3] See S. Hartman, 'Brand Equity Impairment – the Meaning of Dilution', *Trademark Reporter*, 87 (1997) 418, 419–20. There is a neat account of key branding literature as it applies to trade mark law in Gangjee, 'Property in Brands', pp. 34–7.

[4] It should be noted that there is a lively debate as to whether it is desirable for trade mark law to protect brand image. See, e.g., K. Assaf, 'Brand Fetishism', *Connecticut Law Review*, 43 (2010–11), 83 (against); J. Sheff, 'Biasing Brands', *Cardozo Law Review*, 32 (2011), 1245 (somewhere in between); J. Shahar Dillbary, 'Famous Trademarks and the Rational Basis for Protecting Irrational Beliefs', *George Mason Law Review*, 14 (2007), 605 (in favour). The aim of this chapter, though, is to draw attention to how the CJEU is protecting brand image, rather than to condemn or praise this activity.

[5] Case 16/74 *Centrafarm BV and Adriaan de Peijper* v. *Winthrop BV* [1974] ECR 1183, para. 8.

[6] Case 3/83 *Centrafarm* v. *American Home Products Corporation* [1978] ECR 1823, para. 11; Case 1/81 *Pfizer* v. *Enrim-Pharm* [1981] ECR 2913, para. 7; Case C10/89 *SA CNL-SUCAL NV* v. *HAG GF AG* – HAG II [1990] ECR I-3711, para. 29.

> *wishing to take advantage of the status and reputation of the trade mark* by selling products illegally bearing that trade mark.[7]

However, later cases made it clear that the reputation of the mark was not protected per se. Instead, what the Court deemed necessary to protect this seemingly reputation-based specific subject matter was based on examining the 'essential function' of the trade mark, which it said was to:

> guarantee the identity of the origin of the trade-marked product to the consumer or ultimate user, by enabling him without any possibility of confusion to distinguish that product from products which have another origin.[8]

Thus the seemingly image-based statement of the interests of a trade mark owner resulted in confusion-based protection that focussed on not misleading consumers, rather than on protecting the mark's reputation.

Dilution

There was a shift in emphasis with the passing of the Trade Mark Directive,[9] which provides a basic framework of protection that all EU Member States must adhere to. Protection against confusion as to origin remains the most prevalent form of trade mark protection,[10] with its focus on shielding consumers and trade mark owners from the effect of the misleading uses of trade marks. However, the Directive can been seen as protecting brand image through its provisions in Arts 4(4)(a) and 5(2) forbidding blurring, tarnishment and unfair advantage.[11]

Blurring

Blurring is harm to the distinctiveness of a trade mark. On a conceptual level there is some debate as to the nature of this distinctiveness. Some

7 *Ibid.*, para. 8 (emphasis added).

8 Case 102/77 *Hoffmann-La Roche & Co. AG* v. *Centrafarm Vertriebsgesellschaft Pharmazeutischer Erzeugnisse mbH* [1978] ECR 1139, para. 7.

9 The then First Council Directive 89/104/EEC of 21 December 1988 to approximate the laws of the Member States relating to trade marks [1989] OJ L040/1, now Directive 2008/95/EC of the European Parliament and of the Council of 22 October 2008 to approximate the laws of the Member States relating to trade marks [2008] OJ L299/25. There are equivalent provisions in the Community Trade Mark Regulation, what is now Council Regulation (EC) No 207/2009 of 26 February 2009 on the Community trade mark [2009] OJ L78/1.

10 Found at Arts. 4(1)(b) (relative grounds for the refusal of registration) and 5(1)(b) (infringement) of the Directive.

11 On the relationship between branding and dilution see Desai, 'From Trademarks to Brands', 1027 and Hartman, 'Brand Equity Impairment'.

have argued that the damaged addressed by blurring is to the 'commercial magnetism' or 'exclusivity' of the trade mark in a qualitative sense.[12] Others have viewed the harm as only pertaining to the uniqueness of the mark on the market, regardless of the content of any image that the mark communicated to consumers.[13] According to this argument, the mere fact that a mark 'sticks out' and is different to other marks will mean that it more readily triggers in consumers the recollection of previous positive experiences involving the trade mark. These recollections will lead in many cases to repeat purchases. Conversely, if there are many other traders on the market using similar marks, seeing the mark will not automatically trigger consumers' recollection of the senior trade mark, or may trigger it more slowly or in a more muted fashion. This, so the argument goes, will mean that the trade mark will function less effectively as an indication of origin for the senior use and, consequently, seeing the mark will be less likely to motivate or enable consumers to make repeat purchases of the senior goods.

Although the exclusivity-based argument may seem more allied to the idea of protecting a brand's image, the uniqueness argument is also protective of brand image, in that the recollections triggered by a unique mark can include those created by investment in the brand through advertising and so on, as well as those resulting from the physical characteristics of the product.

The European jurisprudence has generally favoured the uniqueness approach. The wording of the Directive is suggestive of this approach, with the harm defined as use of the junior mark that is, or would be 'detrimental to, the distinctive character … of the earlier trade mark'.[14] The leading CJEU case on blurring, *Intel* v. *CPM*, makes no reference to harm to the more ephemeral elements of a trade mark or brand in defining detriment to distinctive character. Instead, borrowing from the US commentaries, the Court explains:

[12] See, e.g., R. Brown Jr, 'Advertising and Public Interest', *Yale Law Journal*, 57 (1947–8), 1165, 1191. For a fuller account of the various explanations that have been offered for blurring, see I. Simon Fhima, 'Dilution by Blurring: A Conceptual Roadmap', *Intellectual Property Quarterly*, [2010], 44.

[13] This would seem to be what is suggested by the 'father' of dilution in his seminal article: see F. Schechter, 'The Rational Basis of Trade Mark Protection', *Harvard Law Review*, 40 (1926–7), 813. See further R. Bone, 'Schechter's Ideas in Historical Context and Dilution's Rocky Road', *Santa Clara Computer & High Technology Law Journal*, 24 (2008), 469.

[14] Arts. 4(4)(a) and 5(2).

> detriment to the distinctive character of the earlier mark, also referred to as 'dilution', 'whittling away' or 'blurring', such detriment is caused when that mark's ability to identify the goods or services for which it is registered and used as coming from the proprietor of that mark is weakened, since use of the later mark leads to dispersion of the identity and hold upon the public mind of the earlier mark. That is notably the case when the earlier mark, which used to arouse immediate association with the goods and services for which it is registered, is no longer capable of doing so.[15]

What appears to matter here is that the senior mark previously reminded consumers about the origin of the goods instantly, but now no longer does so as effectively as it did previously. There is no suggestion that the 'immediate association' should be with any form of qualitative aspect or image relating to the mark or the goods to which it was affixed. The CJEU does not set out a comprehensive test for how detriment to distinctive character can be proven, but it does note that the more 'unique' a senior mark is, the more susceptible it will be to suffering detriment to distinctive character.[16] This again focusses on the distinctiveness per se of the mark, rather than the exclusive image portrayed by the mark. As noted above, distinctiveness can certainly be used as a tool for protecting that image. However, the *Intel* Court stated that in order to prove detriment to distinctive character, the senior user must show a 'change in the economic behaviour' on the part of senior consumers, or at least that such a change is likely to occur.[17] This vague standard is difficult to prove, whatever form the distinctiveness takes. It is unclear how this can be demonstrated and, in particular, how it can be demonstrated that any drop in sales can be attributed to the junior mark, rather than other factors such as changes in market conditions or a decline in the quality of a trade mark owner's offering. Indeed, there has been a sharp decline in the number of blurring cases since *Intel*. Despite the considerable impact that the 'change in economic behaviour' has had, the CJEU recently restated it, emphasising its importance, in *Environmental Manufacturing*.[18]

One small crumb of comfort for brand owners may be that the CJEU has recognised that genericisation (when a mark becomes the name of a category of products, rather than indicating their trade origin), arguably the worst form of harm that a brand can suffer, constitutes a form of

[15] Case C-252/07 *Intel Corp. Inc.* v. *CPM United Kingdom Ltd.* [2008] ECR I-8823, para. 29.
[16] *Ibid.*, para. 74. [17] *Ibid.*, para. 77.
[18] C-383/12 P *Environmental Manufacturing* v. *OHIM* [2013] ECR I-0000, paras. 39–45.

blurring.[19] Moreover, the CJEU has confirmed that the brand owner does not have to wait until the genericisation has already occurred before taking action.[20] However, it has linked genericisation with confusion, giving as its example the situation where consumers, faced with the senior mark used as a keyword for the junior goods, believe (or at least pause to wonder) that the junior offering originates with the senior user, or is part of its network.[21] This approach to genericisation is much narrower than the general understanding of the term.[22]

Tarnishment

Tarnishment is harm to the reputation or image of the trade mark. In protecting these reputational aspects of the mark, the tarnishment action has the potential to be a valuable tool in protecting brand equity and investment in a mark's reputation.[23] The harm involved is also easier to conceptualise than the more ephemeral concept of harm to distinctiveness. It is therefore surprising that tarnishment, or detriment to repute as it is known, has had relatively little impact in Europe.

The influential US commentator McCarthy[24] quotes the First Circuit Court of Appeals' definition of tarnishment to explain the US approach:

> A trademark is tarnished when consumer capacity to associate it with the appropriate products or services has been diminished. The threat of tarnishment arises when the goodwill and reputation of a plaintiff's trademark is linked to products which are of shoddy quality or which conjure associations that clash with the associations generated by the owner's lawful use of the mark.[25]

[19] Case C-323/09 *Interflora Inc. and Interflora British Unit* v. *Marks & Spencer plc et Flowers Direct Online Ltd.* [2011] ECR I-8625, para. 79.

[20] *Ibid.*, para. 77. [21] *Ibid.*, paras. 81–2.

[22] See, for example, R. Folsom and L. Teply, 'Trademarked Generic Words', *Yale Law Journal*, 89 (1979–80), 1323, 1324–5, who attribute genericisation to 'misuse of the mark by its holder in advertising and labeling; insufficient policing of improper use of the trademarked word; or the absence of a short and simple alternative name for the product'. Perhaps even more significant, however, is the propensity of trademark holders to encourage the public to adopt their marks as generic 'household' words.

[23] See Hartman, 'Brand Equity Impairment', 424.

[24] J. McCarthy, *McCarthy on Trademarks and Unfair Competition*, 4th edn, (Eagan, MN: West/Clark Boardman Callaghan, 1998–2014), §24:89, citing *L.L. Bean, Inc.* v. *Drake Publishers, Inc.*, 811 F.2d 26, 13 Media L. Rep. 2009, 1 USPQ2d 1753 (1st Cir. 1987).

[25] *L.L. Bean* v. *Drake Publishers*, p. 31.

The European courts have tended to concentrate on clashing or dissonant goods and have paid less attention to use of goods of shoddy quality. In particular, tribunals have tended to reject the argument that the junior user may, in the future, use the mark in question on poor-quality goods as too speculative.[26] This is particularly so in opposition to registration decisions, where the junior user will often not have started to use the mark in question at all.[27]

Arguments based on dissonant goods have received a warmer reception. Indeed, courts and commentators in Europe have repeatedly cited a pre-harmonisation dissonant goods case as the archetype of tarnishment.[28] In the Benelux case of *Lucas Bols* v. *Colgate Palmolive* the Court found that use owner of the CLAERYN mark for gin could prevent the registration of KLAREIN for an 'all-purpose cleanser' as the latter use would 'appeal to the sensations of the public in such a way that the attraction and capacity of the mark to stimulate the desire to buy the kind of goods which it is registered are impaired'.[29] In other words, no one wants to be reminded of toilet cleaner when they are quaffing their gin.[30]

Subsequent cases have recognised that there can be dissonance where the junior goods are inherently unsavoury or where the goods are not unpleasant per se but are not a good 'fit' with the senior goods. In fact, there are very few of the former category of cases. Most junior users will not be 'brave' enough to engage in blatant use of famous marks on clearly distasteful goods. It is difficult to agree which goods, if any, are inherently unpleasant, and to do so risks engaging in controversial and arguably subjective judgments. The most prominent examples in the UK are

[26] See in particular *Esure Insurance Ltd* v. *Direct Line Insurance plc.* [2008] RPC 6, para. 127. Although the decision was appealed, the finding on tarnishment was not. This ruling has been followed in a number of UK Trade Mark Registry decisions.

[27] See e.g. PEPSI/IPSEI O-326-06 (17 November 2006), para. 175.

[28] See AG Jacobs in Case C-408/01 *Adidas-Salomon AG* v. *Fitnessworld Trading Ltd* [2003] ECR I-12537, para. AG38; C-323/09 *Interflora*, para. AG52. For an early example of the link being made, see A. Kamperman Sanders, 'Some Frequently Asked Questions about the 1994 UK Trade Marks Act', *European Intellectual Property Review*, 67 (1995), 71–2. See also A. Griffiths, 'The Impact of the Global Appreciation Approach on the Boundaries of Trade Mark Protection', *Intellectual Property Quarterly*, 326 (2001), 351–4; *Daimlerchrysler AG* v. *Javid Alavi (T/A Merc)* [2001] RPC 42, para. 91; *Premier Brands UK Ltd.* v. *Typhoon Europe Ltd.* [2000] FSR 767, 788.

[29] *Lucas Bols* v. *Colgate-Palmolive* 7 IIC 420, 423 (1976).

[30] As Gielen puts it, 'It is not funny to drink a good glass of Claeryn Dutch gin while thinking of a cleaning agent at the same time!' – C. Gielen, 'Harmonisation of Trade Mark Law in Europe: The First Trade Mark Harmonisation Directive of the European Council', *European Intellectual Property Review*, 14 (1992), 262, 267.

two cases involving the use of the VISA[31] and EVER READY[32] marks on condoms. In the former decision the association with birth control was found to be negative, while in the latter decision it was not.

Senior users have had somewhat more success in demonstrating detriment to repute where, even though the junior goods are not inherently distasteful, they are dissonant with the nature of the senior goods. The Advocate General in *Intel* describes tarnishment thus:

> I have above given two imaginary examples of unrelated goods sold under the name 'Coca-Cola', or a similar mark: on the one hand, low-grade engine oil or cheap paint stripper; on the other hand, a select range of expensive hand-made jewellery. It seems likely that the former, and unlikely that the latter, would damage the repute of the Coca-Cola Company's trade mark. In each case of alleged tarnishment, it will be necessary to compare the connotations of each mark, in relation either to the goods or services covered or to the broader message which they may convey, and to evaluate the damage entailed.[33]

Although there is nothing inherently bad about engine oil or paint stripper, an association between those goods and a drink is undesirable. In practice though, tribunals have been relatively conservative in finding goods to be dissonant. Perhaps most surprisingly, the Office for Harmonization in the Internal Market (OHIM) First Board of Appeal was unwilling to find detriment to repute based on dissonance where the senior goods were chocolate and the junior goods included 'bleaching products'.[34] The fact pattern here is almost identical to that in *Lucas Bols*, Europe's template for tarnishment. Detriment to repute has been found, though, in other similar cases.[35]

There is perhaps more of an awareness of branding issues in a further, more marginal form of tarnishment. While the above approaches focus on the nature of the parties' goods, there is a line of decisions that take as their starting point the particular image of the senior mark and consider the effect of the junior user on that image. This allows trade mark owners to base their argument on the image that they have invested in through

[31] *CA Sheimer (M) Sdn Bhd's Trade Mark Application* [2000] RPC 484.

[32] *Oasis Stores Ltd's Application* v. *Opposition of Ever Ready plc.* [1998] RPC 631.

[33] C-252/07 *Intel*, para. AG86. See also Case C-487/07 *L'Oréal SA, Lancôme parfums et beauté & Cie SNC and Laboratoire Garnier & Cie* v. *Bellure NV, Malaika Investments Ltd. and Starion International Ltd.* [2009] ECR I-5185, para. 40 and C-323/09 *Interflora*, para. AG92.

[34] *MERSI/MERCI* R 1513/2008-1 (30 July 2009), paras. 41–2.

[35] E.g., GALAXY/GALAXY O-179-00 (19 May 2000).

their branding practices, though it cannot be assumed that the image that the trade mark owner asserts that he has is what the court will find that the image of the mark is. The most prominent example of this approach is the decision of the OHIM Third Board of Appeal in *Hollywood*.[36] The Board accepted the argument that the senior mark had established an image of health, dynamism and youth largely as a result of examining the junior user's advertising and its investment therein. However, the existence of the image was (rightly) not enough to convince the Board that tarnishment had taken place and the Board required the senior user to demonstrate that the image had suffered detriment because:

(a) it is linked with goods of poor quality or which evoke undesirable or questionable mental associations which conflict with the associations or image generated by legitimate use of the trade mark by its proprietor;
(b) it is linked with goods which are incompatible with the quality and prestige associated with the trade mark, even though it is not a matter of inappropriate use of the trade mark in itself; [or]
(c) its word or figurative element is amended or altered in a negative way.[37]

While the senior user did ultimately convince the Board that harm to its image was likely as a result of the junior use on tobacco products, this was by no means an automatic finding, as the Board's careful weighing of the evidence shows.[38]

What unites all the forms of tarnishment from a branding perspective is that while the European courts and tribunals are willing in principle to protect investment in image, in practice the approach is a cautious one that requires the brand owner/senior user to show a relatively exacting standard of harm. This acceptance of the theory but caution towards the evidential standard has much in common with the European approach to blurring.

Unfair advantage

More promising from the brand owner's perspective is the unfair advantage action. Although unfair advantage is not one of the traditional forms of dilution, it shares the fact that it can be used in situations where there is no confusion between the parties' goods and can be used in situations

[36] *Hollywood S.A.S.* v. *Souza Cruz S.A.* R 283/1999-3 [2002] ETMR 64.

[37] *Ibid.*, para. 86. [38] *Ibid.*, paras. 90–7.

where the parties' goods are not similar. Consequently, it can be found in the same provision of the European trade mark legislation as blurring and tarnishment.

The CJEU in *L'Oréal* v. *Bellure* defined unfair advantage as:

> 'parasitism' or 'free-riding' ... the advantage taken by the third party as a result of the use of the identical or similar sign. It covers, in particular, cases where, by reason of a transfer of the image of the mark or of the characteristics which it projects to the goods identified by the identical or similar sign, there is clear exploitation on the coat-tails of the mark with a reputation.[39]

In other words, the CJEU is willing to protect the brand image built up by investment in marketing from being appropriated. Moreover, unlike with blurring and tarnishment, the approach taken to proving that unfair advantage has occurred is one that very much favours trade mark owners. One might expect the unfairness aspect of unfair advantage to provide a significant limitation on the scope of the action. However, the CJEU has interpreted it very widely, stating that there is unfairness:

> where [the junior user] seeks by that use to ride on the coat-tails of the mark with a reputation in order to benefit from the power of attraction, the reputation and the prestige of that mark and to exploit, without paying any financial compensation, the marketing effort expended by the proprietor of the mark in order to create and maintain the mark's image.[40]

Thus the key ingredient of unfairness is merely that the junior user has not paid for the benefit that he has received from the senior mark. One would expect this lack of remuneration to be present in every case that goes to court. Tribunals in the UK have attempted to lessen the effect of this ruling, arguing that in using emotive language such as 'riding on the coat-tails', the CJEU intended to introduce a requirement that the junior user intended to take advantage.[41] This, however, does not seem to be the correct approach in the light of *Interflora*.[42] There the CJEU held that selection of the senior mark INTERFLORA as a keyword for Marks & Spencer's (the junior user's) website exploited the senior user's marketing efforts without paying any financial compensation and so any advantage

[39] C-487/07 *L'Oréal* v. *Bellure*, para. 42.

[40] *Ibid.*, para. 49.

[41] Notably the Court of Appeal in *Whirlpool Corp* v. *Kenwood Ltd.* [2010] ETMR 7, paras. 112–15.

[42] C-323/09 *Interflora*, para. 18.

obtained was unfair.[43] No mention was made of intention and the finding of unfairness seems to have followed essentially automatically from the finding of advantage.

Tribunals have adopted a somewhat more rigorous approach to the 'advantage' element of unfair advantage, with the intention being to establish that the senior mark really will confer a benefit on the junior user. The *L'Oréal* Court suggested that all relevant factors should be considered including the senior mark's reputation, its distinctive character, how similar the parties' marks are and the nature and degree of proximity of the goods or services concerned.[44] Arguably, this is in line with branding concerns as it adopts a flexible, open-ended approach to determining when investment in brand image can be diverted and when it is just too far apart.

What has more potential to limit the scope of the unfair advantage action is the fact that, even where the junior use causes one of the types of detriment or unfair advantage, it will be acceptable if the junior use is with 'due cause'. Until recently, the provision was thought to be something of a 'lame duck', invocable only in cases where the junior user had an earlier right to use his mark, or was compelled to use his mark.[45] However, the growth of unfair advantage has been accompanied by the CJEU's development of the due cause provision as an all-purpose 'get-out clause' for socially useful junior uses. Thus in *Interflora*, the junior use was found to be with due cause, even though it was notionally unfair because the junior user was offering an 'alternative' to the senior products without imitating the senior goods or otherwise harming the senior mark.[46] Following this lead, in *De Vries*[47] the CJEU rejected the narrow interpretation of due cause, emphasising that the wide protection afforded by Art. 5(2) also required significant checks and balances.[48] In that case, it meant that prior use with good faith could amount to due cause.[49] This widening of the scope of due cause could potentially allow uses which are harmful

43 *Ibid.*, para. 89. 44 C-487/07 *L'Oréal* v. *Bellure*, para. 44.

45 This was the approach that had been taken prior to harmonisation in the Benelux countries – see *Lucas Bols* v. *Colgate-Palmolive*, 425. The UK courts assumed that the intention of the drafters of the Directive was to take the same narrow approach – see e.g. *Premier Brands* v. *Typhoon Europe*, 1097.

46 C-323/09 *Interflora*, para. 91.

47 Case C-65/12 *Leidseplein Beheer and Hendrikus de Vries* v. *Red Bull GmbH* [2014] ETMR 24.

48 *Ibid.*, paras. 45–6 in particular.

49 *Ibid.*, paras. 55–60.

to brand images to take place, although there is a debate to be had over whether wider social interests should override those of protecting brand equity in cases like comparative advertising, for example.[50] More broadly, the presently uncertain scope of the due cause provision may be of concern to brand owners.

The alternative track: protection of brand image through trade mark function

Dilution has provided a mixed bag of protection for brand image. Although the wording of the Directive looks promising, the CJEU has undercut that protection with demanding proof standards for blurring, and it looks likely that a similarly narrow approach would be taken for tarnishment. Although unfair advantage has been interpreted widely, that also suffers from a degree of uncertainty in the light of the currently evolving jurisprudence on the meaning of due cause.

In fact, there is a parallel line of protection, focussed largely around Art. 5(1)(a) and parallel importation, that has developed following on from *Centrafarm* v. *Winthrop*. This too appears to offer wide protection at first blush, but once again the CJEU has adopted a cautious approach to translating it into concrete protection.

Protection of reputation, and thus brand image, first appeared in the contemporary cases in the CJEU's 1996 *Bristol-Myers Squibb* v. *Paranova* decision (henceforth, *BMS*).[51] In order to achieve the single internal market, the CJEU has held that where a third party 'parallel imports' trade-marked goods from one EU jurisdiction to another, the default position is that the trade mark owner cannot rely on his trade mark rights to prevent the sale of those goods in the destination country.[52] As part of this process, the importer can repackage the products and reaffix the trade mark owner's mark if this is what is required in order for the goods to be sold on the destination market. However, the repackager must comply with certain conditions, which were laid down in respect of the Directive

[50] Arguably there is an attempt to strike this balance in the CJEU's allowing of socially beneficial uses, but only when they do not cause confusion or blur or tarnish the junior mark.

[51] Case C-436/93 *Bristol-Myers Squibb* v. *Paranova A/S; C. H. Boehringer Sohn, Boehringer Ingelheim KG and Boehringer Ingelheim A/S* v. *Paranova A/S; Bayer Aktiengesellschaft and Bayer Danmark A/S* v. *Paranova A/S* [1996] ECR I-3457.

[52] This is described in detail in D. Keeling, *Intellectual Property Rights in EU Law: Volume I*, (Oxford University Press, 2003), Chapter 7 and pp. 174–213. The rules on exhaustion for trade marks have now been incorporated into the Directive in Art. 7.

in the *BMS* case.[53] Included in these conditions was the requirement that the repackaging must not be such as to damage the reputation of the trade mark owner.[54] This could occur if, for example, the new packaging was defective, of poor quality, or was untidy.[55] In reaching this decision, the Court relied on the trade mark owner's 'legitimate interest' in protecting the specific subject matter of his mark, as adumbrated in *Centrafarm* v. *Winthrop*,[56] and translated it into concrete protection for a mark's reputation.[57] Interestingly, the reputation seems to almost be presumed here, without a need to show that the trade mark owner has established a particular image for his brand.

The CJEU has used this decision as the basis of a gradual expansion of the situations in which it is prepared to consider a mark's reputation. *Dior* v. *Evora*[58] was another parallel importation case, but in that case the trade mark owner objected to the resale of its goods in discount stores, rather than to repackaging. Thus there was no risk to the physical condition of the goods. Nevertheless, the CJEU took account of the specific image that the trade mark owner claimed that it had established – one of prestige and luxury – and found that any reseller must 'endeavour to prevent his advertising from affecting the value of the trade mark by detracting from the allure and prestigious image of the goods in question and from their aura of luxury'.[59] However, the Court was not prepared to unconditionally accept the trade mark owner's assessment of what would damage the image of its mark. Instead, the test appears to be quite an exacting one of use that 'seriously damages' the senior trade mark.[60] In terms of advertising, this meant that use in an advertisement that seriously detracted from the trade mark owner's image would not be acceptable,[61] but use in a style of advertising that differed from the trade mark owner's usual mode of advertising, but which was customary in the trade section in question, would be acceptable.[62] Thus, while the general protection is widely stated, what this translates to in terms of actual protection is narrower and seems to be

[53] C-436/93 *BMS*, paras. 49 onwards. The other conditions are that a failure to repackage would artificially partition the EU market, there must be no change to the condition of the trade mark owner's goods, the repackager must give notice to the trade mark owner of his repackaging and must indicate on the goods that they are repackaged.

[54] *Ibid.*, para. 75. [55] *Ibid.*, para. 76.

[56] 16/74 *Centrafarm* v. *Winthrop*.

[57] C-436/93 *BMS*, para. 75.

[58] Case C-337/95 *Parfums Christian Dior SA and Parfums Christian Dior BV* v. *Evora BV* [1997] ECR I-6013.

[59] *Ibid.*, para. 45. [60] *Ibid.*, para. 47.

[61] *Ibid.* [62] *Ibid.*, para. 46.

pegged to a quasi-objective standard that potentially differs from the trade mark owner's assessment of what is required to protect his brand image.

The implications of *Dior* v. *Evora* were not fully realised until the CJEU's 2009 *Copad* judgment.[63] SIL manufactured Dior products under licence. SIL sought and was refused permission by Dior to sell the products it made outside Dior's selective distribution agreement. SIL nevertheless supplied goods bearing the DIOR trade mark to Copad, a discount retailer. Dior brought trade mark infringement proceeding against both SIL and Copad. This was potentially problematic as Art. 8(2) of the Directive states that licensors can only enforce their trade mark rights (as opposed to their contractual rights under the licence) in a limited set of circumstances, which does not include sale outside of a selective distribution agreement but does include sale of goods of different quality to that agreed in the licence. Dior successfully argued that, although the physical quality of goods supplied by SIL to Copad was identical to 'authorised' products, sale outside the selective distribution agreement could harm the 'aura of luxury' of the goods. In the words of the Court, 'an impairment to that aura of luxury is likely to affect the actual quality of those goods'.[64] Thus the CJEU is equating harm to brand image with harm to the physical quality of the goods and the effect that this has on the ability of the mark to function. Once again, though, while the statement of principle is a broad one, when it comes to translating this into actual protection, the Court is more reserved. Not every sale outside the selective distribution agreement that the trade mark owner objects to is considered to harm the luxury image. Instead, the test is an objective one, taking into account whether each particular discount retailer is likely to cause harm, considering the nature of the luxury goods, the volumes sold, whether the licensee regularly sells to discount retailers and the marketing methods of, and types of goods sold by the discount retailer.[65] Thus a brand's image is respected in theory, but the brand owner actually has little discretion in shaping the scope of that protection.

The CJEU further found that if the trade mark owner could not enforce his trade mark rights as a result of Art. 8(2), the goods had to have been deemed to have been put on the market with the trade mark owner's consent for the purposes of Art. 7(1).[66] However, the trade mark owner would be able

[63] Case C-59/08 *Copad SA* v. *Christian Dior couture SA, Vincent Gladel and Société industrielle lingerie (SIL)* [2009] ECR I-3421.

[64] *Ibid.*, para. 26.

[65] *Ibid.*, paras. 28–32.

[66] *Ibid.*, para. 46.

to object to their resale by the discount retailer if it had 'legitimate reasons' to oppose the sale under Art. 7(2).[67] Following *Dior* v. *Evora*, this included harm to the reputation of the mark. Once again, though, the mere sale outside the selective distribution agreement could not be presumed to be harmful to the brand image, and a further investigation was needed, balancing the trade mark owner's interest in protecting its reputation with the reseller's interest in selling the goods.[68]

Also in 2009, the CJEU brought the protection of brand image into the mainstream of Art. 5 trade mark protection in *L'Oréal* v. *Bellure*,[69] a case that has been discussed above in the context of unfair advantage. Art. 5(1) of the Directive provides protection without the need to show confusion if the parties' marks and the parties' goods or services are identical. Although on its strict wording this protection would appear to be very wide, the CJEU has interpreted it to be limited to situations where the junior use will harm the functioning of the senior mark.[70] The most obvious example of this is where the senior mark's ability to indicate the commercial origin of the goods on which it is used is impaired. However, prior to *Bellure* the CJEU dropped tantalising hints that marks may have other functions that the Court was prepared to recognise.[71] The nature of these functions was confirmed in *Bellure* as 'guaranteeing the quality of the goods or services in question and those of communication, investment or advertising'.[72] The *Bellure* Court did not indicate what sorts of activities would harm those functions, leaving this assessment to the national courts,[73] but it did establish the principle that the CJEU was prepared to protect investment in advertising and brand image through Art. 5.

Clarification of the advertising function came in *Google France*.[74] This is one of a number of cases involving use of trade marks on the Internet in which the CJEU has sought to restate certain fundamental principles

[67] *Ibid.*, para. 55. [68] *Ibid.*, paras. 56–8.

[69] C-487/07 *L'Oréal* v. *Bellure*.

[70] See particularly Case C-206/01 *Arsenal Football Club plc* v. *Matthew Reed* [2002] ECR I-10273, para. 51.

[71] E.g. in C-206/01 *Arsenal* v. *Reed*, para. 51, the Court spoke about harm to the 'functions' of a trade mark, but then proceeded to speak in detail only about the 'essential' function of indicating origin.

[72] C-487/07 *L'Oréal* v. *Bellure*, para. 63

[73] *Ibid.*

[74] Joined cases C-236/08 to C-238/08 *Google France SARL and Google Inc.* v. *Louis Vuitton Malletier SA; Google France SARL* v. *Viaticum SA and Luteciel SARL; and Google France SARL* v. *Centre national de recherche en relations humaines (CNRRH) SARL and Others* [2010] ECR I2417.

of trade mark law. The CJEU defined the advertising function in abstract terms as 'that of using its mark for advertising purposes designed to inform and persuade consumers'.[75] This could be harmed by where the junior use 'adversely affects the proprietor's use of its mark as a factor in sales promotion or as an instrument of commercial strategy'.[76] However, this begs the question: what sorts of junior use would harm the mark in this way? On this the CJEU was not forthcoming, though it did indicate that the fact that a senior user would need to pay more money in order to secure its trade mark as an advertising keyword did not constitute harm to the advertising function.[77] While the Court was willing to recognise the advertising function as protecting trade mark owners' investment in their brands, this is yet another example of the Court's unwillingness to translate that abstract recognition into concrete protection.

The CJEU took a similar approach in *Interflora*[78] in relation to the investment function. It began by confirming the Court's commitment to protecting the non-origin functions of marks.[79] It then reiterated the *Google* Court's definition of the advertising function and noted that the investment function overlapped with this, but was not identical.[80] Instead, the investment function of a mark involves the use of the mark to 'acquire or preserve a reputation' using commercial techniques other than advertising.[81] This function is affected when the junior use 'interferes with the proprietor's use of its trade mark to acquire or preserve a reputation capable of attracting consumers and retaining their loyalty'.[82] In particular, in the context of Art. 5(1)(a) where a mark has a reputation, the investment function is harmed when an identical mark is used on identical goods in a way that jeopardises the maintenance of the reputation.[83] Once again, though, when it came to giving concrete examples of what would harm the investment function, the Court employed only a negative definition, stating what would *not* be enough to harm the investment function, namely that the proprietor of that trade mark has 'to adapt its efforts to acquire or preserve a reputation capable of attracting consumers and retaining their loyalty' or that the senior user loses customers.[84] Thus the establishment and maintenance of a brand image is recognised, but precisely what it can be protected against is not articulated.

[75] *Ibid.*, para. 91. [76] *Ibid.*, para. 92.
[77] *Ibid.*, paras. 94–5. [78] C-323/09 *Interflora.*
[79] *Ibid.*, paras. 37–8. [80] *Ibid.*, para 61. [81] *Ibid.*
[82] *Ibid.*, para. 62. [83] *Ibid.*, para. 63.
[84] *Ibid.*, para. 64.

Clearly, the trend in this line of case law is the recognition of image-related functions of a trade mark as a matter of principle, but a reluctance to recognise concrete examples of such harm. The one exception to this is *L'Oréal* v. *eBay*.[85] The senior user, L'Oréal, argued that various aspects of the sale and advertising of genuine L'Oréal goods by third parties on the eBay online auction website constituted infringement. One of the challenged activities was the sale of L'Oréal perfumes and cosmetics of the same physical quality as authorised products, but without their outer packaging. The CJEU was willing to accept[86] that the removal of such packaging could harm the image of 'prestige and luxury', especially where the packaging was more important to the presentation than the bottle or container in which the product was sold. Such harm would give the trade mark owner legitimate reasons to oppose the sale of its goods on eBay within the European Economic Area (EEA).[87] Although the CJEU noted that harm to reputation would need to be assessed on a case-by-case basis, what is different about this case is that the Court has not couched its answer in the language of equivocation, and has not made the references to balancing the interests of trade mark owners and third parties that are familiar from previous cases. Perhaps this heralds a greater willingness on the part of the CJEU not just to recognise brands in theory, but to protect them in practice.

Brand context

A further, more technical trend that is helpful to brand owners can been be seen in the CJEU's jurisprudence. The general tendency is for trade mark law to examine each aspect of a trade-marked product in isolation. This is especially true when it comes to registrability. To take an example, the name COCA COLA, the shape of the Coca Cola bottle, the red colour and the white cursive script used in packaging and selling Coca Cola would, until recently at least, be treated as separate phenomena.[88] This is at odds with the branding approach, where each of these aspects and

[85] Case C-324/09 *L'Oréal SA* v. *eBay International AG* [2011] RPC 27.

[86] *Ibid.*, paras. 74–83.

[87] If the goods originated from outside the EEA, then there would be no exhaustion and this would be an example of Art. 5(1)(a) identical marks/identical goods infringement unless consent to resale could be demonstrated.

[88] See *O2 Holdings Ltd* v. *Hutchinson 3G Ltd* [2006] ETMR 55 (Ch), para. 7 (cited by D. Vaver, 'Brand Culture: Trade Marks, Marketing and Consumption' – Responding Legally to Professor Schroeder's Paper', Chapter 8 in L. Bently, J. Davis and J. Ginsburg (eds.), *Trade*

the interrelationship between them are all seen as contributing to a single brand image.[89]

The first hint that the CJEU might be open to a more 'in the round' view of trade marks on the registrability side can be seen in *Nestlé* v. *Mars*.[90] Nestlé sought to register the slogan HAVE A BREAK as a UK trade mark. This was found to lack inherent distinctive character. Nestlé argued that the term had acquired distinctive character as a result of the use that it had previously made of the term. The difficulty was that Nestlé had only ever used the applied for mark as part of the longer slogan HAVE A BREAK … HAVE A KIT KAT. Nevertheless, the CJEU found that, as long at the element at issue had been used 'as a trade mark' to distinguish goods, and relevant consumers recognised it as such according to the normal test for acquired distinctiveness, that sufficed. Only the end result matters, not the fact that it had been used as a component of another registered trade mark.[91]

The CJEU went further in *Colloseum* v. *Levi Strauss*.[92] Levi Strauss owned two trade mark consisting of the pocket of a pair of jeans with a red tab. 'Mark number 3' bore the word 'Levis' on the red tag while in 'mark number 6' the red tag had no writing on it. Colloseum sold jeans with a red tab at the side of the pocket and Levi Strauss sued for infringement. Colloseum counterclaimed, arguing that Levi Strauss' mark number 6 should be revoked for lack of genuine use since Levi Strauss had only ever produced trousers with tags marked LEVIS. Applying its finding in *Nestlé* v. *Mars* to the revocation provisions, the Court held:

Marks and Brands: an Interdisciplinary Critique (Cambridge University Press, 2009), pp. 187–8: 'English law does not … protect brands as such. It will protect goodwill (via the law of passing off); trade marks (via the law of trade mark infringement); the use of particular words, sounds and images (via the law of copyright); shapes and configurations of articles (via the law of unregistered design right and so on). But to the extent that a brand is greater than the sum of the parts that English law will protect, it is defenceless against the chill wind of competition.'

89 See for example P. Kotler and G. Armstrong, *Principles of Marketing*, 15th edn (Harlow: Pearson, 2014) p. 255: 'A brand is a name, term, sign, symbol or design, or a combination of these, that identifies the maker or seller of a product or service.' Earlier (p. 249) the authors give the example of the 'Starbucks Experience', which includes 'smells', 'hissing steam' and 'comfy chairs', as well as more conventional brand indicia. Davis explains the distinction between the trade mark and branding approach: J. Davis, 'Between a Sign and a Brand', Chapter 3 in L. Bently, J. Davis and J. Ginsburg (eds.), *Trade Marks and Brands: an Interdisciplinary Critique* (Cambridge University Press, 2009), p. 81.

90 Case C-353/03 *Société des Produits Nestlé SA* v. *Mars UK Ltd.* [2005] ECR I-6135.

91 *Ibid.*, paras. 26–31.

92 Case C-12/12 *Colloseum Holding AG* v. *Levi Strauss & Co.* [2013] ETMR 34.

> regardless of whether the sign is used as part of a registered trade mark or in conjunction with the registered trade mark, the fundamental condition is that, as a consequence of that use, the sign for which registration as a trade mark is sought may serve to identify, in the minds of the relevant class of persons, the goods to which it relates as originating from a particular undertaking.[93]

In *Nestlé* v. *Mars* the mark at issue was arguably a component of the slogan that had been used. Here though, the CJEU is effectively allowing the trade mark owner to combine the effect of the mark at issue (pocket plus tag) with what is arguably a separate mark (the word element) in judging consumer perception. This brings the Court closer to the branding perspective of harnessing the holistic impact of the various different elements of brand image.

The same trend can also be seen in the recent *Specsavers* v. *Asda* case.[94] The senior user had registered the word SPECSAVERS, a figurative depiction of glasses (known as 'the wordless logo') and the combination of the figurative depiction with the word SPECSAVERS superimposed on it as Community trade marks (CTMs). The wordless logo had never been used without the word SPECSAVERS and so the junior user argued that it should be revoked for non-use. The senior user argued that the use of the logo with SPECSAVERS superimposed on it, which was a CTM in itself, was sufficient to amount to genuine use of the logo alone. The Court of Appeal of England and Wales referred this as a question to the CJEU, which answered affirmatively. Under the second paragraph of Art. 15(a), use of a mark in a form that differs from the form registered still amounts to genuine use of the registered mark if the distinctive character of the original mark is not changed.[95] What this meant was that, as a result of the use of the *altered* mark, consumers had to see the *registered* mark as indicating the origin of the goods in question.[96] The fact that the altered mark was itself a registered trade mark had no bearing on the issue.[97] This allows trade mark owners to rely on the combined effect of the logo and naming elements of a brand in order to preserve the individual elements of the brand's identity.

The *Specsavers* case also indicates the CJEU's willingness to take a most holistic approach to judging infringement. It is a well-established principle of EU trade mark law that confusion should be judged via a 'global

93 *Ibid.*, para. 28.

94 Case C-252/12 *Specsavers International Healthcare Ltd* v. *Asda Stores Ltd* [2013] ETMR 46.

95 *Ibid.*, para. 21. 96 *Ibid.*, para. 23. 97 *Ibid.*, para. 25.

appreciation' that takes into account all relevant circumstances.[98] At the same time, though, the comparison was long thought to be between the senior mark as registered and the junior sign as used.[99] Because of the need to reduce signs to a defined graphical representation, this meant that only individual, or perhaps two indicia of a brand would feature in a single registration. Moreover, judicial hostility towards accepting that non-traditional signs could, as a matter of fact, be distinctive meant that the branding elements registered tended to be predominantly words or logos.[100] This meant that the mark as registered, which formed the basis of the comparison, could cover only a narrow category of brand indicia. In *Specsavers*, the CJEU found that, even though the senior mark was registered in black and white, it was acceptable to take into consideration the colours in which the senior user had always used that mark – in this case, green.[101] The fact that the junior user had also used its similar sign in green was relevant to establishing confusion under Art. 9(1)(b) of the CTM Regulation.[102] Additionally, the fact that the junior user had intentionally used a similar colour to the colour that the senior user had always used in its logo (but had not registered for) was also relevant to establishing whether there was an unfair advantage taken under Art. 9(1)(c).[103] By permitting senior users to rely on the context of the use made of their trade marks, the CJEU has opened the door for senior users to pursue an infringement action based on a single element of their brand (such as the word element), but to protect in practice the other elements of the brand image if they have been used alongside the registered element. Thus it seems it could be possible in practice to protect unregistrable combinations of elements that contribute to brand image. It may also be possible to gain some protection for branding elements that are in practice unregistrable, such as smells, or very difficult to register, such as shapes, where they are used in conjunction with more easily registrable elements such as words or logos.[104]

98 See Griffiths, 'The Impact of the Global Appreciation Approach', 326.

99 See D. Keeling *et al.*, *Kerly's Law of Trade Marks and Trade Names*, 15th edn (London: Sweet & Maxwell, 2011) § 14–064. Although there was perhaps a hint at a departure from this in Case C-533/06 *O2 Holdings Limited and O2 (UK) Ltd.* v. *Hutchison 3G UK Ltd.* [2008] ECR I-4231, para. 63, where the mark at issue was a bubble image, but the CJEU found that the junior user of a bubble in a comparative advertisement was not confusing when the advertisement 'as a whole' was considered.

100 Davis, 'Between a Sign and a Brand', especially pp. 70–4.

101 C-252/12 *Specsavers International Healthcare and Others* [2013] ETMR 46, paras. 37–8.

102 *Ibid.*, paras. 44–9.

103 *Ibid.*, para. 40.

104 There is a partial precedent for this in Case C-100/02 *Gerolsteiner Brunnen GmbH & Co.* v. *Putsch GmbH* [2004] ECR I-691, para. 26. There the CJEU was considering whether the junior user's descriptive use of its mark for mineral water was 'in accordance with

Conclusion

There will always be a distinction between trade marks and brands: the needs served and actors concerned with these concepts, while overlapping, are subtly different. What recent jurisprudence demonstrates, though, is that, on the trade mark side, there is a willingness to take on board, and even craft protection for, the branding-led issues encountered by trade mark owners. Although these developments are sometimes slow, and sometimes hesitant (particularly in the case of protecting brand image), it seems likely that branding-led protection will expand as the CJEU gains more experience with these issues and is asked to decide more cases where such issues are implicated.

honest practices', and so could benefit from the Art. 6(1)(b) defence to infringement. The Court found that, in order to make this assessment, all relevant circumstances had to be taken into account, including the shape and labelling of both parties' mineral water bottles. This was despite the fact that it was only the word mark GERRI that was registered. Thus the court was using the fact that the word mark had been used with certain other brand indicia in a way that provided protection beyond the scope of the registered mark.

12

Brands, firms and competition

ANDREW GRIFFITHS

Aims of this chapter

This chapter will consider the legal nature of brands, their role in product differentiation and how they may affect competition and the competitiveness of firms. It will show how the legal entity of the trade mark provides the main legal platform for the marketing entity of the brand and will consider the close but nebulous relationship between these two entities. Firms and other business organisations use brands to compete with each other at the level of marketing,[1] although the brands they use can vary considerably. Some brands provide a personable facade for the firms behind them, but some firms control a range of product-focussed brands, and some brands can appear to be distinct and autonomous entities in their own right. Despite this variety, brands have certain characteristics in common that are relevant when analysing their impact on competition and competitiveness.

This chapter will argue that brands give firms the means and an incentive to compete in terms of product quality, product development and other forms of innovation. However, it will also show how brands can enable firms to gain market power in more controversial ways and will argue that the rights of brand owners need careful calibration to provide an optimal incentive. The chapter will proceed as follows. The following section will make some general observations about branding and competition. The third section will examine the legal basis and nature of a brand. The fourth section will consider how branding has influenced the development of firms and the structuring of economic activity. The fifth section will explain how branding enables firms to provide guidance and assurance about product quality and encourages competition on this

[1] Trade mark law uses the term 'undertaking' to include a firm or any other business organisation that can function as a cohesive unit: *IHT* v. *Ideal-Standard* (C9/93) [1994] 3 CMLR 857 at [38][39]. This chapter will use the term 'firm' in this broad sense unless the context requires otherwise.

basis. The sixth section will show how branding may appeal to consumers for other reasons and encourage less beneficial forms of non-price competition. The final section will draw some conclusions.

Branding and competition

Brands are major assets in the global economy, with the leading ones valued at many billions of dollars.[2] One concern of this book is with how far their value may reflect an ability to gain and maintain excessive market power rather than being a legitimate reward for the beneficial competitive efforts of the firms behind them. The former view sees branding as facilitating product differentiation that is largely artificial or unnecessary with the 'image advantage' that a brand can confer on products as a form of monopoly.[3] The latter view, however, sees branding as valuable guidance and assurance about product quality with the competitive advantage that a brand can confer as a reward for supplying good-quality products and for satisfying consumers' expectations in this respect.[4] Thus, in the latter view, competing products of the same generic kind may differ significantly across a range of characteristics of interest to consumers (or some of them), which can be treated as differences in 'quality' in a broad sense of the term.[5] Branding helps consumers recognise and evaluate these differences, and for many kinds of product consumers have come to regard the variety and differentiation that branding helps to achieve as part of their appeal.[6] Branding therefore serves the public interest by enabling firms to tailor their products to satisfy the variegated desires of consumers as well as encouraging them to ensure that consumers' expectations in terms of quality are not disappointed. Moreover, it can encourage firms to seek to improve the quality of their products and to engage in other forms of

[2] Since 2000, Interbrand has produced an annual ranking of the 'Best Global Brands' by 'brand value' in conjunction with *Business Week* magazine. For 2013, they ranked Apple first at almost $100 billion, with Google second at $93 billion and Coca-Cola (which had been first in all of Interbrand's previous rankings) third at $79 billion. See www.interbrand.com (accessed April 2014).

[3] F. M. Scherer, 'The Posnerian Harvest: Separating Wheat from Chaff', *Yale Law Journal*, 86 (1977), 974–1002 at 996–1000.

[4] N. Economides, 'The Economics of Trademarks', *Trademark Reporter*, *78* (1988), 523–39; W. Landes and R. Posner, 'Trademark Law: An Economic Perspective', *Journal of Law and Economics*, 30 (1987), 265–309.

[5] C. A. Reeves and D. A. Bednar, 'Defining Quality: Alternatives and Implications', *Academy of Management Review*, 19 (1994), 419–45.

[6] W. Streeck, 'Citizens as Consumers: Considerations on the New Politics of Consumption', *New Left Review*, 76 (2012), 27–47 at 31–2.

innovation, which can help to make firms more competitive in the dynamic sense of being able to prosper and survive in a changing environment.[7]

Another concern of this book is with how brands (including the 'private labels' of retailers) have become the focus of consumer attention and demand. A brand gives a common identity to products of a particular kind that are likely to be consistent in quality and to remain so over time. Branding is therefore a convenient device that enables consumers to make judgments and form expectations about product quality based on their own experience or other sources of information without having to ascertain or verify the actual quality of competing products. Consumers can base their searches and decision-making on the perceived quality of competing brands rather than on the actual quality of competing products. This shift of focus is of particular importance in the digital economy where consumers can search for products and information about their likely quality online, and they therefore have to rely on signifiers of these products and on perceptions based on these signifiers. It also means that firms can package and present their products for distribution in ways that ensure they can continue to vouch for the quality of their products, even though they may make inspection prior to purchase difficult if not impossible.

However, the role of branding in product differentiation can go beyond the relatively passive one of providing guidance and assurance about actual differences in quality to the more active one of contributing to these differences. It can give products an emotional dimension, and the distinctiveness of an identity can increase this impact where consumers attach value to differentiation.[8] Branding in effect forms part of the overall quality of branded products.[9] Giving products this kind of appeal is of questionable social value and adds complexity to the relationship between

[7] European Commission (2003), *Innovation Policy: Updating the Union's Approach in the Context of the Lisbon Strategy*, COM (2003), 112 at 5. See generally A. Griffiths, *An Economic Perspective on Trade Mark Law* (Cheltenham: Edward Elgar Publishing, 2011).

[8] B. Beebe, 'Search and Persuasion in Trademark Law', *Michigan Law Review*, 103 (2005) 2020–72; G. B. Ramello, 'What's in a Sign? Trademark Law and Economic Theory', *Journal of Economic Surveys*, 20 (2006), 547–65; G. B. Ramello and F. Silva, 'Appropriating Signs and Meaning: The Elusive Economics of Trademark', *Industrial and Corporate Change*, 15 (2006), 937–63.

[9] The Court of Justice of the European Union (CJEU) has ruled that the overall 'quality' of luxury goods can include certain 'mental' characteristics that result from association with a prestigious image: *Parfums Christian Dior* v. *Evora* (C337/95) [1998] ETMR 26 at [45]; *Copad* v. *Christian Dior Couture* (C59/08) [2009] ETMR 683 at [24]–[26].

branding and product differentiation.[10] In considering how far branding operates in the public interest and justifies legal protection, it is necessary to consider both what it achieves for consumers and how it influences the behaviour of firms. Having exclusive control over a source of emotional appeal to consumers can give a firm significant market power and increase its bargaining power within the streams and value chains in which it operates. The law governing the property rights that determine the extent of a brand owner's exclusive control has to strike a balance that takes into account both the socially useful and the more questionable effects of the product differentiation that it facilitates and encourages. The subsequent sections of this chapter will therefore examine the issues relevant to this balancing exercise in more detail.

What is a brand?

The marketing term 'brand' is not defined in law and its relationship with the legal term 'trade mark' is therefore hard to specify with precision.[11] A brand roughly means a distinctive and exclusive identity that a firm can establish and control through registering (or using) a sign (or signs) as a trade mark and that the firm can confer on its products to facilitate their marketing to consumers. A brand is therefore the identity that a trade mark (or set of trade marks) signifies and represents, and that provides a clear and convenient focus for a firm's marketing efforts and for consumer attention and demand.[12] A firm can gain exclusive rights over a sign that it uses or intends to use for this purpose through registering it as a trade mark, but may acquire certain rights simply through using the sign as a trade mark.[13]

[10] Ramello and Silva, 'Appropriating Signs and Meaning', pp. 951–3, 956–9.

[11] Section 1 of the United Kingdom's Trade Marks Act 1994 defines a trade mark as 'any sign capable of being represented graphically which is capable of distinguishing goods or services of one undertaking from those of other undertakings'.

[12] The International Trademark Association has defined a brand as 'a trade mark (or combination of trademarks) that, through promotion and use, has acquired significance in distinguishing the source or origin of the goods or services offered under the trademark from those offered by others in the marketplace ... Brands are intellectual property and, as such, are part of the assets or "goodwill" of a company, and may be bought or sold like any other asset or property': see www.inta.org/TrademarkBasics/FactSheets/Pages/BrandValuation.aspx (accessed April 2014).

[13] In the European Union, the law governing registered trade marks has been substantially harmonised pursuant to Directive 2008/95/EC, which codified Directive 89/104/EEC (as amended) (hereinafter 'the Directive'). In the United Kingdom, signs used as trade marks also enjoy some legal protection regardless of registration under the tort of passing off.

A trade mark has to be registered for a particular kind (or kinds) of products on the basis that it is being or will be used for the marketing of products of this kind (or kinds). However, the rights conferred on the owner of a trade mark can extend to cover use for products that are not of the same or even of a similar kind as those for which the trade mark has been registered.[14]

The potential value of a brand as a marketing resource lies in its capacity to acquire a reputation, an image and other associations in the minds of consumers. There is mutual dependence in the relationship between a brand and a trade mark that signifies it inasmuch as the distinctiveness, salience and intrinsic connotations of a brand's name and other signifiers can contribute to its capacity to gain a reputation and other associations and to its emotional appeal; and the reputation and other associations of a brand underlies the strength of its signifiers.[15] Specifying the relationship between a brand and a trade mark that signifies it with greater precision can be complicated because a firm may use more than one trade mark to signify a particular brand and may establish more than one brand for marketing its products.[16] In either or both of these cases, the firm may vary the combination of trade marks that it uses and may use particular trade marks for particular purposes such as signifying the connection between its brands. The owner of a brand may change the brand's name or its other signifiers, but do so in a way that ensures the brand's continuity as an identity along with its reputation and any other associations it has acquired. A brand therefore has a flexible and protean character and the capacity to evolve as a marketing resource.

The exclusive property rights that the owner of a trade mark enjoys over the sign in question extend to cover similar signs that relevant consumers may confuse with the trade mark. These include signs that these consumers are likely to perceive as signifying the same commercial 'origin' as the trade mark (in effect, as the same brand) and signs that they are likely to perceive as signifying an economic link with the trade mark (in effect, as a connected brand).[17] These ancillary rights give flexibility to the signification of a brand and increase the scope for it to evolve.

[14] The Directive, Arts. 5.1 and 5.2.

[15] P. G. Sandner and J. H. Block, 'The Market Value of R & D, Patents and Trademarks', *Research Policy*, 40 (2011), 969–85.

[16] *Andrew (John)* v. *Kuehnrich* (1913) 30 RPC 677(CA).

[17] *Sabel* v. *Puma* (C-251/95) [1998] ETMR 1; *Canon* v. *MGM* (C-39/97)[1999] ETMR 1; *Lloyd Schuhfabrik* v. *Klijsen Handel* (C-342/97) [1999] ETMR 690; *Medion* v. *Thomson Multimedia* (C-120/04) [2006] ETMR 164.

Trade marks therefore provide the main legal anchor for brands and the exclusive rights of trade mark owners are the main determinant of the potential value of a brand as a marketing resource. A trade mark should be distinctive as a sign and is exclusive to its owner as a marketing resource. It should be distinctive in the sense that relevant consumers should readily recognise it as exclusive to one firm in particular and should be able to distinguish the branded products from others of the same kind without any risk of confusion.[18] A trade mark should therefore give the branded products an identity that is convenient, memorable and readily recognisable and be capable of entering the minds of consumers with this special meaning along with its associations as the identifier or signifier of a brand. Where the trade mark is or includes a word, it may also provide a name for the brand and the branded products. Consumers can use this in searches and enquiries. It provides a basis for defining the branded products in transactions and a reference point for conveying and acquiring information about the products and for use in marketing activity designed to attract demand for them.

The exclusivity of a brand as a marketing resource is essential to its capacity to acquire a reputation and other associations concerning the branded products and to provide guidance and assurance concerning their likely quality. A trade mark's owner has the exclusive right to use it (or authorise its use) for marketing purposes and therefore to profit from its power to attract consumers.[19] A trade mark gives consumers a legal guarantee that branded products have a specific commercial 'origin', which means that the owner must also be in a position to vouch for the quality of the marked products.[20] This alignment of exclusive interest and unitary control supports the trade mark's 'economic guarantee' concerning the likely quality of the branded products.[21] The branding of a product

[18] The CJEU has defined the 'essential function' of a trade mark, as being to 'guarantee the identity of the origin of the trade-marked product to the consumer or ultimate user, by enabling him without any possibility of confusion to distinguish that product from products which have another origin': *Hoffmann-la-Roche* v. *Centrafarm* (C-102/77)[1978] 3 CMLR 217 at [7]; *Arsenal FC plc* v. *Matthew Reed* (C-206/01) [2003] ETMR 19 at [48].

[19] 'In relation to trade marks ... [the owner] has the exclusive right to use that trade mark for the purpose of putting a product into circulation for the first time': *Hoffmann-la-Roche* v. *Centrafarm* (C-102/77) [1978] 3 CMLR 217 at [7]. See also *Major Bros.* v. *Franklin* [1908] 1 KB 712 (HC); and *Primark* v. *Lollypop Clothing* [2001] ETMR 334 (HC).

[20] *Hag II* (C-10/89) [1990] 3 CMLR 571 at [13]; *IHT* v. *Ideal-Standard* (C9/93) [1994] 3 CMLR 857 at [38]–[39]. See also *Aristoc* v. *Rysta* [1945] AC 68 (HL).

[21] The CJEU has ruled that a trade mark 'must constitute a guarantee that all the products bearing it have been manufactured under the supervision of a single enterprise to which responsibility for their quality may be attributed': *Hag II* (C-10/89) [1990] 3 CMLR 571 at [13]; *IHT* v. *Ideal-Standard* (C-9/93) [1994] 3 CMLR 857 at [38]–[39]. See also the Opinion

can be viewed as signifying an assumption or acceptance of commercial responsibility for its quality.[22]

As a marketing resource established and signified through trade marks, a brand has the same characteristics of distinctiveness and exclusivity. A brand may be perceived as synonymous with the firm that uses it, or as a distinct component of a firm or even as an autonomous and opaque firm-like entity. However, even a brand that appears to be relatively simple and straightforward can be complex and mutable in terms of the legal structure and organisation that may lie behind the mask of apparent stability that its signifiers can provide.[23] A brand can mask radical changes both as regards its own ownership and control and as to how its owner organises the production, procurement or provision of the branded products.[24] A brand is a firm-like entity because it is exclusive and subject to unitary control: there is a single decision-maker in control with discretionary powers over its use and development as a marketing resource and which can exercise judgment on 'its' behalf.[25] This controller has an interest in exercising its discretion in a way that maintains or increases the brand's value as an asset, which means maintaining or increasing its power to attract consumers to the branded products. However, there is no legal guarantee that a brand's controller will always do this.

A brand provides a platform from which its owner can engage in marketing to attract demand for the branded products and secure 'brand loyalty'. The owner's exclusive right to use a trade mark signifying the brand for this purpose, and its exclusive control over the quality of the

of Advocate General Jacobs in *Hag II*: 'although trade marks do not provide any form of legal guarantee of quality … they do in economic terms provide such a guarantee, which is acted upon daily by consumers':[1990] 3 CMLR 571 at 583.

22 *Aristoc* v. *Rysta* [1945] AC 68 at 101–2; *Scandecor Development* v. *Scandecor Marketing* [2001] ETMR 800 at [19].

23 See C. Hays, *Pop: Truth and Power at the Coca-Cola Company* (London: Arrow, 2005), pp. 8–47 on how the production and distribution arrangements behind the 'Coca-Cola' brand have changed.

24 For brief accounts of the histories of 222 of 'the most intriguing and visually compelling' well-known brands, including details of changes in their ownership and organisation, see D. Newton, *Trademarked: A History of Well-Known Brands from Aertex to Wright's Coal Tar* (Stroud: Sutton Publishing, 2008).

25 A key characteristic of a firm is the centralisation of control over a set of resources (including intangible resources) and personnel in a decision-making body that can exercise judgment in response to opportunities and threats, including changes in the firm's environment, and that can engage in strategic planning so that the firm can survive and prosper: R. N. Langlois, 'The Vanishing Hand: The Changing Dynamics of Industrial Capitalism', *Industrial and Corporate Change*, 12 (2003), 351–85.

branded products, is reinforced by various supplementary rights that enable it to ensure that any use of the trade mark for post-marketing or 'downstream' transactions does not affect the brand's reputation concerning product quality or other aspects of its attractive power. In particular, the owner can prohibit a party's use of the trade mark for downstream transactions after unauthorised interference with marked products (such as repackaging or relabelling), unless the party complies with a stringent set of conditions that are designed to protect the owner's legitimate interest in the reputation and appeal of its trade mark.[26] The owner of a brand can also use its signifiers in advertising and other promotional activity, and thereby reach over retailers and other downstream intermediaries to communicate directly with consumers and secure or strengthen specific demand for the branded products. Again, the owner has a supplementary right to control the use of a trade mark in the marketing activity of downstream parties in order to protect the trade mark's reputation.[27]

There is one other characteristic of the trade mark that increases the value and versatility of the brand as a marketing resource. It was noted above that a firm may use a trade mark not as the signifier of a specific brand, but to signify an economic link of some kind with a firm or another brand. The legal rights conferred on trade mark owners take account of this possibility and, in effect, support and facilitate the scope for using signs to do this. The Court of Justice of the European Union (CJEU) has ruled that the right of a trade mark owner to prohibit the use of an identical or similar sign, because this creates 'the likelihood of confusion' with the trade mark, applies where relevant consumers are likely to think that the products in question 'come from the same undertaking, or, as the case may be, economically linked undertakings'.[28] The CJEU has indicated that this can arise where a third party

[26] *Hoffmann-la Roche* v. *Centrafarm* (C-102/77) [1978] 3 CMLR 217; *Bristol-Myers Squibb* v. *Paranova* (C-427/93) [1996] ETMR 1; *Boehringer Ingelheim (No. 2)* (C-348/04) [2007] ETMR 1164; *Wellcome* v. *Paranova* (C-276/05) [2009] ETMR 363; *Portakabin* v. *Primakabin* (C-558/08) [2010] ETMR 930; *L'Oréal* v. *eBay* (C-324/09) [2011] ETMR 971. See also the owner's right under Article 8 of the Directive to prohibit the use of its trade mark to identify products that a licensee has put on the market after breach of certain conditions of its licensing agreement, in particular after breach of any condition relating to the 'quality' of the products: *Copad* v. *Christian Dior* (C59/08) [2009] ETMR 683.

[27] *Parfums Christian Dior* v. *Evora* (C-337/9) [1998] ETMR 26 at [44].

[28] *Canon* v. *MGM* (C-39/97) [1999] ETMR 1 at [29], citing *Sabel* v. *Puma* (C-251/95) [1998] ETMR 1 at [16]–[18]. See also *Lloyd Schuhfabrik* v. *Klijsen Handel* (C-342/97) [1999] ETMR 690 at [17]; *Medion* v. *Thomson Multimedia* (C-120/04) [2006] ETMR 164 at [26]; and *O2 Holdings* v. *Hutchison 3G* (C-533/06) [2008] ETMR 853 at [59]. Article 5.1 of the Directive provides that the owner of a trade mark 'shall be entitled to prevent all third

uses a composite sign that includes the owner's trade mark or a distinctive element of that trade mark.[29] The CJEU has provided further support for this capacity in its rulings on the scope of the owner's other protective rights and on the scope of the defences.[30] Among other implications, this capacity provides a legal platform for the practices known as 'brand extension' and 'brand stretching', which involve making use of the attractive power of a familiar brand in new markets.[31]

A brand is therefore an exclusive resource that a firm can own and use to market its products, to provide a focus for consumers' attention and to secure or strengthen specific demand for the products. Its exclusivity as an asset and its distinctiveness as a marketing identity are secured through the owner's rights over the trade mark (or marks) that signifies and represents it and that can be used to refer to it. A brand is, in effect, a valuable intangible input that its owner can add to products to increase its return from them. Moreover, as the next section will show, having exclusive control over this input can also provide a platform for organising the production, procurement or provision of the branded products.

Branding and business organisation

The emergence of the brand as a marketing resource and of marketing as a distinct form of economic activity coincided with the rise of the 'modern corporation', which provided an efficient structure for acquiring and organising the capital, resources and capabilities necessary for large-scale mechanised production.[32] This development led to there being much greater distance between producers and consumers. Consumers

parties not having his consent from using in the course of trade … (b) any sign where, because of its identity with, or similarity to, the trade mark and the identity if similarity of the goods or services covered by the trade mark and the sign, there exists a likelihood of confusion on the part of the public, which includes the likelihood of association between the sign and the trade mark'.

29 *Medion* v. *Thomson Multimedia* (C-120/04) [2006] ETMR 164 at [31].

30 See, for example, *Portakabin* v. *Primakabin* (C-558/08) [2010] ETMR 930;*Interflora* v. *Marks & Spencer* (C-323/09) [2012] ETMR 1; *Viking Gas* v. *Kosan Gas* (C-46/10) [2011] ETMR 58. On defences, see *BMW* v. *Deenik* (C-63/97) [1999] ETMR 286 at [51]; *Gillette* v. *LA-Laboratories* (C-228/03) [2005] ETMR 825 at [42].

31 These terms tend to be used loosely and interchangeably in the literature on marketing: J. P. Choi, 'Brand Extension as Informational Leverage', *Review of Economic Studies*, 65 (1998), 655–69; L. M. Pepall and D. J. Richards, 'The Simple Economics of Brand Stretching', *Journal of Business*, 75 (2002), 535–52.

32 M. Wilkins, 'The Neglected Intangible Asset: The Influence of the Trade Mark on the Rise of the Modern Corporation', *Business History*, 34 (1992), 66–95.

could no longer rely on the reputation of a familiar local firm for guidance and assurance about product quality and other matters and were instead presented with the products of remote and impersonal entities.[33] Whilst retailers and other intermediaries could provide some guidance and assurance, this would increase their bargaining power over producers.[34] The lack of any capacity to provide assurance and secure demand in other ways could have undermined the efficiency of the modern corporation, but branding enabled a firm to give its products a personable identity with the potential to acquire a reputation that could provide assurance to consumers.[35] In other words, branding gave firms the capacity to develop humanistic relationships with consumers and other stakeholders and to do so remotely.[36]

As a marketing resource, a brand can therefore be of great value to producers and other 'upstream' firms. However, in the second half of the twentieth century branding also contributed to the decline of the 'Fordist' modern corporation and the rise of disaggregated systems of production involving fluid networks of producers associated with 'Post-Fordism'.[37] Changes in technology and communication, especially digitalisation, increased the efficiency of smaller scale production and enabled much greater flexibility. This enabled firms to adapt production to exploit or respond to innovation much more rapidly.[38] It also increased the scope for customising products and upgrading them rapidly to meet consumer demand for greater variety and differentiation.[39] Branding has helped to shape this development, because having the capacity and capabilities to engage in marketing and secure specific demand is a good platform

33 R. Marchand, *Creating the Corporate Soul: The Rise of Public Relations and Corporate Imagery in American Big Business* (Berkeley and Los Angeles: University of California Press, 2001).

34 Langlois, 'The Vanishing Hand', pp. 355–8.

35 Wilkins, 'The Neglected Intangible Asset', pp. 68–70, 82–7.

36 Marchand, *Creating the Corporate Soul*, pp. 7–47.

37 S. Berger, 'Toward a Third Industrial Divide?', in P. Osterman (ed.), *Economy in Society: Essays in Honour of Michael J. Piore* (Cambridge, MA: MIT Press, 2012), pp. 65–88; R. N. Langlois, 'Modularity in Technology and Organization', *Journal of Economic Behaviour and Organization*, 49 (2002), 19–37; R. Murray, 'Fordism and Post-Fordism', in S. Hall and M. Jacques (eds.), *New Times: The Changing Face of Politics in the 1990s* (London: Lawrence and Wishart, 1990), pp. 38–53; M. Piore and C. Sabel, *The Second Industrial Divide: Possibilities for Prosperity* (New York: Basic Books, 1984); C. F. Sabel and J. Zeitlin, 'Neither Modularity nor Relational Contracting: Inter-Firm Collaboration in the New Economy', *Enterprise & Society* 5 (2004), 388–403.

38 Berger, 'Toward a Third Divide?', pp. 74–5.

39 Streeck, 'Citizens as Consumers', 28–36.

from which to organise production and orchestrate a network of producers. Ownership of a brand enables a firm to develop and exploit an attractive marketing presence, even where it outsources production and in effect acts as an intermediary between producers and consumers. The main constraint is that the firm should be able to exercise adequate control over the quality of the branded products, but changes in technology and communication have increased the scope to do this through contractual mechanisms. Moreover, where there is scope to market products on a large scale and potential value in an attractive marketing reputation, and where production can be efficiently organised through a fluid network of suppliers, branding has enabled so-called 'weightless' firms to evolve.[40] These firms engage only in activities such as research and development, design, marketing and reputation management along with the orchestration of production. A manufacturing firm with an established marketing capability may be able to evolve in this direction through outsourcing some or all of its production to focus more on marketing and the other 'weightless' activities.[41] A brand provides a flexible resource that can facilitate this kind of organisational transformation and may help mask it from consumers.

The capacity of a brand to enable the marketing of products to be organised separately from their production is due to the open and unspecified nature of the commercial 'origin' that a trade mark signifies and guarantees. A trade mark signifies that its owner has authorised its use for marketing products of the relevant kind sold under it and that the owner (or a superior controller) is in a position to exercise ongoing control over their quality.[42] The right to use trade marks has never been restricted to firms that produce the marked products in-house, but has been available to intermediate or downstream firms that procure, select or commission 'their' products from other firms on the basis that they are also in a position to vouch for the quality of the marked products and to assume commercial responsibility for them accordingly.[43] The CJEU has ruled that the owner of a trade mark can have the requisite ongoing 'possibility' of

[40] N. Klein, *No Logo* (London: Flamingo, 2000), p. 4.

[41] On the transformation of Clarks Shoes into a global marketing firm, see P. Barkham, 'How the Chinese fell in Love with Clarks Shoes', *The Guardian*, 9 March 2011, available at www.guardian.co.uk/lifeandstyle/2011/mar/09/chinese-love-clarks-shoes (accessed April 2014).

[42] *IHT* v. *Ideal-Standard* (C-9/93) [1994] 3 CMLR 857.

[43] *Major Bros.* v. *Franklin* [1908] 1 KB 712 (HC); *Aristoc* v. *Rysta* [1945] AC 68 (HL); *Primark* v. *Lollypop Clothing* [2001] ETMR 334 (HC).

control over product quality through a variety of mechanisms including licensing.[44] This means that firms operating quite far downstream, including retailers, can use branding to develop a marketing presence and reputation, and use this to compete directly with upstream firms at the level of marketing, as long as they have some basis for attracting consumers to their products, such as being able to provide credible quality assurance. Retailers can therefore use private labels to appropriate more of the potential rewards for providing quality assurance where they have sufficient bargaining power with suitable upstream suppliers.[45]

A brand is therefore an intangible firm-like entity that a firm can use as a platform for marketing and developing a resource that attracts consumers to its products, and also for organising or orchestrating production. A system for allocating and protecting exclusive property rights over signs is essential for brands to exist and perform these functions. To this extent, the economic case for this system is analogous to that for awarding exclusive property over scarce tangible resources, namely to ensure their efficient use through preventing conflicting or 'rivalrous' use of signs and through encouraging investment in the maintenance and development of the brands they signify.[46] Accordingly, the law's main concern should be with ensuring that firms can only appropriate signs that can perform the required function, and cannot appropriate signs that have some pre-existing meaning or significance in the relevant market that would give them an unfair advantage over other traders. Moreover, the law should limit the scope of the property rights that firms can acquire over signs to what is necessary for them to function as the signifiers of brands. The case for any further protection depends on the social value of the additional value that it would be required to secure. This in turn depends on the basis of the power of brands to attract consumers.

Branding and quality assurance

The CJEU has claimed that trade marks are an essential element of a system of 'undistorted competition' because they enable firms to attract and retain customers by the quality of their products.[47] This claim presumes

[44] *IHT* v. *Ideal-Standard* (C9/93) [1994] 3 CMLR 857 at [38]–[39].

[45] A. Ezrachi and D. Bernitz (eds.), *Private Labels, Brands and Competition Policy: The Changing Landscape of Retail Competition* (Oxford University Press, 2009).

[46] H. Demsetz, 'Towards a Theory of Property Rights', *American Economic Review*, 57 (1967), 347–59.

[47] See, for example, *Loendersloot (Frits)* v. *Ballantine* (C349/95) [1998] ETMR 10 at [22].

that branding differentiates products in a way that gives consumers a reliable basis for taking account of product quality in their searches and decision-making and that branded products appeal to consumers primarily for this reason. It also implies that branding serves the interest of consumers by giving firms an incentive to meet their preferences and satisfy their expectations in terms of product quality. This is consistent with the Chicago School's economic rationale of the trade mark system, which argues that it benefits consumers through reducing search and communication costs, through encouraging firms to invest in product quality and through discouraging the kind of opportunistic behaviour that leads to consumer disappointment.[48] This section will examine this claim and consider how branding can provide guidance and assurance about product quality.

Products of the same kind can differ in various ways that consumers (or some of them) regard as significant and that can be viewed as differences in 'quality' in a broad sense of the term.[49] These differences are positive and negative inasmuch as consumers value certain attributes in products but expect them to be free of others.[50] The initial concern of consumers is likely to be with attributes relating to the functionality and material condition of products, such as their reliability, durability, serviceability and conformance to specification. Consumers may also attach importance to the design and aesthetic appeal of some products.[51] Beyond this, consumers may value variety and differentiation and the emotional impact of certain kinds of product.[52]

The fact that products of a particular kind can differ significantly in terms of quality gives firms supplying products another dimension in which they can compete.[53] However, it also raises two economic problems for suppliers and consumers. First, there is the difficulty of specifying and communicating the quality of a particular product (whether offered or

[48] Landes and Posner, 'Trademark Law', pp. 268–70. See also G. Akerlof, 'The Market for "Lemons": Quality Uncertainty and the Market Mechanism', *Quarterly Journal of Economics*, 84 (1970), 499–500; Economides, 'The Economics of Trademarks', pp. 525–7.

[49] A. Griffiths, 'Quality in European Trade Mark Law', *Northwestern Journal of Technology and Intellectual Property*, 11 (2013), 621–41.

[50] J. M. Juran, *Juran's Quality Control Handbook* (New York: McGraw-Hill, 1988), pp. 2–3.

[51] D. A. Garvin, 'What Does 'Product Quality' Really Mean?', *Sloan Management Review*, 26 (1984), 25–43; D. A. Garvin, 'Competing on the Eight Dimensions of Quality', *Harvard Business Review*, 65 (1987), 101–9.

[52] See above nn. 8–10.

[53] L. Abbott, *Quality and Competition: An Essay in Economic Theory* (New York: Columbia University Press, 1955).

desired) with precision. This causes various search and communication costs including the risks of error and subsequent disappointment. Second, there is the difficulty of verifying the actual quality of an offered product at the time of purchase or consumption, which also causes various search costs including the risk of 'adverse selection'.[54] For some products, adequate specification and verification may be possible in theory but prohibitively costly in practice, and for many products, including services, they may not be possible at all.[55] Moreover, for some products the two problems can be intertwined: consumers look to producers or suppliers for diagnosis and guidance on their requirements as well as confirmation that an offered product has the requisite 'credence' characteristics.[56] If not combated, these two problems would also undermine the incentives for competing firms to offer consumers the best overall value and would instead give unscrupulous firms the opportunity to supply low-quality or unsuitable products.[57]

A private mechanism for providing reliable guidance and assurance about product quality can therefore benefit and encourage firms to meet consumers' desires and expectations in this respect. Trade marks and the brands they signify provide such a mechanism, although they do not give consumers any legally binding guarantee about product quality. A trade mark merely guarantees that one firm has authorised its use as a product identifier and that this firm is in a position to control the quality of those products.[58] This means that consistency is possible, but the likelihood of that depends on the strength of the brand owner's economic interest in ensuring that branded products meet consumers' expectations in terms of quality and minimising their risk of disappointment. This gives a trade mark's 'guarantee' of quality a flexible and dynamic character, which can work both for and against the interest of consumers. An important supplement to this economic guarantee is the fact that branding links products on the market to a specific commercial source. Giving products this organisational context brings a range of other matters into the frame of

[54] C. Wilson, 'Adverse Selection', in J. Eatwell, M. Milgate and P. Newman (eds.), *The New Palgrave: Allocation, Information and Markets* (London: The Macmillan Press, 1989), pp. 31–4.

[55] P. Nelson, 'Information and Consumer Behaviour', *Journal of Political Economy*, 78 (1970), 311–29.

[56] M. R. Darby and E. Karni, 'Free Competition and the Optimal Amount of Fraud', *Journal of Law and Economics*, 16 (1973), 67–88.

[57] Akerlof, 'The Market for "Lemons"'.

[58] '[T]he decisive factor is the possibility of control over the quality of goods, not the actual exercise of that control': *IHT* v. *Ideal-Standard* (C-9/93) [1994] 3 CMLR 857 at [38].

potential interest to consumers, including the behaviour of the brand owner, its response to problems and setbacks, and the identity and track record of other firms in the supply chain.

A brand therefore mitigates the problem of specifying product quality through providing a convenient reference point based on likely consistency. This can be an efficient basis for communication, since it is not necessary for a product's quality to be specified and ascertained in full detail, even if this were possible. It also enables consumers to make use of prior experience where appropriate. This can be especially useful in searching for and requesting products where consumers' preferences are variable and highly subjective, such as food and drink. Moreover, by giving products an organisational context, branding enables consumers to evaluate their likely quality in this context and take account of the organisational track record. This may show how product quality has stabilised, improved or varied in other ways over time. It can also enable consumers to recognise and seek out products with unusual characteristics that may be hard, if not impossible, to specify and that may reflect the particular combination of knowledge, skills and other capabilities that a firm has acquired and developed.[59]

Moreover, the fact that the branding of a product does not guarantee a specific standard of quality can be an advantage to firms and consumers. Whilst this flexibility means that brand owners can let product quality decline or take risks with quality, it also creates scope for product improvement or applying other forms of innovation that a legal obligation to maintain a specific standard of quality could hinder or preclude. Predicting how consumers will respond to product innovation or the effects of other innovation is difficult, and innovation can involve a process of trial and error in this respect as well. Giving an organisational context to a new product or a product that reflects some other form of innovation can provide valuable assurance because it enables consumers to take account of the organisation's overall track record, including its behaviour in response to previous problems and setbacks.[60] A brand does not just provide a salient focal point for incidents of negative publicity, but also one for publicising a firm's response to negative publicity and for putting such incidents into a broader organisational context. This may be

[59] On the value of the 'tacit' knowledge and skills of an organisation, see M. Polanyi, *Personal Knowledge: Towards a Post-Critical Philosophy* (London: Routledge and Kegan Paul, 1962) (corrected edition), pp. 49–65.

[60] For examples, see N. F. Koehn, *Brand New: How Entrepreneurs Earned Consumers' Trust from Wedgwood to Dell* (Boston, MA: Harvard Business School Press, 2001), pp. 321–6.

sufficient to restore or even to strengthen consumers' trust in the brand as a source of guidance and assurance. In other words, branding enables reputation to be managed at the organisational level.

A brand's capacity to provide assurance about product quality rests on its owner's interest in ensuring that the brand retains or increases its power to attract consumers. As the exclusive beneficiary of this power, the owner has an incentive to ensure that a brand acquires a good reputation and to minimise the impact of problems or negative publicity. The brand provides consumers as individuals (where appropriate) and consumers as a class with a means of retaliation in the event of disappointment.[61] And this can include their response to the behaviour of the firm behind the brand as well as to the track record of the branded products. The strength of the owner's incentive should increase in line with the investment made in building up and maintaining the good reputation that underlies the strength of the brand's quality assurance.[62] The competitive advantage and market power that this capacity generates can be viewed as the owner's return on the investment, and this has a self-reinforcing effect inasmuch as the increasing size of this return further increases the owner's incentive to maintain or increase the brand's attractive power.[63]

The private and institutional nature of a brand's quality assurance that a brand provides means that it is possible to increase this through other kinds of investment focussed on the brand, as long as this can be seen to increase the owner's stake in the brand's continuing power to attract consumers.[64] This includes expenditure on advertising and other promotional activity such as sponsorship and securing endorsements for the brand, which may have the additional benefit of increasing its emotional appeal. Whilst the social value of this appeal is questionable, investing in boosting it should nevertheless increase the brand's quality assurance insofar as it is related to the functional and material quality of the branded products and is therefore vulnerable to any disappointment or negative

[61] Akerlof, 'The Market for "Lemons"', p. 500.

[62] B. Klein and K. B. Leffler, 'The Role of Market Forces in Assuring Contractual Performance', *Journal of Political Economy*, 89 (1981), 615–41; C. Shapiro, 'Consumer Information, Product Quality and Seller Reputation', *Bell Journal of Economics*, 13 (1982), 20–35; C. Shapiro, 'Premiums for High Quality Products as Returns to Reputations', *Quarterly Journal of Economics*, 98 (1983), 659–79.

[63] Landes and Posner, 'Trademark Law', 270. See further I. Png and D. Reitman, 'Why Are Some Products Branded and Others Not?', *Journal of Law and Economics*, 38 (1995), 207–24; and S. Wiggins and D. Raboy, 'Price Premia to Name Brands: An Empirical Analysis', *Journal of Industrial Economics*, 44 (1996), 377–88.

[64] Klein and Leffler, 'The Role of Market Forces', pp. 629–33.

publicity in this respect. The owner can also increase the brand's quality assurance by linking it to other brands through 'brand extension' and 'brand stretching', since these also increase its apparent value as a stake.[65]

However, the strength of a brand's quality assurance ultimately depends on how far the owner considers that the net overall benefits of maintaining a good reputation for the brand exceeds the potential net overall benefits of courses of action that would reduce product quality, or would at least increase the risk of inconsistency and incidents of negative publicity. In other words, the owner does not have an unqualified incentive to do everything that is required to meet or exceed the expectations of consumers in terms of product quality, and may well have an incentive to take risks in this respect in order to reduce costs or increase output.[66] Nevertheless, subject to this qualification, the owner has good reason to maintain or improve the brand's reputation concerning likely product quality. The fact that the brand's reputation can encompass the owner's response to any previous setbacks or problems gives the owner some leeway for experimentation and innovation, especially since a reputation based on innovation can be a factor that attracts consumers.[67] However, the balance of incentives can be a fine one and a firm's desire to protect a good reputation may discourage radical forms of innovation.[68]

A brand's institutional ability to link specific products on the market to a specific firm, and to the behaviour of this firm and in the relevant supply chain, can be of further value to consumers, since it enables them to give weight to organisational detail and behaviour in their decision-making as if these matters formed part of the overall quality of the branded products. A familiar brand can provide a salient target for publicising incidents and behaviour within an entire stream of economic activity, thereby giving its owner an incentive to enforce standards within the stream.[69] This can include ensuring the observance of regulation applicable to upstream firms, thereby increasing its effectiveness, and ensuring the observance of standards or codes of ethics or social responsibility.[70]

65 On these practices, see above at n. 31.

66 Economides, 'The Economics of Trademarks', 529–30.

67 G. S. Carpenter and K. Nakamoto, 'Consumer Preference Formation and Pioneering Advantage', *Journal of Marketing Research*, 26 (1989), 285–98.

68 R. Cole and T. Matsumiya, 'Too Much of a Good Thing? Quality as an Impediment to Innovation', *California Management Review*, 50 (2007), 77–93.

69 M. P. Vandenbergh, 'The New Wal-Mart Effect: The Role of Private Contracting in Global Governance', *UCLA Law Review*, 54 (2007), 913–70.

70 A brand owner's ability to enforce standards downstream depends on the downstream rights that enable it to protect a trade mark's reputation being calibrated accordingly: see

Whilst it is questionable as to how much weight consumers are likely to give such matters in practice, familiar brands provide a 'transmission mechanism' that enables consumers to respond to behaviour and incidents that could otherwise seem remote and disconnected from products on the marketplace.[71]

The view that trade marks and brands promote beneficial competition therefore rests on an elegant economic theory in which their power to attract consumers is a legitimate reward for meeting consumers' desire in terms of product quality, and for providing guidance and assurance about this. It supports an economic case for conferring exclusive property rights on brand owners that are sufficient to protect the exclusivity and distinctiveness of brands as marketing identities. However, a brand may attract consumers and influence their perceptions in other ways, and here the impact of branding on competition is of much more questionable value.

The emotional and cognitive appeal of branding

Marketing involves identifying consumers' desires and preferences concerning products and their quality, and informing and persuading consumers that a particular brand can meet them.[72] However, marketing can also be active and creative, and seek to influence the preferences of consumers and appeal to their emotional desires.[73] Branding is relevant to this creative side of marketing because the identity that a brand confers on products gives a context to an individual act of consumption that may increase its emotional impact and turn it into the basis of a continuing relationship.[74] The fact that this can increase or stimulate demand for products has been attributed to an evolution in the preferences of consumers

A. Griffiths, 'Trade Marks and Responsible Capitalism', *International Review of Intellectual Property and Competition Law*, 43 (2012), 798–824 at 818–20.

[71] S. Hilton, 'The Social Value of Brands', in R. Clifton and J. Simmons (eds.), *Brands and Branding* (London: The Economist in association with Profile Books, 2003), pp. 47–64 at 55. See, for example, the impact of the Rana Plaza disaster on various 'fast fashion' brands: J. Burke, 'Rana Plaza: One Year on from the Bangladesh Factory Disaster', *The Guardian*, 19 April 2014, available at www.theguardian.com/world/2014/apr/19/rana-plaza-bangladesh-one-year-on (accessed April 2014).

[72] P. F. Drucker, 'Marketing and Economic Development', *Journal of Marketing*, 22 (1958), 252–9; G. T. Gundlach and W. L. Wilkie, 'The American Marketing Association's New Definition of Marketing: Perspective and Commentary on the 2007 Revision', *Journal of Public Policy and Marketing*, 28 (2009), 259–64.

[73] J. B. Swann, 'An Interdisciplinary Approach to Brand Strength', *Trademark Reporter*, 96 (2006), 943–76.

[74] Ramello and Silva, 'Appropriating Signs and Meaning', pp. 947–8.

once they have satisfied their main functional needs.[75] A brand can also increase the emotional impact of consumption by associating a product with a particular image of quality, or an image relating to the consumer, or with a particular set of values. In effect, branding can transform a product into a source of self-assurance or a means of self-expression, or a symbol of status or of adherence to certain values.[76] However, the social value of this kind of appeal is debatable.[77]

The capacity of a brand to attract consumers through increasing the emotional appeal of products makes it more like the intangible subject matter of other forms of intellectual property right. Rather than providing guidance and assurance about the branded products, such a brand becomes an object of desire in its own right with the branded products becoming media through which consumers can gain access to it. This is relevant to assessing the economic case for the legal protection of brands and calibrating the scope of their protection. The fact that a brand has emotional appeal to consumers and can therefore boost demand for branded products may appear to justify its legal protection. It may also appear to justify more extensive legal protection, because emotional appeal can be vulnerable to discordant imagery and associations that may intrude when something reminds consumers of the brand, even though it does not suggest or imply any economic link with the brand.[78] Moreover, strength of emotional appeal can also derive from the singularity of a brand's signifiers.[79]

However, the case for extending the legal rights of trade owners to protect the emotional impact of their brands is far from clear, especially given its questionable social value.[80] Depending on how far its appeal is independent of its messages and assurances concerning product quality,

[75] It has also been related to the progression of human needs and desires identified in the humanistic psychology of Abraham Maslow: D. A. Aaker and E. Joachimsthaler, *Brand Leadership: The Next Level of the Brand Revolution* (New York: The Free Press, 2000), pp. 48–9; J. B. Swann, D. A. Aaker and M. Reback, 'Trademarks and Marketing', *Trademark Reporter*, 91 (2001), 787–832 at 796–7.

[76] B. Beebe, 'Intellectual Property Law and the Sumptuary Code', *Harvard Law Review*, 123 (2010), 809–89; D. Holt and D. Cameron, *Cultural Strategy: Using Innovative Ideologies to Build Breakthrough Brands* (Oxford University Press, 2010).

[77] R. Brown, 'Advertising and the Public Interest: Legal Protection of Trade Symbols', *Yale Law Journal*, 57 (1948) 1165–206 at 1169; A. Offer, 'The Mask of Intimacy: Advertising and the Quality of Life', in A. Offer, *The Challenge of Affluence: Self-Control and Well-Being in the United States and Britain since 1950* (Oxford University Press, 2006), pp. 103–37.

[78] *Colgate-Palmolive* v. *Erven Lucas Bols* [1979] ECC 419 (Benelux HC); *Sheimer (C.A.)'s Trade Mark Application* [2000] RPC 484 (AP).

[79] Beebe, 'Search and Persuasion in Trademark Law', 2043–6.

[80] See n. 10.

such a brand can give its owner a form of monopoly power. As the exclusive supplier of its emotional appeal, the brand's owner enjoys some important competitive advantages: it can be conferred on products at a low marginal cost and consumers may find the corresponding emotional desire harder to satisfy than their need or desire for the products as products.[81] Moreover, differentiating products in this way can distort competition by creating additional emotional 'switching costs' for consumers.[82] These competitive advantages not only increase the brand owner's market power, but may give it much greater scope to reduce or take risks with the other elements that contribute to the overall quality of the marked products. Emotional appeal may therefore ultimately weaken the brand's capacity to provide reliable guidance and credible assurance about product quality. Trade mark law therefore has to strike a careful and pragmatic balance in specifying the scope of the exclusive rights of trade mark owners to limit their incentive to invest resources in cultivating and exploiting emotional appeal.

There is another factor contributing to the market power of some brands and their signifiers that justifies setting limits on the exclusive rights of trade mark owners to ensure effective competition. This is the 'cognitive availability' that a brand enjoys once its signifiers have become established in the minds of consumers as salient and familiar reference points. Consumers can use the signifiers of such brands to simplify what might otherwise be a complex and time-consuming process of evaluation and comparison.[83] The school of behavioural economics has argued that human actors tend to behave intuitively in this way and that this can lead their behaviour to diverge significantly from the predictions based on the assumption of rational wealth-maximising behaviour underlying economic theory.[84] This suggests that consumers may favour a familiar brand

[81] Ramello and Silva, 'Appropriating Signs and Meaning', pp. 946–9.

[82] P. Klemperer, 'Markets with Consumer Switching Costs', *Quarterly Journal of Economics*, 102 (1987), 375–94; P. Klemperer, 'Competition when Consumers Have Switching Costs: An Overview with Applications to Industrial Organization, Macroeconomics, and International Trade', *Review of Economic Studies*, 62 (1995), 515–39.

[83] A. Ehrenberg, N. Barnard and J. Scriven, 'Differentiation or Salience', *Journal of Advertising Research*, 37 (1997), 7–14.

[84] T. Gilovich, D. Griffin and D. Kahneman (eds.), *Heuristics and Biases: The Psychology of Intuitive Judgment* (Cambridge University Press, 2002); D. Kahneman, 'Maps of Bounded Rationality: Psychology for Behavioral Economics', *American Economic Review*, 93 (2003), 1449–75.

without significant negative connotations, not because it assures them of better value, but simply because it is convenient for them to do so.[85]

Trade mark law therefore has to calibrate the exclusive property rights of brand owners to curb the potentially anti-competitive effects of the emotional appeal and cognitive availability of certain brands. However, it also has to take account of the fact that the capacity of a familiar brand to provide quality assurance may depend on its singularity and salience as a focal point for investment and that the confidence it inspires in consumers may derive from its emotional impact.[86] In European trade mark law, this balancing exercise has to be performed in applying the additional right conferred on the owners of trade marks with 'a reputation' to prohibit unauthorised third parties from using signs that are identical or similar to their trade marks, if these cause detriment to or take 'unfair advantage' of the 'distinctive character' or 'repute' of their trade marks and do so without 'due cause'.[87] This additional right needs to be qualified to ensure that it does not insulate a brand with significant emotional appeal from effective competition.[88] The balancing exercise is also required in applying the core right of a trade mark owner to prohibit unauthorised parties from using an identical sign to market products of an identical kind. Here, the owner must show that the sign in question is liable to affect one of the functions of its trade mark, though the CJEU has ruled that these include its 'advertising' and 'investment' functions as well as its 'essential' function of signifying commercial 'origin'.[89]

To curb excessive market power based on cognitive availability, the exclusive rights of the owners of salient brands should be qualified to enable competitors to make use of the brands' signifiers as long as the competitors do not mislead consumers about the commercial origin of their products. A qualification of this kind can be seen in the CJEU's rulings concerning the use of the signifiers of familiar brands in making requests and as keywords for online searching.[90]

[85] Ramello, 'What's in a Sign?', 556–9.

[86] *Boehringer Ingelheim (No. 2)* (C-348/04) [2007] ETMR 1164 at [43]–[44].

[87] The Directive, Art. 5.2. *L'Oreal* v. *Bellure* (C-487/07) [2009] ETMR 987; *Interflora* v. *Marks & Spencer* (C-323/09) [2012] ETMR 1.

[88] *Specsavers International* v. *Asda* [2012] EWCA Civ 24.

[89] *L'Oreal* v. *Bellure* (C-487/07) [2009] ETMR 987; *Google France* v. *Louis Vuitton* (C-236/08-238/08) [2010] ETMR 503; *Interflora* v. *Marks & Spencer* (C-323/09) [2012] ETMR 1.

[90] *Hölterhoff* v. *Freiesleben* (C-2/00) [2002] ETMR 917; *Google France* v. *Louis Vuitton* (C-236/08238/08)[2010] ETMR 503; *Portakabin* v. *Primakabin* (C-558/08) [2010] ETMR 930; *Interflora* v. *Marks & Spencer* (C-323/09) [2012] ETMR 1.

Conclusions

The capacity of brands to attract consumers to products is an incentive for firms to use and develop them as marketing resources. According to the CJEU, trade marks (being the signifiers of brands) reinforce the incentive that firms have to improve and maintain the quality of their products and to compete in terms of product quality. However, brands give firms a broader incentive to seek a competitive advantage at the level of marketing and this can involve much more than producing good-quality products and having a good reputation for product quality. It has been seen that brands provide a private, institutional and dynamic form of quality assurance that can encompass the behaviour of the firms behind them concerning product quality and other matters, and which gives branded products an organisational context. Brands give firms the scope to engage in product development and other forms of innovation and to compete at this level as well. Brands enable and incentivise firms to develop a good reputation as a valuable strategic asset and to engage in reputation management. This can include regulating standards and behaviour within the supply chains and other streams in which the firms operate.

Moreover, the ability to develop brands as marketing resources and strategic assets is not limited to upstream firms engaged in production. Midstream and downstream firms can also use brands as a basis for building a reputation and using this to achieve a competitive advantage, provided that they can exercise adequate control over the quality of the products that they brand. Branding therefore facilitates some separation of marketing from production (or service provision), and this allows these activities to develop according to their own economic logic in terms of scale, scope and organisation. This can give a strategic advantage to firms able to compete effectively at the level of marketing and has implications for consumers and other firms in the same stream. For example, where upstream firms are not well placed for marketing and promoting their products directly to consumers, they can be vulnerable to the bargaining power of the downstream firms able to compete effectively at that level. Here, the effect of branding is to intensify competition within a stream in terms of price and reliability, but not necessarily to the benefit of consumers who are dependent on the effectiveness of competition further downstream at the level of marketing and retail.

It has also been seen that there are other ways in which firms can use brands to attract consumers and these may enable them to gain excessive market power, with implications for consumers and for the balance of power within streams. The intangible and inexhaustible nature of emotional appeal as a form of output means that firms may find that it offers them an easier route to achieving a sustainable competitive advantage and may therefore prefer to invest resources in cultivating this kind of appeal, rather than directing investment and competitive effort at improving product quality and at building and maintaining a good reputation for product quality. The property rights conferred on brand owners therefore require careful calibration to ensure that they provide an optimal incentive.

INDEX